Ermolao Barbaro's *On Celibacy*
3 and 4 and *On the Duty of
the Ambassador*

BLOOMSBURY NEO-LATIN SERIES

Series editors: William M. Barton, Stephen Harrison, Gesine Manuwald and Bobby Xinyue

Early Modern Texts and Anthologies
Edited by Stephen Harrison and Gesine Manuwald

Volume 6

The 'Early Modern Texts and Anthologies' strand of the *Bloomsbury Neo-Latin Series* presents editions of texts with English translations, introductions and notes. Volumes include complete editions of longer single texts and themed anthologies bringing together texts from particular genres, periods or countries and the like.

These editions are primarily aimed at students and scholars and intended to be suitable for use in university teaching, with introductions that give authoritative but not exhaustive accounts of the relevant texts and authors, and commentaries that provide sufficient help for the modern reader in noting links with classical Latin texts and bringing out the cultural context of writing.

Alongside the series' 'Studies in Early Modern Latin Literature' strand, it is hoped that these editions will help to bring important and interesting Neo-Latin texts of the period from 1350 to 1800 to greater prominence in study and scholarship, and make them available for a wider range of academic disciplines as well as for the rapidly growing study of Neo-Latin itself.

Also available in this series:
An Anthology of British Neo-Latin Literature by Gesine Manuwald, L. B. T. Houghton and Lucy R. Nicholas
An Anthology of European Neo-Latin Literature edited by Gesine Manuwald, Daniel Hadas and Lucy R. Nicholas
An Anthology of Neo-Latin Literature in British Universities edited by Gesine Manuwald and Lucy R. Nicholas
Ermolao Barbaro's On Celibacy 1 and 2 edited by Gareth Williams
Japan on the Jesuit Stage by Akihiko Watanabe
Roger Ascham's Themata Theologica by Lucy R. Nicholas

Ermolao Barbaro's *On Celibacy* 3 and 4 and *On the Duty of the Ambassador*

Edited by Gareth Williams

BLOOMSBURY ACADEMIC
LONDON • NEW YORK • OXFORD • NEW DELHI • SYDNEY

BLOOMSBURY ACADEMIC
Bloomsbury Publishing Plc
50 Bedford Square, London, WC1B 3DP, UK
1385 Broadway, New York, NY 10018, USA
29 Earlsfort Terrace, Dublin 2, Ireland

BLOOMSBURY, BLOOMSBURY ACADEMIC and the Diana logo are trademarks of Bloomsbury Publishing Plc

First published in Great Britain 2024
Paperback edition published 2025

Copyright © Gareth Williams, 2024

Gareth Williams has asserted his right under the Copyright, Designs and Patents Act, 1988, to be identified as Author of this work.

Cover image: Vittore Carpaccio, *St. Ursula's Arrival in Rome*, part of his *Saint Ursula* cycle, 1488–95. Gallerie dell'Accademia, Venice. Photo by Fine Art Images/Heritage Images/Getty Images

All rights reserved. No part of this publication may be reproduced or transmitted in any form or by any means, electronic or mechanical, including photocopying, recording, or any information storage or retrieval system, without prior permission in writing from the publishers.

Bloomsbury Publishing Plc does not have any control over, or responsibility for, any third-party websites referred to or in this book. All internet addresses given in this book were correct at the time of going to press. The author and publisher regret any inconvenience caused if addresses have changed or sites have ceased to exist, but can accept no responsibility for any such changes.

A catalogue record for this book is available from the British Library.

A catalog record for this book is available from the Library of Congress.

ISBN: HB: 978-1-3503-9893-1
PB: 978-1-3503-9892-4
ePDF: 978-1-3503-9894-8
eBook: 978-1-3503-9895-5

Typeset by RefineCatch Limited, Bungay, Suffolk

To find out more about our authors and books visit www.bloomsbury.com and sign up for our newsletters.

Contents

List of Illustrations	vi
Preface	vii
List of Abbreviations	ix
Introduction	1
Note on the Texts and Translations	4
On Celibacy Book 3: Text and Translation	8
On Celibacy Book 4: Text and Translation	94
Introduction to *On the Duty of the Ambassador*	167
I: To Milan	167
II: The text: its history, completeness and content	168
III: The originality of *De officio legati*	170
IV: Behind the mask	174
On the Duty of the Ambassador: Text, Translation and Notes	184
Bibliography	209
Index of Passages	219
General Index	226
Index of Latin Words	234
Index of Greek Words	235

Illustration

1 *De coelibatu* 3.6.52-4.1.3, here reproduced from MS Classe II 9, Biblioteca Comunale Ariostea, Ferrara, with the permission of the Servizio Biblioteche e Archivi del Comune di Ferrara   5

Preface

The modest aim of this volume and its companion-piece in the *Bloomsbury Neo-Latin Series* is to do what they can to enhance the modern visibility, especially in Anglophone circles, of a truly remarkable figure in the history of Italian humanism: Ermolao Barbaro (1454–93). After our coverage of Books 1 and 2 of Barbaro's *De coelibatu* (*On celibacy*, 1472–3) in the first volume, we turn in this second volume to *On celibacy* 3 and 4 and then to the short treatise *De officio legati* (*On the duty of the ambassador*, probably written in mid- to late-1489). My motivation in juxtaposing these two texts in this combined study is set out briefly in the introduction below, and more fully in that to the first volume.

The preface to that first volume also contextualizes this project within the modern editorial history of these two important but still relatively unheralded works of Barbaro. The two were first juxtaposed in Vittore Branca's pioneering textual edition of 1969: this was the first printed edition of *De coelibatu*, and only the second (after Hrabar 1906) of *De officio legati*. The texts as presented in my paired volumes are based on my own examination of the sole extant manuscript of *De coelibatu* and, in the case of *De officio legati*, on Branca's edition, which itself relies on the ten manuscripts that were known to Branca. Quite apart from the practical difficulties posed by the Covid-19 pandemic in the preparation of this study, I make no claim to the editorial competence that *ab initio* construction of the text of *De officio legati* would now require.

The two volumes of this edition present what is, to my knowledge, the first complete translation into English (or any other language) of *De coelibatu*, and the first complete English version of *De officio legati* (cf. in Italian Rinaldi 2013–14). But Branca supplied relatively little in the way of annotation that would reveal the richness of Barbaro's learned allusiveness and the complexity of his engagement with the literary and philosophical storehouse on which he prolifically draws, especially in *De coelibatu*.[1] Hence the notes that accompany the present translations are designed to shed some useful light on the sheer breadth of learning that the young Barbaro already had at his disposal in *On celibacy* – and on his ability to apply that learning with an easy

---

[1] Cf. in review Scaglione 1972: 339: 'The only criticism one could offer to this otherwise admirable publication concerns the very limited scope of the exegetic apparatus. The text is usually plain enough, but not always; several passages demand explanation or interpretation, and literary or historical references are frequent.'

touch, an enviable fluency in a vast range of sources, and a keen eye for wit and sparkle.

I elaborate in the preface to the first volume on the further motivations that have spurred this project, and I also declare there the multiple debts that I owe to the many friends and colleagues whose help has been invaluable in the preparation of this study. The two volumes of this edition are designed to be stand-alone productions as much as possible: in both cases, the Abbreviations and Notes on the Text(s) and Translation(s) are pertinent only to the given volume, and the Bibliography and Indices in each are volume-specific. Much cross-reference is nevertheless made between the two volumes in the annotations to *De coelibatu*: in such cases, simple reference is made in the annotations in the second volume to (e.g.) '2.3.9 n. 56' in the first volume, and vice versa; outside the annotations, cross-referencing follows volume and page number (e.g., 'See Vol. 1 Intro. p. 18'). At all times, in the annotations to both *De coelibatu* and *De officio legati* and in my introduction to the latter work, all translations are my own unless otherwise stated.

New York City
May 2023

Abbreviations

Ael.	Aelian (*c.* 170–235 CE)
VH	*Varia historia*/Historical miscellany
Apul.	Apuleius (b. *c.* 125 CE)
De dog. Plat.	*De dogmate Platonis*/On Plato and his doctrine
Arist.	Aristotle (384–322 BCE)
De an.	*De anima*/On the soul
De somn.	*De somno et vigilia*/On sleep and waking
EE	*Ethica Eudemia*/Eudemian ethics
EN	*Ethica Nicomachea*/Nicomachean ethics
Gen. an.	*De generatione animalium*/On the generation of animals
Hist. an.	*Historia animalium*/History of animals
Metaph.	*Metaphysica*/Metaphysics
Part. an.	*De partibus animalium*/On the parts of animals
Poet.	*Poetica*/Poetics
Pol.	*Politica*/Politics
[Arist.]	
Oec.	*Oeconomica*/Household management
Pr.	*Problēmata*/Problems
Arr.	Arrian (*c.* 86–160 CE)
Anab.	*Anabasis of Alexander*
Artem.	Artemidorus of Ephesus (late 2nd to early 3rd century CE)
Oneir.	*Oneirocritica*/The interpretation of dreams
Ath.	Athenaeus (*fl. c.* 200 CE)
Deipno.	*Deipnosophistae*/The learned banqueters
August.	Augustine (354–430 CE)
De bon. coni.	*De bono coniugali*/On the good of marriage
Brun.	Leonardo Bruni (1370–1444)
De stud. et litt.	*De studiis et litteris*/The study of literature
Catul.	C. Valerius Catullus (*c.* 84–54 BCE)
Cels.	A. Cornelius Celsus (*fl.* 1st century CE)
Med.	*De medicina*/On medicine
Cic.	M. Tullius Cicero (106–43 BCE)
Ac.	*Academica*
Brut.	*Brutus*
Cat.	*In Catilinam*/Against Catiline

De or.	*De oratore*/On the orator
Div.	*De divinatione*/On divination
Fin.	*De finibus*/On ends
Flac.	*Pro Flacco*/For Flaccus
Har.	*De haruspicum responso*/On the response of the soothsayers
Leg.	*De legibus*/On the laws
Luc.	*Lucullus*
Mur.	*Pro Murena*/For Murena
Nat. D.	*De natura deorum*/On the nature of the gods
Off.	*De officiis*/On duties
Orat.	*Orator*
Rep.	*De republica*/On the republic
Top.	*Topica*/Topics
Tusc.	*Tusculanae disputationes*/Tusculan disputations
Verr.	*In Verrem*/Against Verres
Curt.	Q. Curtius Rufus (*fl.* mid-1st century CE), author of *Historiae Alexandri Magni*/Histories of Alexander the Great
Dio Cass.	Dio Cassius (*c.* 164–after 229 CE), author of an 80-book history of Rome down to 229 CE
Diod. Sic.	Diodorus Siculus (*fl.* 1st century BCE), author of a universal history from mythical times down to 60 BCE
Dion. Hal.	Dionysius of Halicarnassus (*fl. c.* 20 BCE)
Ant. Rom.	*Antiquitates Romanae*/Roman Antiquities
DK	H. Diels and W. Kranz, eds. *Die Fragmente der Vorsokratiker*. 6th edn. 3 vols. Berlin, 1952.
D. L.	Diogenes Laertius (*fl.* 3rd century CE), biographer of the ancient philosophers from Thales to Epicurus
DMLBS	R. K. Ashdowne, D. R. Howlett, and R. E. Latham, eds. *Dictionary of Medieval Latin from British Sources*. 3 vols. Oxford, 2018.
Enn.	Q. Ennius (239–169 BCE), Roman epic poet, dramatist and satirist
Ann.	*Annales*/Annals
Gal.	Galen (129–*c.* 210 CE), Greek physician
Ars med.	*Ars medica*/The art of medicine
De const. art.	*De constitutione artis medicae*/On the constitution of the art of medicine
De san. tuen.	*De sanitate tuenda*/On the preservation of health

In Hipp. Prog. comment.	*In Hippocratis prognosticum commentarii*/*Commentary on Hippocrates'* Prognostic
Gell.	Aulus Gellius (2nd century CE), Roman miscellanist and author of the 20-book *Noctes Atticae* (*Attic nights*)
Guar.	Battista Guarino (1434–1503[?])
De ord.	*De ordine docendi et studendi*/*A program of teaching and learning*
Hdt.	Herodotus of Halicarnassus (b. *c.* 485 BCE)
Hipp.	Hippocrates (*c.* 460–375 BCE)/Hippocratic Corpus
Epid.	*De morbis popularibus*/*Epidemics*
Nat. hom.	*De natura hominis*/*Nature of man*
Progn.	*Prognosticon*/*Prognostic*
Vet. med.	*De vetere medicina*/*Ancient medicine*
Hom.	Homer (*c.* 8th century BCE)
Il.	*Iliad*
Od.	*Odyssey*
Hor.	Horace (Q. Horatius Flaccus, 65–8 BCE)
Ars P.	*Ars poetica*/*Art of poetry*
Carm.	*Carmina*/*Odes*
Joseph.	Flavius Josephus (b. 37/38 CE)
B. Jud.	*Bellum Judaicum*/*Jewish War*
Just.	Justin (M. Iunian[i]us Iustinus, 2nd century CE[?])
Epit.	*Epitome* of the otherwise lost *Liber historiarum Philippicarum* (*Philippic histories*) of Pompeius Trogus (time of Augustus)
Juv.	Juvenal (D. Iunius Iuvenalis, 1st–2nd century CE), satirist
Liv.	Livy (Titus Livius, 59 BCE–17 CE)
LM	A. Laks and G. W. Most, eds. *Early Greek Philosophy*. 9 vols. Loeb Classical Library Volumes 524–32. Cambridge, MA, and London, 2016.
[Long.]	'Longinus' (author unknown; 1st century CE[?])
Subl.	*De sublimitate*/*On the sublime*
LS	C. T. Lewis and C. Short, eds. *A Latin Dictionary*. Oxford, 1879.
LSJ	H. G. Liddell and R. Scott, eds. *A Greek-English Lexicon*. 9th edn, rev. H. Stuart Jones. Oxford, 1925–40.
Luc.	Lucan (M. Annaeus Lucanus, 39–65 CE)
Lucr.	Lucretius (Ti. Lucretius Carus, *c.* 94–55 BCE)
Mart.	Martial (M. Valerius Martialis, *c.* 40–101 CE)
Nonn.	Nonnus of Panopolis, Egypt (*fl.* 5th century CE)

Dion.	Dionysiaca
OLD	P. G. W. Glare, ed. *Oxford Latin Dictionary*. Oxford, 1982.
Ov.	Ovid (P. Ovidius Naso, 43 BCE–17 CE)
Met.	*Metamorphoses*
Pers.	Persius (A. Persius Flaccus, 34–62 CE), satirist
Piccol.	Aeneas Sylvius Piccolomini (1405–64, Pope Pius II from 1458)
De lib. educ.	*De liberorum educatione*/*On the education of boys*
Pl.	Plato (*c*. 429–347 BCE)
Ap.	*Apologia*/*Apology*
Ep.	*Epistulae*/*Epistles*
Resp.	*Respublica*/*Republic*
Tht.	*Theaetetus*
Tim.	*Timaeus*
Plaut.	Plautus (T. Maccius Plautus, d. 184 BCE)
Aul.	*Aulularia*/*The pot of gold*
Plin.	Pliny the elder (C. Plinius Secundus, *c*. 23–79 CE)
NH	*Naturalis historia*/*Natural history*
Plut.	Plutarch (L.[?] Mestrius Plutarchus, *c*. 46–after 120 CE)
Hom. stud.	*Homērikai meletai*/*Homeric studies*
Mor.	*Moralia*
Vitae	*Lives*
Alex.	*Alexander*
Caes.	*Caesar*
Cat. min.	*Cato minor*/*Cato the younger*
Cic.	*Cicero*
Dem.	*Demosthenes*
Luc.	*Lucullus*
Num.	*Numa*
[Plut.]	
De lib. educ.	*De liberis educandis*/*On the education of children*
Porph.	Porphyry (234–*c*. 305 CE)
Vit. Pyth.	*Vita Pythagorae*/*Life of Pythagoras*
Quint.	Quintilian (M. Fabius Quintilianus, *c*. 35–after 96 CE)
Inst.	*Institutio oratoria*/*The orator's education*
Sall.	Sallust (C. Sallustius Crispus, 86–*c*. 34 BCE)
Cat.	*Catilina*/*The war with Catiline*
[Sall.]	
Cic.	*In Ciceronem*/*Invective against Cicero*

Sen.		Seneca the younger (L. Annaeus Seneca, c. 4 BCE–65 CE)
	Ben.	De beneficiis/On benefits
	Dial.	Dialogi/Dialogues
	Ep.	Epistulae/Letters
	Q. Nat.	Quaestiones naturales/Natural questions
Sext. Emp.		Sextus Empiricus (fl. 3rd century CE)
	Pyr.	Pyrrhoniae hypotyposes/Outlines of Pyrrhonism
Suet.		Suetonius (C. Suetonius Tranquillus, b. c. 70 CE)
	Vitae Caesarum	Lives of the Caesars
	Claud.	Claudius
	Dom.	Domitianus
	Iul.	Iulius [Caesar]
	Ner.	Nero
Tac.		Tacitus (Cornelius Tacitus, c. 56–120 CE)
	Ann.	Annales/Annals
	Dial.	Dialogus de oratoribus/Dialogue on oratory
Tert.		Tertullian (Q. Septimius Florens Tertullianus, c. 155–220 CE)
	De an.	De anima/On the soul
Theophr.		Theophrastus (c. 372–287 BCE)
	Char.	Characters
V. Fl.		C. Valerius Flaccus (d. c. 92 CE), poet of an epic Argonautica
V. Max.		Valerius Maximus (fl. early 1st century CE), author of the 9-book Facta et dicta memorabilia/Memorable doings and sayings
Verg.		Pier Paolo Vergerio (1370–1444)
	De ingen. mor.	De ingenuis moribus et liberalibus adulescentiae studiis/The character and studies befitting a free-born youth
Virg.		Virgil (P. Vergilius Maro, 70–19 BCE)
	Aen.	Aeneis/Aeneid
	Ecl.	Eclogae/Eclogues
	G.	Georgica/Georgics
Xen.		Xenophon (c. 430–350 BCE)
	Mem.	Memorabilia
	Symp.	Symposium

Introduction

Central to the storyline that dominates this study of the eminent Venetian humanist Ermolao Barbaro (1454–93) is the life-long drama of his divided loyalties to the self and to the state: on the one hand, he faced the pressure of conformity to the traditional obligations, expectations, and career path of his patrician class at Venice; and, on the other, he felt the gravitational pull to an existence devoted to his beloved literary studies. Much of Barbaro's life consisted of an uneasy compromise between these different callings until matters came to a head when, in early 1491, he was nominated as the Patriarch of Aquileia by Pope Innocent VIII. At the time Barbaro was serving as Venice's ambassador to the Papal Curia in Rome. He accepted the nomination to Aquileia in obedience to the Pope but without Venetian consultation or permission. The Venetian Senate was quick to express its displeasure at what it perceived as an egregious act of disloyalty. Summarily stripped of his ambassadorial office, Barbaro remained in Rome, resentful of the Republic's treatment of him and distressed at the disgrace brought upon the family name; but he nevertheless absorbed himself in his beloved humanistic studies. Matters remained at an impasse until Barbaro died, probably of the plague, in late July 1493, at the age of only thirty-nine. On November 4 1493 Pope Alexander VI named Nicolò Donato, Venice's nominee, as the new Patriarch of Aquileia; and so ended the convoluted saga that had dragged on for almost three years.

Such is the background to our treatment of *De coelibatu* (*On celibacy*) and *De officio legati* (*On the duty of the ambassador*) in the paired volumes of this edition of both works. In his *On celibacy* of 1472–3, the young Barbaro is committed to a life that proudly renounces civic engagement in the name of self-discovery and inner fulfillment. Yet a very different Barbaro asserts himself in *On the duty of the ambassador*, which he probably penned in mid- to late-1489: he now presents himself as a committed public servant in a work that is ahead of its time in theorizing the nature of 'modern' Renaissance diplomacy. This work was composed only shortly before Barbaro caused outrage in Venice by his perceived act of betrayal over Aquileia: how to reconcile the public face that he shows in *On the duty of the ambassador* with his private yearning for an existence unhampered by official service? And how to view his sermon on fidelity to the state in *On the duty of the ambassador* in light of the message that he preaches in *On celibacy* – that the celibate's self-fulfillment at a remove from the Venetian *cursus* is an eminently worthy and justifiable life-path that is endorsed by divine sanction? To what extent had the more mature Barbaro of 1489 left behind the youthful aversion that he showed in *On celibacy* to the life-trajectory and career path that were traditionally incumbent on the patrician class at Venice?

These questions are examined in detail in the introduction to *On celibacy* 1 and 2 in the companion volume to this treatment of *On celibacy* 3 and 4 and *On the duty of the ambassador*. The present volume traces to its conclusion Barbaro's detailed examination of the natural aptitudes and the educational formation that the young celibate-to-be needs to equip himself – or, indeed, *herself*[1] – for an existence free of marriage and sexual engagement of any kind. After a brief summary of the topics covered in the first two books (3.2), and after concise coverage of what it is to live chastely both within and then outside marriage (3.3–4), Book 3 is dominated first by the forms of behaviour that are to be scrupulously avoided by the celibate-to-be: sensory pleasure, overindulgence in food and drink, consorting with the opposite sex, and an irregular pattern of sleep (3.5). Self-control is all, the Aristotelian golden mean its guiding principle.[2] But after first expatiating on the precautions to be taken by the celibate, Book 3 focuses secondly on the treatments to be applied so as to keep him safe from contamination: moderation of his appetites in accordance with his own needs and nature, an appropriate degree of detachment from social intercourse, and properly regulated sleep (3.6).

The first part of Book 4 is more abstract in feel, as if Barbaro's exploration there of the nature of contemplation (4.1) elevates the treatise, and the celibate himself, to a more ethereal plane. After the social distancing that Barbaro recommends in Book 3, he enforces a different but complementary distance in 4.1 between lofty contemplation on the one hand and, on the other, the everyday values (e.g., desire for wealth, social position, material pleasure, etc.) that predominate in life at ground level, so to speak. This distance is again discernible in Barbaro's tailoring in 4.2 of the familiar humanistic curriculum to the rarified needs of the celibate-to-be: by turning his mind to geometry, music, arithmetic, and the visual arts/optics, the young man acquires a mathematical grasp that equips him for his higher studies, not least in the astronomical branch of natural science (cf. 4.2.4–5). The study of eloquence is hardly a priority (4.2.10–20), given the celibate's detachment from the civic arena where rhetorical skill comes into its own. In requiring the student to pay close attention to dialectic (4.2.26–30), Barbaro eschews the sophistic quibbling and sleight of hand that too often blight the discipline, at least as he finds it habitually practiced; the celibate's dialectical training instead sharpens the intellect for his high-minded immersion in moral philosophy and natural science (the latter including 'the investigation of matters pertaining to the gods and to mortals,' 4.2.31). Beyond this customized shaping of the humanist curriculum to serve the celibate, Barbaro also reverts to Cicero's *De officiis* (*On duties*) in an extended section (4.2.37–56) that importantly complements and rounds out his appropriation of that work in Book 1.[3]

As Book 4 hurries on to its conclusion, Barbaro neatly forestalls any impression that the celibate shaped in his pages must be a model of pinched severity and earnest self-containment; hence the appealing dash of colour with which Barbaro pictures him as vivacious and cheerful in outlook, affably enjoying the company of friends, vibrant in spirit as in body (4.2.72–87), and even 'a kind of likeness on earth, and an attestation, of the blessedness of God' (4.2.88). Just before the close, Barbaro goes out of his way to add a brief but important coda that is strikingly forward-looking for its time: he explicitly states that women are no less capable than men of achieving the end-goal of celibacy as set out in his four books (4.2.91–6) – a radical departure from the male-oriented asceticism and frequent misogyny of medieval writing on monastic celibacy.[4]

On the duty of the ambassador receives its own dedicated introduction later in this volume in advance of my annotated translation of the work.[5] Much important light has been cast in recent scholarship on the originality of this short treatise in the history of Renaissance writing on diplomacy, not least because of Barbaro's focus on the permanent or 'resident' ambassador as opposed to the envoy sent on short-term, ad hoc missions. Beyond its relation to *On celibacy*, much effort is therefore made in this volume to view *De officio legati* on its own terms as a charter of sorts for a 'modern' diplomatic ethos and practice that were far removed from the world of medieval diplomacy. To avoid excessive repetition, the general character and tendencies of Barbaro's Latinity in both *On celibacy* and *On the duty of the ambassador* are surveyed in section IV ('Style and technique') of the introduction to my companion volume on *On celibacy* 1 and 2; and that introduction offers much else in the way of historical, socio-cultural, and literary contextualization for the approach taken below to *De coelibatu* 3 and 4 and *De officio legati*.

Notes

1 See p. 3 and Vol. 1 Intro. pp. 8–9.
2 See 3.6.15 and n. 224.
3 See on this Ciceronian dimension Vol. 1 Intro. p. 19 and 4.2.39 n. 137.
4 See further Vol. 1 Intro. p. 14–15.
5 Pp. 167–83 below.

Note on the Texts and Translations

In keeping with the different life-stages at which Barbaro wrote *De coelibatu* and *De officio legati*, and given his very different thematic and literary agendas in the two works, the translations offered in this volume are cast in different registers. The stylistic panache and versatility of *De coelibatu* 3 and 4 demand in a translation at least the attempt at a matching liveliness of tone, a brisk pace that is in step with Barbaro's own accelerations, and adjustments of mood according to the shifting contours of his narrative. In particular, I have incorporated features of spoken English, especially contractions, in my version of *De coelibatu*, but not in that of *De officio legati*, where a more formal tone seems appropriate, and also a plainer uniformity of voice. The section divisions as marked in the Latin texts and their respective translations (3.1.1, 2, 3, etc.) follow those deployed by Branca in his 1969 edition. In the case of *De coelibatu*, I have also incorporated references to the page sequence in the sole extant manuscript of the work,[1] i.e., 53*v*[*erso*], 54*r*[*ecto*], 54*v*, etc.; the elegance of that manuscript is sampled in Figure 1.

The text of *De officio legati* as given in this volume reproduces with minimal adjustment[2] that in Branca's 1969 edition; his apparatus remains indispensable, as does his survey of the manuscripts on which his text is based.[3] Unless otherwise noted, the text of *De coelibatu* 3 and 4 reproduces Branca's. His departures from the MS are listed below my text, as are my own departures from Branca's printed readings, including the correction of MS misreadings in his text. Spaces left blank in the MS (usually presupposing the insertion of one or more Greek words) are duly noted; and my apparatus also registers those places where my text departs from Branca's in matters of orthography and punctuation. For clarity, more notable departures from Branca and/or the MS are reasoned as follows:

Book Three

3.3.3   *Nero, humani generis fax*: *fax* MS; Br. 101 n. 1 conjectures *faex* (cf. *OLD* 3a: '[of persons] The dregs, scum'), but for the MS wording cf. of Caligula and Nero Plin. *NH* 7.45 *faces generis humani*.

---

[1] For which see Vol. 1 Intro. pp. 5–6.
[2] See p. 196 n. 32 on §30 *ultro* †*seset*†.
[3] 1969: 25–51; see further p. 168 below.

Note on the Texts and Translations 5

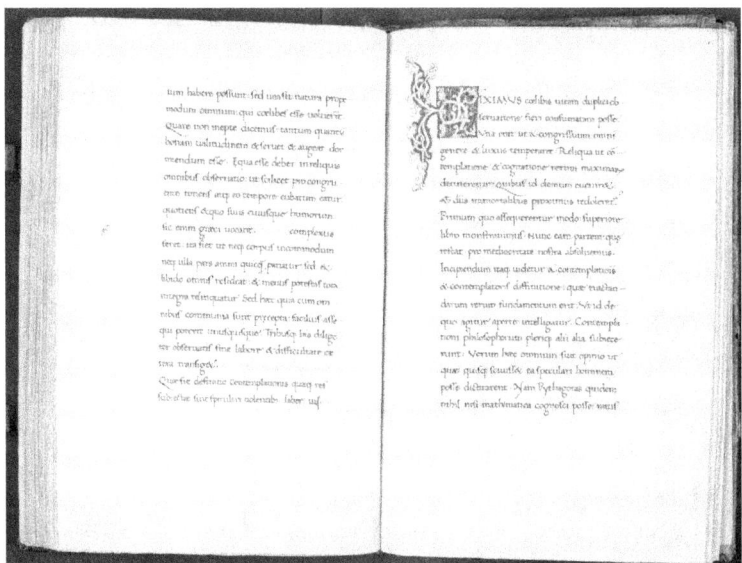

Figure 1 *De coelibatu* 3.6.52-4.1.3, here reproduced from MS Classe II 9, Biblioteca Comunale Ariostea, Ferrara, with the permission of the Servizio Biblioteche e Archivi del Comune di Ferrara.

3.3.6   *Sanctum est enim ut*: *sanctum* MS; for Br. 101 n. 3, *sancit-* (in the same hand in the right margin) 'perhaps the right reading,' but for the idiom *sanctum est ut*... cf., e.g., Cic. *Har.* 32, *Off.* 3.65, 69.

3.5.31 *ea* [sc. *aegritudine*] *nunc maxime quae ad luxum et gulam pertinet*: *pertinent* MS, Br., but *quae* is fem. sing., not neut. plur.

3.5.67 *suus coelibatui locus destinetur*: *-etur* after Br.'s conjecture (115 n. 1); MS *-aretur* printed by Br., but *-etur* conforms to the sequence of present verbs earlier in the sentence.

3.5.77 *quovis alio homine vel deo, saepe belua*: Br. 117 n. 1 conjectures *sive* for *saepe*, but Barbaro follows Cic. *Div.* 1.60 *cum quovis alio vel homine vel deo, saepe belua*.

3.5.81 *ea dumtaxat a nobis* †*dum*† ... *decursa cognosces*: †*dum*† Wi.; *dum* MS with space after it, whence *dum<modo>* read by Br., but *dummodo* is then hard to construe in relation to *dumtaxat*. Dittography after *dumtaxat* until the scribe recognized the error and jettisoned the repetition?

3.6.7   *in continuo corporis ex<er>citu*: MS *excitu* is suspect because of the required sense ('exertion,' but cf. *OLD excitus* 'A summons to appear';

excitus is in any case v. rare); Br. 120 n. 1 conjectures *esercitio*, but *exercitu* (cf. *OLD exercitus*² 1) presupposes a simpler slip of the pen to yield *excitu*.

Book Four

4.2.55 *neque consentaneum est eum qui nullo metu frangatur aut labore vincatur vel capi voluptatibus vel cupiditate aliqua irretiri*: *eum esse qui* MS, Br., but *esse* distorts the flow of the indirect statement in *eum . . . vel capi . . . vel irretiri*. Accepting *esse*, Br. punctuates after *vincatur*; but the two infs. in *vel capi . . . vel irretiri* are then left syntactically uncoordinated within the overall sentence structure.

4.2.63 *quantum* [sc. *ruboris et verecundiae*] *me hercle putas . . . contraxisse*: *quantum, mehercle, putas* Br., but in the indirect statement introduced by *putas*, word separation supplies the subj. acc. (*me*) governing *contraxisse*; for Barbaro's use of stand-alone *hercle* cf. *De off. leg.* 42, 48.

Tertius liber qui de offitio caelibis pertractabit

[1] Prologus.

1.1 Hactenus quae requirantur in puero pro nostra imbecillitate monstravimus. Praeterea de tota vita et offitio maius quidem opus aliquanto et spetiosius persequemur. Quod si in medio orationis, ut plerique[1] fecerunt, invocare deorum opem liceret, id esset mihi hoc loco maxime faciendum. **2** Nam et poetae et historiarum scriptores non solum initio operum suorum praesentiam numinum promereri votis aut laudibus conabantur, verumetiam et quom progressi longius in difficiliorem quendam [**53v**] locum incidissent usque adeo deorum favoribus exorandis non parcebant, ut nova etiam precatione uterentur. **3** Quorum exemplo nos quoque Deum optimum maximum atque simillimam illius mentem aeternamque et pientissimam maiestatem obsecramus, ut ingenio adsit, auxilietur, aspiret, efficiatque ut quemadmodum divinae felicitatis exemplar caelibatum effingi ad suum decus et gloriam non ignorat, ita pro rei amplissimae dignitate quae optima sint et necessaria maxime explicentur. Ordiamur itaque volentibus diis atque initium hunc in modum auspicemur.

---

[1] *plaer-* MS, Br., but cf. Br. *pler-* for MS *plaer-* at 2.6.3, 15, 17.

Book Three, which will treat the duty of the celibate

[1] Prologue.

1.1 Thus far I have shown, insofar as my feeble capacities allow, the qualities looked for in the boy. Beyond this, I shall set about a considerably greater and more imposing task on the entirety of the [celibate's] life and duty.[2] But if it were permissible to summon the gods' help in the middle of a discourse (as very many have done), I would very much have to take such action at this point.[3] **2** For both poets and historical writers not only used to try to win the supportive presence of the gods through prayers or praises at the commencement of their works, but also, even when they'd advanced a good way and had come upon some rather tricky passage, they were so unsparing in their entreaties for divine support that they would resort even to a fresh prayer.[4] **3** On this model, I too beseech God who is best and greatest, and His mind that is very much like Him,[5] and His eternal and most righteous grandeur – [I beseech Him] to support my abilities, to give aid, to breathe favour, and to bring it about that, just as He is not unaware that celibacy is fashioned as an illustration of divine blessedness for His own glorious distinction, so its most estimable and essential features are set out to the fullest extent in keeping with the prestige of a most magnificent topic. Accordingly, let's begin with divine consent, and make a favourable start in the following manner.

---

[2] In embarking on his 'greater task' (*maius opus*) by moving from part to whole (boyhood to the 'entire life') at this mid-point in *De coelibatu*, Barbaro pointedly echoes Virgil's transition at the epicenter of the *Aeneid* to 'the greater task' (*maius opus*, 7.45) of recounting the wars and struggles that await Aeneas after his arrival in Italy: the stage is set for the truly 'epic' phase of Barbaro's undertaking.

[3] On the classical phenomenon of such prayerful 'proems in the middle' see Conte 1992.

[4] Cf. in classical/post-classical verse Lucr. 4.1-25; Virg. *Ecl.* 6.1-12, *G.* 3.1-48, *Aen.* 7.37-45; V. Fl. 5.217-24; Nonn. *Dion.* 25.1-10, 253-70; in historical epic verse, Enn. *Ann.* 206-12 Sk. For historical prose see Livy's hypothetical invocation to the gods in his preface (§13) – an invocation in fact 'unparalleled in historical prefaces and hence highly challenging' (Moles 1993: 156), and not repeated in the prefaces to later books (so 6.1.1-3, 21.1.1-3, 31.1.1-5).

[5] I.e., 'best and greatest' like God Himself.

[2] Epilogus dictorum.

2.1 Dictum est unam esse rerum substantiam omnium quae mundo continentur, differre autem ab altero unumquodque proprietatibus adiunctis conna[**54r**]tisque: quo fit ut a reliquis animantibus sit id animal separatum quod rationis est particeps. Sed et hominem ab homine dissidere naturae diversitate[6] declaratum est: quare hic quidem in negotiis vivit, ille vero speculando. **2** Ostensum est etiam illud vivendi genus, quod est in actione positum et ad communem utilitatem accommodatum, tametsi non negligendum, esse tamen inferius longe quam alterum. Praeterea, quod ex priori questione pendere videbatur, demonstratum est iocundiorem esse vitam eorum qui vivunt in caelibatu quam qui uxorem duxerunt. **3** Post haec probatum est quatuor exigi, quae adesse ei puero debent qui in hunc finem educabitur: quorum duo, robur scilicet et ingenium, in ipsa protinus infantia elucescant[7] oportet et intrinsecus sint ac [**54v**] maxime genuina, reliqua vero extrinsecus; horum aliqua, ut valitudo, opes, ingenium, per totam vitam requiruntur. Recurrendumque erit ad ea praecepta,[8] quae retro locavimus, si scire illa oportebit.

4 Hunc in modum institutus atque his muneribus ornatus puer de se iam spondere quod volumus poterit, iam sua sponte illicitas voluptates et omne congressuum genus effugiet honestatisque appetentissimus et decori studiosissimus fiet, ad contemplandum quoque magno animo et ardentissima cupiditate feretur: talem sese demum exhibebit ut et iuvare consilio et erigere institutis sine parentum industria se ipsum possit. Quare non amplius de iis verba faciemus, quae ad curam parentum attineant, sed ea incohabimus

---

[6] *-em* MS, corrected to *-e*.
[7] *-at* MS.
[8] *-repta* MS.

[2] A summary of what has been said.

2.1 It's been stated[9] that all things that are contained in the world have a single essential nature, but that each individual entity differs from another in its associated or innate properties; hence the living being that shares in reason is distinct from all other creatures. But it's also been shown[10] that human differs from human through natural divergence; hence one person leads a busy and active life, but another a life of contemplation. **2** It's been demonstrated, too,[11] that the kind of existence that is located in action and applied to the common good, even if it's not to be disregarded, is nevertheless far inferior to the other. Moreover (the corollary that seemed to hang from that previous issue), it's been shown[12] that the existence of those living in celibacy is more pleasurable than that of those who've married. **3** Thereafter, it was established[13] that there are four requirements that must be present in the boy who will be brought up towards this end-goal. Of these, two, namely physical robustness and natural ability, should be apparent right from the start of early childhood. They should come from within and be very much inborn, but the others[14] from without; some of them, such as health,[15] resources,[16] and natural abilities,[17] are needed throughout the whole of life. And we'll have to go back to the strictures I laid out before[18] if a [refreshed] understanding of them will be required.

4 The boy trained in this way and equipped with these gifts will now be able to guarantee of himself what we desire, and now, of his own accord, he will avoid forbidden pleasures and every kind of intercourse; he will become most desirous of respectability and very eager for propriety,[19] and he will also be moved to contemplation by high-mindedness and the most burning passion. In sum, he will show himself to be the sort who, without the diligent attention of his parents, can help himself through sound judgment and elevate himself through his training. Hence I shall say no more about the matters relating to

---

[9] 1.1.1-3, but the point summarized in 3.2.1 'all things ... nature' evidently belongs to the lost portion at the start of Book 1, on which see Vol. 1 Intro. p. 6.
[10] 1.1.4-11.
[11] In 1.3 and 1.4.
[12] In 1.5 and 1.6.
[13] 2.3.2.
[14] In 2.3.2, devoted parenting (then elaborated upon in 2.3.3-27) and adequate resources (taken up in 2.4).
[15] The subject of 2.5.
[16] 2.4, esp. §§7-12.
[17] 2.6.
[18] In Books 1-2 generally.
[19] For symmetry with *honestatis* above, *decori* gen. from *decorum -i* n. (cf. OLD *studiosus* 1a, w. gen.), not dat. from *decus -oris* n.

maxime quae ad eam aetatem, quae paternum ius sit [55r] praetergressa, pertinere videbuntur.

5 Noster itaque coelibatus duobus offitiis expleri posse monstrabitur, ne si cui fortasse magna exigere videamur, saltem non multa videamur postulare: id enim operis dignitatem ostendit, quae magnitudine non multitudine extimatur. Nam in vilissimis quibusque artibus tot et tam multa requiruntur, ut ex hoc uno patere potissimum debeat esse quid infimum et inperfectum: quicquid tot partibus et tam oblique in usus diversissimos explicatis cohaerere vix possit. **6** Ut enim quaeque artium liberalissima est, ita plerunque paucissimis indiget instrumentis: nam et pennicillo pictor et caelo caelator opus suum consummatum[20] reddit, nam color huic, illi marmor haud scio an in artis varietatem ascribenda sint: materiam enim subiec[55v]tam oportuit esse quandam artifici. **7** Aliae vero artes, ut minus ingenuae sunt, ita multiplices magis et abiectiores adhibent modos, veluti aegrum corpus et morbis obnoxium quod fomentis crebrioribus et varia medicamentorum ope substentatur. Nam et natura quoque rerum generibus ut perfectioribus praestantioribusque alioqui et immortalibus et sempiternis numerum quendam assignavit, particularium vero, ut nullam esse scientiam, ita etiam neque numerum voluit.

---

[20] *consumm-* Br. for MS *consum-*, as at 4.1.1; cf. 2.1.2 and n. 2 and 4.2.56 and n. 178.

parental attention, but will begin to deal above all with the concerns that will seem to apply to the life-stage that has passed beyond fatherly authority.[21]

5 Accordingly, my notion of celibacy can be fulfilled, it will be shown, by two obligations[22] – so that if to anyone I perhaps seem to be demanding much, I at least don't seem to be making *many* demands; for that scale of task[23] demonstrates a worth that's based on weight of importance, not of number. For in all the most trifling forms of craftsmanship, so many and such manifold components are needed that something wholly lacking in worth and finish must be very evident from this single consideration: whatever is constituted from so many parts that are so indirectly deployed to very different purposes can hardly have any overall unity.[24] **6** Why? Because the more ennobling each of the arts is, the fewer pieces of equipment it generally needs. Both the painter with his brush and the engraver with his burin bring their own works to completion: I'm not sure whether colour in the former's case and marble in the latter's are to be attributed to any variety of art; for a given material *had* to be placed at the artist's disposal.[25] **7** As for other arts, however, just as they're of a lesser standing, so they apply a greater number of rather lowly methods – in the way an ailing body that's liable to diseases is kept going by rather frequent curatives and by the motley help of medications. For nature too also allocated a certain number to classes of things, as being more complete and in other respects superior, and immortal and everlasting; as for the individual components [of those classes], however, just as nature wanted there to be no special branch of knowledge associated with them, so she also wanted no fixed number of them either.[26]

---

[21] In moving to a more advanced stage in the young celibate's development in Books 3 and 4, the work itself grows and 'matures' in tandem with its subject – a growth factor with teasing implications for Barbaro's authorial positioning in relation to his addressee father, now that Ermolao has himself suggestively reached 'the life-stage that has passed beyond fatherly authority.'

[22] Defined in 3.2.8.

[23] I.e., one limited to stressing two key obligations.

[24] Barbaro touches here on the traditional classical idea of the unity of artistic conception and execution (cf. esp. Arist. *Poet.* 8 1451a16-35, Hor. *Ars P.* 1-37); his wording in 3.2.5 'whatever ... unity' is also strikingly reminiscent of Quint. *Inst.* 2.11.7 *unde fit ut dissoluta et* ex diversis *congesta oratio* cohaerere non possit ('Consequently, the fragmented speech, made up of such diverse elements, cannot hold together'; tr. Russell 2001: 335).

[25] I.e., the tool (brush or burin) is all-important, its skillful deployment primary, the material in/on which it works secondary; pigment or marble here offer no 'variety' in the sense that the artistic agency lies solely with the tool/the hand that applies it.

[26] Rather than a Platonizing vision of the relationship between the defining Forms and the innumerable particular instantiations of them (cf. 1.4.21 and n. 87), Barbaro here invokes a classificatory system that is Aristotelian in colour, with nature ordaining sets of categories that are distinct from the indefinite number of constituents within each category (so, e.g., the subdivision of animal types at *Hist. an.* 1.6 490b8-14, 2.15 505b26-32, 4.1 523a32-b22, 4.8 534b12-15).

8 Divisimus itaque haud indecenter in partis duas caelibatus offitium: harum prima est perpetua observatio castitatis, altera contemplandi voluntaria et constans ratio. Et de ea quidem parte, quae propria esse videtur, quodammodo prius est perscrutandum: nam primo quidem quid ca[56r]ste sit vivere et quid inceste dicemus, postmodum quae sit circa id cura adhibenda pro viribus explanare tentabimus.

[3] Quid sit caste vivere in coniugio.

3.1 Caste vivitur aut in coniugio aut extra coniugium: in coniugio cum nulli praeterquam uxori et illi quidem honeste et moderate congreditur, qualem fuisse Lelium antiquitas omnis attestatur. Nam Socrates, alioqui oraculo Apollinis sapientissimus iudicatus, non solum inceste vixisse comprehensus dicitur, verumetiam duas uxores eodem tempore habuisse memoratur. Quarum tamen usus minus est accusatus, quia lege Atheniensium tenebatur: Romae poena multatus est qui primus uxorem dimisit. **2** Sed et plurimum impietatis habuit aetas illa quae civilia bella praecessit. Nam et Ci[56v]cero Terentiam ex inani suspitione vel nimia in filiam indulgentia thoro seiunxit, et

8 So in no unseemly fashion I've divided the duty of celibacy into two parts: of these, the first is the ceaseless safeguarding of chastity; the second is a willing and unwavering regard for contemplation. And somewhat of a priority for investigation is the aspect [of celibacy] that seems to be its defining feature: I shall speak first of what it is to live chastely, and what to live unchastely; afterwards, I'll try to set out, to the best of my abilities, the serious attention that is to be applied in this matter.

[3] What it is to live chastely in marriage.

3.1 People live chastely either in marriage or outside it: in marriage, when intercourse happens with no one apart from one's wife, and with her in a becoming and measured way[27] – the way in which ancient writers universally assert that Laelius had behaved.[28] Again, Socrates, who was otherwise adjudged the wisest of all by Apollo's oracle,[29] is not only said to have been caught living unchastely,[30] but is also reported to have had two wives at the same time.[31] However, his dealings with them drew less accusation, because they were upheld by Athenian law;[32] at Rome, the first man to divorce his wife was visited with punishment.[33] **2** But the period preceding the civil wars also had the greatest degree of disloyal behaviour. Cicero both excluded Terentia from the marriage bed through groundless suspicion or through excessive fondness for his daughter, and after he eventually took Publi[li]a as his wife

---

[27] In line with Francesco Barbaro's injunction on marital intercourse in *De re uxoria* XVI Griggio 2021: 266–71 (Gnesotto 1915–16: 83.6-86.6; tr. King 2015: 112-14).
[28] Gaius Laelius (*c.* 190–after 128 BCE, cos. 140), nicknamed 'the wise' (e.g., Cic. *Nat. D.* 3.5, *Off.* 2.40, *Tusc.* 5.54), is frequently hailed for his virtuous equanimity, temperance, affability, etc. (so, e.g., Cic. *Fin.* 2.24-5, *Off.* 1.90, *Top.* 78).
[29] See Pl. *Ap.* 21a, D. L. 2.37; a Platonic invention (cf. Montuori 1990)?
[30] With the implication of pederasty (Ath. *Deipno.* 5 219b, Ael. *VH* 4.21; cf. also D. L. 2.19 for report that he was Archelaus' catamite). For Socrates' more general reputation in the Italian Renaissance, and for attempts to make him 'safe for Christianity,' Hankins 2006.
[31] See 2.2.19 and n. 42.
[32] Cf. D. L. 2.26: to expand their population, the Athenians 'decreed that a man could marry one Athenian woman and have children by another; and ... Socrates accordingly did so' (tr. Mensch 2018: 76). For the historical background (the ban on illegitimate offspring lifted during the Peloponnesian War of 431–404 BCE), Wolff 1944: 85–6.
[33] By one tradition, allegedly Sp. Carvilius Ruga (cos. 234, 228) in 231 BCE (albeit chronological variation in the sources), on the grounds of his wife's barrenness (so, e.g., Gell. 4.3.2, 17.21.44, Plut. *Mor.* 267c); but for reports that he was reviled for his action cf. V. Max. 2.1.4, Dion. Hal. *Ant. Rom.* 2.25.7. But for some evidence of divorces before Carvilius' case cf. V. Max. 2.9.2 (L. Annius expelled from the senate after divorcing his wife in 307/6 BCE), 6.3.10-12 with Dixon 1985: 357 and n. 9.

Publiam novissime superinductam eadem animi mollitie dispulit. Quid quod Catoni visum est id esse probabile? is enim suam uxorem Hortensio, illius amore flagranti, concessit neque scelus id esse unquam est ab aliquo animadversum. **3** A quo, ut in non nullis feris est observatum, abhorrere beluae consueverunt: nam aliae quidem iugalia novere vincula, a quibus nullo unquam tempore dissolvuntur; aliae vero cognationis intellectum habent. Quod Nero, humani generis fax,[34] est aspernatus. **4** Is enim et sororum et quamlibet attinentium nuptias fieri posse concessit, legemque impiam senatus auctoritate sancitam voluit, id certe quod in equis et aliis ferme compluribus brutis abominabile et monstruosum est. Fertur [**57r**] equum quandoque adopertis oculis, ut sua stabulariorum industria est, cum matre coiisse: quod ubi deiectis luminum operimentis animadvertisset, veluti infandissimum scelus non ignoraret, praerupta petiit poenamque, quam mereri ex culpa putaverat, sibi ipsi morte sancivit.

5 Nos vero, ut in plerisque aliis, christianae religionis iuvamur institutis, ex quibus qualibet[35] ante inscitia et vanitate obcaecati mirum est quantum

---

[34] *fax* MS; see p. 4 above.
[35] *quam-* MS.

in replacement, he got rid of her with that same weakness of mind.[36] What of the fact that such behaviour seemed to Cato to be acceptable? For he made over his own wife to Hortensius when the latter was burning with love for her, and that was never perceived by anyone to be a criminal act.[37] **3** Wild animals customarily recoil from such behaviour, as is observed in a number of beasts: for some recognize matrimonial bonds from which they're never released at any time; others, moreover, have an understanding of blood relationship – which Nero, the firebrand of the human race, treated with contempt. **4** For he made it possible for marriage to happen with sisters and with relatives to whatever degree, and he wanted the ungodly law sanctioned by senatorial approval[38] – to be sure, a phenomenon that's a detestable monstrosity among horses and, as a rule, many other animals.[39] It's said that a horse had at some point had its eyes covered and – in accordance with the stable-keepers' own deliberate purpose[40] – mated with its mother; when it perceived as much after its eye-coverings were removed, it made for a precipice, as if it were all too aware of a most unspeakable crime, and by its death ratified the punishment that it had thought it deserved because of its crime.[41]

5 We, however, as in most other matters, are helped by the teachings of the Christian religion: it's remarkable how much benefit we take from those teachings after being blinded[42] beforehand by all sorts of ignorance and

---

[36] Cf. for these events 1.2.2 and n. 26. Cicero was crushed by the death in 45 BCE of his beloved daughter, Tullia; he allegedly divorced Publilia not least because of her lack of sympathy for his loss (cf. Plut. *Cic*. 41.5). For the hint of incest in 'excessive fondness for his daughter' cf. [Sall.] *Cic*. 2, Dio Cass. 46.18.6.

[37] For the saga of Marcia's divorce from the sternly Stoic M. Porcius Cato (Cato the younger, 95–46 BCE), her marriage to the orator and statesman Q. Hortensius Hortalus (114–50 BCE), and her subsequent remarriage to Cato after Hortensius' death, see Luc. 2.326-80, Plut. *Cat. min*. 25.

[38] Barbaro appears to modify Francesco Barbaro's allusion in his *De re uxoria* (V.8 Griggio 2021: 204–6 [Gnesotto 1915–16: 44.9–12]; tr. King 2015: 81) to *Claudius Nero* extorting from the senate a decree to legitimize marriage between uncles and their brothers' (but not their sisters') daughters. Francesco refers to the emperor Claudius, whose original name down to his accession in 41 CE was Tiberius Claudius Nero Germanicus; Claudius used such legislation to facilitate his marriage to Agrippina, his niece, in 49 CE (cf. Tac. *Ann*. 12.5-7, Suet. *Claud*. 26.3). In referring to the emperor Nero instead (his full name Nero Claudius Caesar Augustus Germanicus), Ermolao builds on Claudius' initial excess by having Nero shockingly expand the permissible range of incestuous unions in 'with sisters... degree.' At sixteen Nero married his step-sister, Octavia; for allegations also of incestuous union with his mother, Agrippina, cf. Tac. *Ann*. 14.2, Suet. *Ner*. 28.2.

[39] So, e.g., camels and horses in Arist. *Hist. an*. 9.47 630b32-631a8, albeit the incestuous mating of horses is recognized at 6.22 576a18-21.

[40] After Nero's example, the perversity of the keepers' intention is implied.

[41] The anecdote is Aristotelian (cf. *Hist. an*. 9.47 631a1-8), but Barbaro's immediate source appears (given verbal overlaps) to be Plin. *NH* 8.156.

[42] The metaphor in *obcaecati* aligns the misguided with the blinkered horse of 3.3.4.

utilitatis capiamus. His enim non modo a parentum et consanguineorum congressu revocamur, verumetiam matrimonii dignitatem honestissimo sacramento illustramus. **6** Sanctum[43] est enim ut, nisi quis honestam afferat causam et manifestam, eam, quae semel placuit, uxorem nemo dimitteret, et priore dimissa coniuge viva illa nequeat nuptias alias reparare. Quo facto genus humanum ab [**57v**] usus illius impurissimi et more beluarum[44] indiscretissimi dedecore liberatum est atque in aliam quandam praestantiorem consuetudinem revocatum.

7 Quare is caste vivere credendus erit, qui nihil extra thorum maritalem concupiscet, neque ductam semel uxorem a se dimittet; qui vero contrarium horum aliquid[45] faciet, vivet inceste.

[4] Quid sit caste vivere extra coniugium.

4.1 Extra coniugium quoque honeste vivitur et inhoneste. Primo libro, quom de vita iugali et coelibe tractaremus, duo esse genera diximus eorum qui uxore carerent. **2** Hi enim, ut turpissimam vitam ducant et licentiosius peccent, ad omnem libidinis rabiem et quidem ferarum ritu indiscretam proni, carere sotia et teste volunt. Huiuscemodi pestem a civitatibus [**58r**] sapiens rei publicae gubernator exterminabit: inficit et quidem contagio huiuscemodi genus et coinquinat iuventutem, facitque ut suo exemplo, prima quidem facie liberali et in quod leves animi facile respiciant, impudentissimus quisque rem publicam deserat vitiisque nefandissimis implicetur.

---

[43] *sanctum* MS; see p. 5 above.
[44] *bael-* MS.
[45] *-quui* MS.

futility. For we're not only restrained by them from intercourse with parents and blood relatives, but we also give luster to the intrinsic worth of marriage through its most honourable sacrament.[46] **6** For it was laid down that, unless a man puts forward a clear and creditable reason,[47] no one would divorce the wife who had once found favour; and that no one could establish another marriage as long as that former wife he'd divorced still lived.[48] By this development the human race was delivered from the disgrace of that most abominable and (in beastly fashion) indiscriminate malpractice, and summoned to a certain different and superior mode of behaviour.

7 Hence the husband who will have no desire beyond the marital bed and will not divorce the wife he's taken once and for all will have to be considered as living chastely; but the man who does anything contrary to this will live unchastely.

[4] What it is to live chastely outside marriage.

4.1 Outside marriage as well, there is a decent existence, and an indecent one. In the first book, when I was dealing with the married and the celibate life, I said that there were two categories of those who were unmarried.[49] **2** The one group, in order to lead a most shameful life and to sin with a rather wanton abandon (inclined as they are to every conceivable frenzy of passion, and an indiscriminate passion at that, in the manner of wild animals),[50] wants to be without a marriage partner and witness. The prudent state ruler will banish this sort of scourge from communities: to be sure, this sort of stock affects the young with disease and contaminates them, and brings it about that by its own example – with its initially appealing appearance, the kind of example to which fickle minds easily pay heed – all the most shameless men abandon the state and become embroiled in the most unspeakable moral failings.

---

[46] The Christian view of marriage taken in 3.3.5-6 is close in language and thought (esp. on its indissoluble permanence) to Francesco Barbaro's characterization of the Christian way (*Christiana constitutio*) early in *De re uxoria* (I.7-8 Griggio 2021: 184–6 [Gnesotto 1915–16: 30.23-31.15]; tr. King 2015: 70).

[47] Esp. sexual infidelity.

[48] So Matthew 19.9 ('And I say to you: whoever divorces his wife, except for unchastity, and marries another, commits adultery'), Mark 10.11-12; cf. August. *De bon. coni.* 3 (a husband or a wife cast out by the other cannot remarry while the other yet lives).

[49] 1.5.3.

[50] This first group of the unmarried is aligned by verbal similarity with the beastly type in 3.3.6 (cf. *more beluarum indiscretissimi* there and *ferarum ritu indiscretam* here).

3 Quantae auctoritatis Bion sua aetate fuit, cum ob doctrinae opinionem, tum vero maxime ex hac ipsa vita quam detestamur? Is enim hac umbra potissimum adolescentium innocentiam puritatemque corrupit foedavitque. Quod si tum Graecia tantum moribus indulsisset, quam inclinatis ad disciplinarum amorem favoribus curam bene vivendi neglexit, tulissentque fortasse minorem in docendo sciendoque praerogativam, maiorem certe laudem assequuturi fuissent si prius bene facere quam bene dicere [58v] didicissent. 4 Contra romanus fuit mos ut prius fortitudini virtutique operam darent, quam laxatis evulsisque viribus sub scelestissima praeceptoris[51] cura languescerent. Agris enim cultu sano opus est, non fuco aut domibus circum astructis: alioquin sterilescunt. Nam quid dicere similius possum? quando praesertim nihil est sterilius animis iis qui, ad bene vivendum nati, non solum id non praestant, sed etiam fertilitate sublata in lolium fruges convertunt suas.

5 Alterum genus esse diximus huic longe diversum: qui quanvis uxore carere velint, non tamen ad male vivendum ea utuntur occasione, sed ex divinae cuiusdam in terris vitae similitudine, congressus omnes fugiunt et honestissimis cogitationibus detinentur. Primum ergo genus impudice et inceste, proximum pudice et caste degit.

6 Diximus quid inceste, quid caste sit [59r] vivere: nunc quae sit ratio caste vivendi, quis modus in caelibatu adhibendus. Reliquum est ut ostendamus quae esse praecepta debeant ad caste vivendum in caelibatu.

---

[51] -orei MS.

3 How much prestige did Bion command in his own time, not just because of his reputation for learning, but especially as a result of this very existence I abhor?[52] For he, above all through this empty appearance [of greatness], polluted and perverted the unsullied blamelessness of the young. But if at that time Greece had shown as much regard for good morals as it did disregard for attending to living well because their enthusiasms were drawn to a passion for specialized learning – and if they'd perhaps acquired a less privileged status in teaching and knowledge – they would surely have been set to win greater praise if they'd learnt to act well before speaking well. **4** By contrast, it was the Roman way to devote attention to courage and moral excellence[53] rather than to become enfeebled through the slackening and uprooting of one's strength under a teacher's most villainous attention. For fields need sensible cultivation, not fancy embellishment or houses built around them; otherwise they lose their fertility. What can I say that's more apposite – especially since there's nothing more barren than those minds that, though born to live well, not only don't produce that result, but also lose their fertility and transform their own yield into weeds?[54]

5 I've said that the other sort is far different from this one – the sort who, though they want to be free of a wife, nevertheless don't exploit that circumstance to live improperly, but – in imitation of a certain divine existence on earth – avoid all sexual unions and are preoccupied by the most upright forms of reflection. The first group lives, then, in a sinful state of sexual impurity, the one just mentioned, in chaste purity.

6 I've said what it is to live unchastely, and what chastely; and, now, what the guiding principle is of living chastely, and what mode of life is to be adopted in celibacy. It remains for me to set out the precepts that necessarily apply to living chastely in celibacy.

---

[52] For Bion, 2.3.12-13 and nn. 59-61. After an early period in Athens, he wandered throughout the Greek world, an itinerant lecturer and teaching for money; as if a super-spreader of pollution in his wanderings, he here prepares the way for Barbaro's vision below of Greece pervaded by moral corruption.

[53] For such quintessential Roman values defined by contrast with Greek ways cf. esp. Virg. *Aen.* 6.847-53 – values portrayed by moralizing Roman historians as corrupted by the effects of Rome's rise to prosperity (so, e.g., Sall. *Cat.* 9.1-12.5, Liv. Pref. 11-12). In stressing Roman virtue here, Barbaro exploits, and indirectly endorses, the myth of Venice as the new Rome (see Vol. 1 Intro. p. 10).

[54] Powerfully ironic: if the unmarried reprobate is 'barren' of mind like the sterile field, the contemplative celibate is a model of 'sensible cultivation' and productive fertility.

[5] Praecepta ad caste vivendum in coelibatu.

5.1 Duo auxilia sunt reperta, quibus homines quae volunt assequi possunt et tueri: unum ut quae utilia et conducentia sunt admoveantur, alterum ut contraria et repugnantia evitentur. In morbis enim aegritudinibusque non modo ea solet adhiberi curatio, quae pharmacis aut medicamentis opituletur, sed vel tum[55] maxime perspici consuevit ne adversis aut cibo aut potu utatur aegrotus. **2** Servandae quoque valitudinis ratio non solum habebitur si corpus aut lucta aut cursu aut saltu exerceatur, verumetiam si ea fugiantur quae adversari videbuntur. Sed et materiarius faber non modo quae ad usum [**59v**] suum faciant, ut lignum et lapides, comparat, sed et a ventis[56] et imbribus quantum potest operam suam defendit. **3** In brutis quoque non possumus eam diligentiam desyderare; in plerisque enim tantus est rerum suarum intellectus, ut foetus suos non solum cibatu sustentent, sed etiam a contrariis frigoribus et inimicis animalibus tueantur, neque ad pascua prius proficiscantur quam in tuto domum suam et natos collocarint.

4 Signum autem eorum quae dicta sunt est id quod medici, tum demum quum desperata est aegri salus, nihil iubent vetari amplius quod ille concupiscat, quo manifestius sit iis quibus spes est aliqua convalescendi plurimum esse laborandum ne a contrariis laedantur. Quod si ea est cura adhibenda iis qui aegrotant, haud scio an maiorem [**60r**] iis adhibendam[57] putem, qui sani sunt et valentes. Quanvis enim aegroti periculo propius videantur, saepe tamen evenit ut, admotis iis quae contrariabantur, sani sint repente facti: ex iis vero qui boni habitus essent, nemo fuit unquam cui[58]

---

[55] *vel tum* Br. 103 n. 1 for MS *vultum*.
[56] *comparat sed et ventos et imbres quantum potest ab opere suo defendit sed et a ventis* MS: a fusion of alternative readings (one a marginal variant?) in the antigraph (cf. Br. 103 n. 2)?
[57] *-am* MS; *-a* Br.
[58] *qui* MS.

[5] Principles for living chastely in celibacy.

5.1 Two sources of help are found by which people can attain what they want and safeguard it: one is the application of beneficial expedients, the other the avoidance of their harmful opposites.[59] For in diseases and illnesses the treatment usually applied isn't just the sort that helps through drugs or medications, but even then very close attention is usually given to ensuring that the patient experiences nothing harmful in food or drink. **2** Also, a systematic way of maintaining good health will be established not just if the body gets exercise through wrestling, running, or jumping, but also if things that will seem to oppose it are avoided. But the builder, too, not only prepares the materials that are suited to his own purpose, such as wood and stones, but also protects his day's work from the winds and rain as much as he can. **3** In animals as well, we can't find any lack of that careful attitude; for in most of them, their consciousness of their own circumstances is so great that they not only provide their own young with food, but also protect them from conditions of harmful cold and hostile predators, and they don't head out to feed before they've made their own dwelling and offspring safe.

4 Evidence of what's been said is the fact that only at the point when a patient's health is beyond hope do doctors give instructions for nothing he craves to be forbidden any longer; [they do so] for it to be clearer to those with some hope of recovery that every possible effort is to be made for them not to be harmed by opposite influences. But if such treatment is to be applied to the sick, I'm not sure I think it's to be applied in any greater measure to the hale and hearty. For though the sick seem closer to danger, it's nevertheless often happened that they were suddenly made well when antithetical measures were applied to them;[60] but of those of a healthy disposition, there was never anyone who gained benefit from things that do harm. **5** I'll be

---

[59] Barbaro touches lightly on the instinct for self-preservation that was fundamental to the Stoic doctrine of 'affiliation' (*oikeiōsis*), extending outward from the newborn's impulse to preserve itself to the mature animal's care for its offspring (cf. 2.4.17 and n. 99; hence the pertinence of Barbaro's allusion to animals protecting their young in 3.5.3). Central to that impulse are (i) the young animal's desire for things conducive to its health and wellbeing, and (ii) the rejection of their opposites; see, e.g., Cic. *Fin.* 3.16, Sen. *Ep.* 121.17-21 with Inwood 2007: 332–3, 342–5.

[60] That opposites are a cure for opposites is already stated as a general principle in several parts of the Hippocratic corpus (see, e.g., *Nat. hom.* 9 [6.52 Littré] with Schiefsky 2005: 225-6 on *Vet. med.* 13.2 τῷ ὑπεναντίῳ προσήκει λῦσαι); and the implication of a 'balanced treatment' in Barbaro's account (i.e., a degree of 'opposite' applied in proportion to the degree of deviation from normal health) is also ancient, as in, e.g., Galen's second-century CE *De const. art.* 16 (1.283-4 Kühn = Johnston 2016: 102–5).

inimicae res profuerint. **5** Contentus ero uno illo exemplo Pheraei,[61] qui, quom vomica laboraret iamque a medicis deploratus mortem in acie quaereret, ea parte pectoris, qua morbus inerat, vulneratus, medicinam invenit. Rara sunt aut nulla prorsus experimenta quae diversum probent.

6 Quare et in virtute acquirenda, et ea maxime quae difficilior est et, ut ita loquar, supra naturam, magis diligentius est insudandum ne ab adversis puritas nostra laedatur. Quamobrem primum quidem naturae ritu, quae prius contrarias vires expellit quam novas inducat, quid [**60v**] cavendum sit iis, qui pudice victuri sunt, aperiemus; ordine deinde suo quid faciendum ut id assequantur processu docebimus.

7 Sensus in nobis sunt, quorum diversae sunt actiones: ut enim auribus sonos, oculis colores, olphactu odores, gustu cibum et potum, tactu calidum frigidum et reliqua huiuscemodi complura percipimus, ita variae sunt et multiplices sensuum potestates. **8** Sequitur autem sentientem voluptas vel dolor, quibus pro usu rei affici solemus: voluptatis autem et doloris quidam est modus, ut neque nimium delectari neque dolere vehementer sine vitio et reprehensione possimus. Quom enim bene et male uti sensibus in nostra potestate positum sit, virtutem et vitium, decus et dedecus, laudem et vituperationem nos ipsi generamus.

9 Sensuum vero pernitiosissimus gustus et tactus. Erramus [**61r**] et per visum et auditum, sed minus et rarius: nam olfactus minima est gratia

---

[61] *phalerei* MS.

satisfied with the single well-known example of the man from Pherae:[62] when he was ill with an abscess and the doctors had already despaired of him, he sought death in battle; wounded in the part of his chest where the malady was lodged, he found his cure. Examples that demonstrate the opposite[63] are scarce or altogether non-existent.

6 Hence in both the acquisition of virtue, and especially that branch of virtue that's harder to attain and, so to speak, beyond nature, the more attentively we must sweat at the task of preventing our chasteness from being harmed by opposite influences. Therefore, in the manner of nature, which dispels harmful influences before bringing different ones to bear, I'll first explain what needs to be guarded against by those who are set to live chastely; then, in its due order, I'll demonstrate what must be done so that they successfully attain that goal.

7 We possess senses that operate in different ways: for just as we perceive sounds with our ears, colours with the eyes, odours through smell, food and drink through taste, hot and cold through touch, and all the many other things of this sort, so the capacities of the senses are many-sided in their variety. **8** When the senses are engaged, pleasure or pain ensues, and we are usually affected by them in proportion to our experience of a given circumstance. But there's a certain limit of pleasure and pain, so that we can neither enjoy ourselves to excess nor feel grievously pained without blemish and censure.[64] For since we have it in our power to use our senses for good and ill, we ourselves give rise to virtue and vice, honour and dishonour, praise and recrimination.

9 Certainly, the most harmful of the senses are taste and touch.[65] We also go wrong through sight and hearing, but to a lesser extent and more rarely.

---

[62] Jason, fourth-century BCE tyrant of Pherae in Thessaly. For the following anecdote cf. Cic. *Nat. D.* 3.70, V. Max. 1.8 ext. 6, Sen. *Ben.* 2.18.8, but close verbal overlaps identify Plin. *NH* 7.166 as Barbaro's precise reference-point. Of these four sources, all but Seneca name Jason; despite not specifying Jason, Barbaro perhaps quietly exploits the irony of his name here (Gk. *Iāsōn* linked to *īaomai* 'heal': Mackie 2001), in that Jason inadvertently heals himself when seeking death in battle.

[63] I.e., the healthy helped by antithetical means.

[64] This limit is differently achieved in different philosophical systems. In Stoicism, pleasure and pain are two (of four) types of passion, and to assent to these impulses is irrational – in contrast to the reasonable affective responses (*eupatheiai*) that are joy (*chara*), caution (*eulabeia*), and wish (*boulēsis*; further, Inwood 1999: 699–705). In Epicureanism, assessment of whether or not to pursue a given pleasure ('the hedonistic calculus') weighed its future effects/consequences for better and worse and moderated action accordingly (further, Tsouna 2017: 59–65). The self-control exercised by Barbaro's celibate in 3.5 is Stoic in colouration, while the pleasure seeking he condemns smacks of hedonism of the most extreme kind, philosophical (cf. the examples in 3.5.14-16) or otherwise.

[65] The two basest sources of sensory pleasure because animals, too, derive pleasure from them, but not from the other three senses in the aesthetically discerning way humans do (cf. nn. 70–1 below): see Arist. *EE* 3.2.9-11 1230b36-1231a7, *EN* 3.10 1118a23-6, [Arist.] *Pr.* 28.2 949b6-12, 28.7 949b37-950a16 (the latter cited by Gell. 19.2.5).

paucissimisque id peccandi genus obesse consuevit et perditissimi quique vix ea gaudent voluptate. At gustus et tactus fons est communium scelerum et publicae pestis fomentum, in homine praesertim, cui, quom a multis in reliquis superetur, ex sensibus tactus et gustus deinde ante omnia melior est. Altero Veneris faces imbibimus, altero Venerem experimur: quorum utrunque[66] nostro abegimus coelibatu. **10** Nam cibi et potus eam velim curam adhiberi, ut nihil sit pertimescendum magis quam impleti ventris dominatus.[67] Ferimur enim quo ducit appetitus, mente devincta et sensibus abdicatis manibus pedibusque a suo deiectis munere; nullus rationi locus, nullae monitis aures, nulla conscientiae refragatio; ducuntur una spiritus, animi sensus, voluntas: [61v] omnia ad scelus administrant. Consentiunt membra venis oppletis, corpus omne pronum et inclinatum iacet. **11** Quid plura? Nulla spes libidinis refrenandae: furens, amens et concitatus, quo vadat quid moliatur ignarus, praerupta petit, et in caput ruit suum, gladium et arma furiosus in suam comparat necem et iugulum ultro petit; neque consistit prius enerve illud et temporarium robur quam impurissimae cupiditatis, utcumque[68] obvius feratur, turpitudinem expleat.

---

[66] *utrun-* MS; *utrum-* Br.
[67] *-atum* MS.
[68] *utcumque* Br. 105 n. 1 for MS *utrunque*.

Smell has the least influence; blundering in that way usually does harm to very few people, and all the most depraved types hardly take delight in that source of pleasure.[69] But taste and touch are the origin of commonplace outrages and the instigator of a general pestilence, especially in man; even though he's surpassed by many creatures in all the rest,[70] of the senses touch and then taste are better developed in him before all the species.[71] With the one we drink in the flames of love, and with the other we have tangible experience of love;[72] each of them I've banished from our state of celibacy. **10** Moreover, such is the attention that I'd want to be applied to food and drink that nothing is more to be feared than the tyranny of a stuffed stomach.[73] For we're carried where desire leads us, with the mind in fetters, and, our senses disowned, our hands and feet are deposed from their usual function;[74] there's no place for reason, no ears for advice, no resistance from moral consciousness; the spirit, mental self-awareness, and freewill are led away in company together; everything works towards villainy. The limbs comply with their stuffed veins, and the entire body lies face down and sunken. **11** Why go on? There's no hope of reining in lust: crazed, out of his mind, and all shaken up, [such a type] doesn't know where he's going and what he's doing, he's heading for the cliff edge[75] and rushing to attack his own life, madly making his sword and weapons ready for his own death and voluntarily reaching for his own jugular; nor does that weak and transitory burst of strength come to a halt before it fulfills the foulness of his filthiest lust, however he's brought to confront it.

---

[69] Presumably because their sense of smell is blunted by their debauched ways.

[70] I.e., in the three senses apart from touch and taste – an interpretation confirmed by Barbaro's explicit recourse to Plin. *NH* 10.191: *ex sensibus ante cetera homini tactus, dein gustatus; reliquis superatur a multis* ('Among the senses, that of touch in man ranks before all the other species, and taste next; but in the remaining senses he is surpassed by many other creatures'; tr. Rackham 1983: 413–15).

[71] '[B]etter developed' in terms not necessarily of the pitch or keenness of physical sensation, but of aesthetic discernment and enjoyment. Humans are said by Cicero at *Nat. D.* 2.145 to excel the lower animals in *all* the senses, but human superiority is more usually asserted in only certain of them, esp. taste and touch (see nn. 65, 70 with Pease 1955–8: 2.927-8).

[72] I.e., the food and drink we taste induce the heat of lust (cf. 3.5.17-18); to stress the erotic challenge to the celibate, Barbaro directs both taste and touch to the same sexual end, not to gluttony and lust respectively (as in, e.g., Gell. 19.2.3 after [Arist.] *Pr.* 28.7 949b38-950a2).

[73] The link between the sated belly and lust is underscored by the wordplay in *Veneris/Venerem* and *ventris*.

[74] The tyranny of desire over reason is here cast in Stoic terms: Latin *appetitus* (Gk. *hormē*) is a 'too vigorous impulse ... which varies widely from the consistency of nature' (Cic. *Tusc.* 4.47; tr. Graver 2002: 56) unless tamed by reason; cf. 1.4.23 and nn. 88, 91.

[75] Like the suicidal horse in 3.3.4 *praerupta petiit*.

12 Neque solum haec ipsa crapulandi luxuries magna et praeclara contemplaturis adversatur, mentemque a divinissimo et praestantissimo munere alienat, verumetiam et minora tractaturis plurimum detrimenti affert; neque solum animi offitiis adversatur et corporis, sed etiam valitudinem quatit et vegetationem. **13** Ut enim a minoribus [**62r**] exempla non petantur, philosophorum maximi, quos honoris causa libentius nominarem, hausto licentius mero et conviviis supramodum frequentatis decessisse produntur; quo minus etiam valet apud nonnullos Platonicae[76] sanctitatis fides, quam dicta et praecepta Socraticae[77] integritatis facere certissimam potuissent, nisi repugnantia scriptis, ut aiunt, facta et symposia mirifice adamata e sententia homines exturbassent. **14** Nam de Aristippo, tametsi eiusdem magistri scholis uso, minus est mirum, quom incontinentiam palam amplecteretur: is enim, quom nihil tantum caveret quam ne sensus ullius periret voluptas, utpote ad quam omnia, ut ea Cyrenaicorum opinio est, referre tentaret, ita cibi et potus intemperans fuit, ut sitim aut famem, ut aiunt, senserit nunquam. Sed parum in hoc errabat [**62v**] et alioqui laudari solet haec cura, praesertim[78] vero a medicis, a quibus haec omnia impetrantur. **15** At nulla erat excusatio amplius,

---

[76] *Plat-* MS; *plat-* Br.
[77] *Socr-* MS; *socr-* Br.
[78] *cura praesertim* Br.

12 Not only does this gluttonous overindulgence in drunkenness itself adversely affect those aiming to reflect on ideas of great grandeur, estranging the mind from its most divine and preeminent function, but it also does a very great deal of damage to those who are set to embark on lesser matters as well; nor does it adversely affect just the functions of the mind and body, but it also shatters good health and energetic vitality. **13** For (so as not to seek examples from a lesser order) the very greatest of philosophers – I'd more than gladly name them for the sake of honouring them – reportedly died from drinking wine with abandon and from excessive attendance at feasts. Hence quite a few people have less strength of confidence in Plato's integrity: his words and teachings could have generated the surest faith in Socrates' moral uprightness, were it not that the contradiction (as they say) between his actions and writings and his amazing passion for symposia had driven people to change their thinking.[79] **14** Again, although he was associated with the followers of that same teacher,[80] there's less surprise about Aristippus,[81] since he openly embraced self-indulgence. He took pains to ensure more than anything that the pleasure of no sensory experience was ever lost – since (in conformity with the Cyrenaic belief) he tried to evaluate everything in terms of pleasure.[82] So lacking in self-control was he in food and drink that he never, they say, experienced thirst or hunger.[83] But in this respect he wasn't particularly misguided: in other circumstances this concern [to have no want of food or drink] is usually praised, and in fact especially by doctors, from whom permission is granted for all such things.[84] **15** But there was no longer any justification when it came to

---

[79] An extreme caricature of Socrates, who is portrayed in the Platonic *Symposium* as relatively abstemious in his drinking habits, and never visibly drunk when he does imbibe (220a; cf. Xen. *Mem.* 1.3.5-6, *Symp.* 2.24-6). Drunkenness is strictly forbidden among the Guardian class in Plato's *Republic* (3 398e, 403e), and allowed but carefully controlled in the *Laws* (cf. 1 637a-650b, 2 666a-e, 671c-672a with Belfiore 1986: 424–5); for Plato's position in the *Laws* distorted into a license for indulgence, Gell. 15.2.1-3 (a distortion corrected in 15.2.4-8). For Plato's own alleged modesty of appetite and opposition to intoxication cf. Cic. *Tusc.* 5.100, D. L. 3.39 with Swift Riginos 1976: 123–4 Anecdote 78.
[80] Socrates.
[81] For whom 1.4.18 and n. 80, 2.3.9-10.
[82] For the Cyrenaic system encapsulated cf. Cic. *Fin.* 2.39-41, *Off.* 3.116 (they 'placed all good in pleasure and considered that virtue should be praised only on the grounds that it was productive of pleasure'; tr. Griffin and Atkins 1991: 145), D. L. 2.86-90.
[83] With the implicit critique that self-control is necessary for pleasure (cf. Xen. *Mem.* 4.5.9): such control (*enkrateia*), not its opposite (*akrasia*), leads to pleasure because enduring hunger, thirst, etc., generates desire for pleasurable eating, drinking, etc. – desires annulled by permanent gratification of the Aristippean kind (further, Johnson 2009: 219–20).
[84] I.e., concerning the adequate intake of food and drink. Bitingly ironic: Barbaro paradoxically aligns Cyrenaic hyper-satisfaction of hunger and thirst with medically tempered satiation.

quom ad ebrietatem, ad[85] lassitudinem veniebat; sed neque hoc omni supplicio dignum esset, nisi deterius sequeretur et in venerem pronior post saturitatem cuiusque mens fieret. Repit enim violenta quaedam et inexpugnabilis incitatio pedetentim[86] iacensque animi minime repugnantis robur armata confodit, resurgentes igniculos fugat, pallentes spiritus et dormientes passim libera populatur, agit in praedam omnia: turpissimo demum et miserabili modo captivam temperantiam secum absportat et rapit.

16 Non ea mollitie Xenocratis Atheniensis animus intabuit, quippe quem non solum turpissima haec culinae sagacitas nunquam a continentiae virtutisque, quam semel praesumpsit concepitque, opinione [**63r**] discussit, verumetiam neque Phrynes illius pulchritudo, quam tota admiratur antiquitas, laudatissima scilicet et ad omnia libidinum incitamenta sufficiens, neque alia ulla impuritas contaminavit. Noverat enim vir praestantissimus posse homine indignum videri si cupiditatibus passim obviis et abiectissimae illarum servituti nobilissimam rationis particulam, ferarum more, summisisset.

17 Sed his ita tractatis, iam ad praecepta veniamus, ea scilicet quae ad cibi et potus abstinentiam pertinent. Tria sunt quae intemperantiam in esu faciant et quae ad libidinem et corpus et mentem inflamment: primum est frequenter, alterum admodum, tertium adversa comedere. Interest enim plurimum quo quis utatur cibo; ciborum enim alii ex inflatione, alii ex caliditate vescentibus nocent. **18** Nam et conchylia et tubera vene[**63v**]rem cient membris vento turgentibus, et Pythagoricis ex eo interdictum est ne faba uterentur; inflat enim is cibus et mentis tranquillitati contrariatur; idem quoque, ut inquit

---

[85] *ad lass-* Br. 105 n. 2 for MS *ad ebrietatem lass-*.
[86] *peded-* MS.

drunkenness and heavy fatigue; but not even *this* would warrant full punishment, if there weren't a worse consequence and everyone's mind didn't become more eager for sex after an abundance [of food and drink]. For a certain aggressive and unassailable arousal gradually creeps in and transfixes with its weapons the dormant strength of our mind, whose resistance is virtually non-existent; it dispels the sparks[87] that rise again, and freely ravages our pale and somnolent spirits on all fronts, seizing everything as plunder; in the end, in the most shameful and wretched manner, it makes self-control its captive, carrying it off and snatching it away. **16** The mind of Xenocrates the Athenian[88] wasted away through no such softness, as is to be expected of one who was not only never shaken from his reputation for virtuous self-restraint (qualities he chose and adopted for himself once and for all) by this most shameful keenness of culinary wit, but also never corrupted by the beauty of that famous Phryne,[89] who is universally admired by the ancients (her beauty was praised to the skies, to be sure, and well capable of every conceivable arousal of lust), or by any other form of defilement. For that most excellent man recognized that it could seem unworthy of a human if, in the manner of wild animals, he'd subjected that most uplifting element of reason to desires that are encountered everywhere, and to the most sordid slavery to them.

17 But after dealing with these matters in this way, let's now come to precepts; I mean, of course, those having to do with restraint in food and drink. There are three factors that cause a lack of self-control in eating and inflame both body and mind towards lust: the first is eating often; the second is eating in large amounts; the third is eating what's bad for you.[90] For it very much matters what food a person consumes: some foods are harmful to those eating them because of flatulence, others because of the hotness [they induce]. **18** For instance, both shellfish and truffles[91] rouse up sexual feeling in limbs swollen with wind, and for that reason Pythagoreans were forbidden to consume beans (for that food causes flatulence and is antithetical to calmness of mind);[92] as Aristotle says and Plutarch recalls, Pythagoras is also

---

[87] *igniculos* is markedly Ciceronian in the positive sense of a 'spark' of virtue vel sim. (cf. *Fin.* 5.18, *Leg.* 1.33, *Tusc.* 3.2).
[88] For whom 2.5.11 and n. 124; cf. also 3.5.28, 4.2.6.
[89] For this famed courtesan's failure to seduce the indomitable Xenocrates, V. Max. 4.3 ext. 3a-b, D. L. 4.7 (where another courtesan, Lais, is also thwarted).
[90] Barbaro's treatment of sleep shows a similar tripartite division of categories at 3.5.69.
[91] Delicacies (so, e.g., Sen. *Dial.* 1.3.6, *Ep.* 89.22, Plin. *NH* 19.33-5, Juv. 5.116-19, 14.7), their luxuriousness itself implying moral corruption.
[92] Cf. for the Pythagorean prohibition Plin. *NH* 18.118, Tert. *De an.* 48.3 (with Waszink 2010: 511–12). But Barbaro alludes explicitly to Cic. *Div.* 1.62 (cf. also 2.119), albeit seemingly via the Ciceronian quotation in Gell. 4.11.3, given Barbaro's reliance on that same Gellian source immediately below (see n. 95).

Aristoteles et Plutarchus meminit, a vulva, corde et marina urtica fertur abstinuisse. Piper vero et aromatum genera, calefactis intestinis, iacentem quasi materiam et quodammodo algescentem pertinaciter excitant: quo fit ut torpescentes igniculi veluti silvis admotis suscitentur, furentibus deinde flammis pars quaeque cedat atque succumbat.

19 Superius autem, quom comedere diximus, cibum et potum intelligi volumus: non enim est ita[93] imprudens quispiam ut eum qui multum devoret multum etiam absorbere non putet, nisi forte mihi multos obieceris qui vino non utantur, plerosque etiam qui omnino nihil epotent. [**64r**] **20** Iulium Viatorem accepimus, quom aquae sub cutem fusae morbo laboraret, humoribus omnibus abstinuisse, in senectute etiam verso in naturam usu potu caruisse. Sed quota horum portio? Aut quis vinum aut potum, praeterquam ex nausea aut aegritudine motus, non virtute ulla, contempsit? **21** Sed, age, etiam plerique ultro id fecerint; nobis minor cura relinquetur, si potandi usum abiicere caelebs voluerit. Quod si carere potu decreverit unusquisque, quod tamen non penitus approbo, nos saltem bene diximus in comedendo multum aut frequenter aut quae contrariantur gulae vitia esse compraehensa.

22 Cavendum est igitur, ut ad propositum revertamur, ne nobis ipsis nostra cupiditas obsit. Id vero facile assequemur si tria haec, compendio absoluta, velut inimica pernitiosaque caveamus. Sciant autem [**64v**] inprimis[94] necesse est, qui adhibere animum ad instructionem hanc volent, nihil esse perditissimo homine dignius quam gulae servire. **23** Is morbus tantae vilitatis est et habetur, ut praeter hanc culpam singula scelera veniam aliquam apud diversas nationes impetrarint. Nam reliqua peccatorum genera partem aliquam et similitudinem virtutis prae se ferunt, aut fragilitate humana

---

[93] *ista* MS.
[94] *inprimis* MS; *in primis* Br.

said to have steered clear of sow's womb, heart, and sea-anemone.[95] Moreover, by warming the guts, pepper and the various kinds of spices resolutely stir up the bodily matter (as it were) that just lies there, growing somewhat cold; hence the tiny sparks that languish listlessly are roused as if by a supply of kindling, and each part [of the guts] subsequently gives way in surrender to the raging flames.[96]

19 Above, when I said 'eat,' I meant both food and drink to be understood; for no one's so obtuse as not to imagine that the glutton who gobbles up a lot also gulps down a lot – unless perhaps you cite as counter-examples against me the many who don't consume wine, and also the oh-so-many who drink absolutely nothing at all. **20** We're told that Julius Viator, when he was suffering from the malady of water spreading under his skin, refrained from liquids of every kind, and that in old age he went against natural practice by doing without drinking.[97] But how many such cases are there? Or who disdained wine or drinking except one moved to do so as a result of nausea or illness, not any virtue? **21** But come, suppose even most people did this of their own accord: I'll be left with a reduced responsibility if the celibate wants to give up his practice of drinking. But if each and everyone decided to do without drinking (a circumstance, however, that I don't altogether commend), I've at least fittingly stated that flaws are observed in eating a lot, or often, or what goes against natural appetite.

22 We must therefore ensure – to get back to the point – that our desire doesn't work to our own disadvantage. We shall doubtless easily achieve as much if we guard against these three factors as being (in brief summation) harmful and destructive. But those who'll want to apply their minds to this training have to know above all that nothing more befits the most dissolute of people than slavery to appetite.[98] **23** That affliction is – and is regarded as – of such baseness that every single act of villainy apart from this cause of reproach has won some measure of forgiveness among different peoples. Why? Because the other categories of wrongdoing exhibit some degree of virtue and a resemblance to it, or they find excuse in human frailty;

---

[95] Barbaro draws on Gellius' report (4.11.11-13) of Plutarch's own quotation from Aristotle (*Hom. stud.* fr. 122 Sandbach 1969: 238–9; Ross 1955: 133 fr. 4); further, D. L. 8.19, Plut. *Mor.* 670d, Porph. *Vit. Pyth.* 45.

[96] I.e., despite the positive connotation of the sparks (*igniculi*) here (cf. n. 87 above), they are over-stimulated by the warming effects of pepper, etc.

[97] The condition is dropsy. Barbaro draws explicitly on Plin. *NH* 7.78; if the first-century CE Ti. Julius Viator is meant, he may have been personally known to Pliny (Beagon 2005: 262).

[98] The well-worn slavery metaphor (e.g., Sen. *Dial.* 7.4.4, *Ep.* 39.6, 110.9, *Q. Nat.* 4b.13.11) complements and extends that of the soul incarcerated by the body (cf. 2.5.6 and n. 113).

excusantur: haec una gulositatis et ventris et gutturis lues imago est simulachrumque ignobilitatis. **24** Quo fit ut haud immerito tam iacens luxus et resupinum malum nulla virtute aut generositate tolerabile videatur, sed sine advocato et defensore contumeliis omnium et probris expositum quottidie miserabiliter fatigetur. Beluis propemodum incognitum est hoc vitium, ut mirum sit quor, quom eo sensu non careant, carere nihilominus [**65r**] vitio possint, sed et a caeteris quoque peccatis naturae beneficio liberatae sunt.

25 Nobis id est negatum et innumerabilibus hostibus obiectus est cuiusque animus: incerta victoria est, sed speranda et viribus omnibus de manu inimicorum extorquenda; fragile est et caducum robur, sed in animi potestate positum et substentatum. Si flumen impetu ruat, obicibus obstruendum est ostium,[99] alioqui vorabit omnia; ego, si procella in mari iactabor, navem anchoris infrenabo: si opus erit pluribus, agam pluribus. **26** At hoc melius succurrere nobis ipsis possumus quam nautae sibi: ii enim, si gravior tempestas invaserit aut si rudentes exesi fluctibus defecerint,[100] una cum navigio summergentur; nobis vero ea conditio est ut nunquam volentibus animi desint, nunquam auxilia intervertantur; semper adest vegeta illa vis [**65v**] et quidem recentissima spiritus animalis, qui quom lubet ab obsidione protinus hostem pellit, quom parum etiam audet fugat.

27 Iram nos et fastum, invidiam, odia, luxum, avaritiam nos ipsi contra nos alimus et armamus: si rursus poeniteat, eosdem exarmabimus quos ultro nostris telis instruximus. Nemo cogitur ad ulciscendum vindictae libidine,

---

[99] *host-* MS; but for *ost-*, Br. 107 n. 1.
[100] *defic-* MS.

but this plague alone, of gluttony of both stomach and throat, is the picture and image of vileness. **24** Hence such sluggish super-indulgence and slothful sinfulness seem for good reason beyond toleration by any high-minded nobility of character; but since they're exposed on a daily basis, without a supporting counsel for the defense, to the insulting reproaches of all-comers, they are wretchedly worn out. This vice is virtually unknown to wild animals, so that it's surprising why, since they don't lack that sensory capacity [of taste],[101] they can nevertheless be free of the vice; but by nature's kindness they are also freed from the other sins[102] as well.

25 That kindness is denied to us humans, and everyone's mind is exposed to countless enemies. Whether we can win is uncertain, but victory must be hoped for and wrenched from the enemies' hands with all vigor; our strength is impermanent and frail, but located and sustained in the power of the mind. If a river rushes on headlong with a violent surge, its mouth is to be blocked by obstacles; otherwise it will devour everything.[103] For my part, if I'll be tossed by a storm at sea, I shall make fast[104] the ship with anchors; if more anchors are needed, I'll do so with more. **26** But in this matter we're better able to help ourselves than can sailors help themselves; for if too severe a storm assails them, or if the ropes fail after being worn away by the waves, they will be sunk along with the ship. *Our* situation, on the other hand, is such that, so long as we want it, our spirits never fail, and forms of help are never misapplied: ever-present is that vigorous – and yes, that most freshly energized – force of living spirit that right away, when it pleases, repulses the enemy from his state of siege, and puts him to flight when it's even not particularly venturesome.[105]

27 We, we ourselves, nurture and arm against ourselves anger and pride, envy, hatred, self-indulgence, and greed; if, on the other hand, we feel regret, we shall disarm the same agencies we've voluntarily equipped with our own weaponry. No one is forced to take revenge out of a passion for vengeance, and no one is constrained by a desire to incur, against his will, feelings of guilt

---

[101] See 3.5.9 and nn. 65, 70–1.
[102] I.e., 'the other categories of wrongdoing' in 3.5.23.
[103] The mouth metaphor in *ostium* (cf. *OLD* 2b) is apt, the river's voracious appetite (*vorabit omnia*) matching the glutton's (cf. 3.5.19 de*voret*).
[104] *infreno -are* lit. 'put a bridle on a horse' (*OLD* 1), but also used fig. of mooring a boat; hence aptly applied here, complementing the 'reining in' (*refreno*) of lusty appetite in 3.5.11, 30.
[105] Beyond their dramatic effect, the comparisons with struggling against the stormy seas and repulsing the besieging enemy give different nuance to the contemplative celibate as 'active' (cf. 1.4.14 and n. 74; Vol. 1 Intro. pp. 18–19, 21, 23–4): by analogy, he now actively battles against the billowing assaults of vice.

nemo impellitur cupidine ad culpas scelerum invitus contrahendas. **28** Si thesaurum videro, aut eum qui in arce Atheniensium adservabatur aut eum qui in templis Flaviae gentis tam pretiosus et largus vulgo ferebatur, si Darii gemmas illas orientales et indicas opes in oculis manibusque habuero, fieri potest ut, si nolim, quicquam absportem? Xenocrates atque Pericles Athenienses ambo Alexandri pecunias ultro aspernati sunt, ego illas invitus [**66r**] rapiam? **29** Si ad lautissimam coenam, quales fuisse L. Luculli memorantur, cibis, inquam, pretio et sapore praestantibus et omni luxuriae copia affluentem invitabor, implebo ventrem ad summum et ferri sinam gulae imperio adversante animo et repugnante? At in convivium semel vocatus Menedemus domumque ingressus, quom splendidissimos apparatus animadvertisset, quam primum qua venit regressus est.

 30 Frustra nobis inesset ea ratio, qua a coeteris animantibus segregamur, nisi et insitas libidines refrenare et insurgentes animi morbos tollere aut sedare possemus. Tueantur itaque se homines suamque vitam vendicent a

for crimes committed. **28** If I saw a treasure-trove, either that kept under guard on the Athenian acropolis[106] or that which, by common report, was so valuable and copious in the temples of the Flavian family,[107] or if I beheld and handled those fabulous jewels from the East, Darius' Indian riches[108] – can it be that, if I didn't want to, I'd make off with anything? The Athenians Xenocrates and Pericles both of their own accord spurned Alexander's money:[109] would I grab it against my will? **29** If I'm invited to a most sumptuous dinner of the sort that Lucius Lucullus reportedly held[110] – a dinner overflowing, I mean, with foods that are exceptional in price and taste, and with all possible abundance of luxury – shall I fill my stomach to the maximum degree and allow myself to be carried away by the dictates of my belly when my mind opposes and resists it? But Menedemus was invited just once to a dinner party:[111] when he entered the house and noticed the extremely showy sumptuousness of the occasion, he retreated as soon as possible by his route of entry.

30 To no purpose would we possess that capacity for reason that separates us from all other creatures,[112] unless we were able both to rein in[113] our innate passions and to remove or relieve the diseases of mind when they rise up. And so people should look after themselves and free their own existence

---

[106] There were in fact several distinct treasuries on the Acropolis: see van Rookhuijzen 2020.

[107] The *templum gentis Flaviae* was built under the emperor Domitian in the mid-90s CE on the site of his birthplace on the Quirinal Hill (Suet. *Dom.* 1.1). Barbaro's plural *templis* finds metrically convenient poetic precedents in, e.g., Mart. 9.3.12, 9.34.2, but his use of the plural is perhaps more knowing: the structure in fact consisted of both a shrine to the *gens Flavia* and a dynastic Mausoleum of the Flavians (see Dąbrowa 1996, esp. 153, 156).

[108] If Darius I, see 1.2.4 and n. 27, and cf. for his fabulous wealth Hdt. 3.89-98; if Darius III, 2.5.9 and n. 117 with Plin. *NH* 7.108.

[109] See for Xenocrates 2.5.11 and n. 124 (cf. also 3.5.16, 4.2.6); for his refusal of Alexander's largesse, Cic. *Tusc.* 5.91, V. Max. 4.3 ext. 3b, Plut. *Mor.* 333b, D. L. 4.8. Barbaro takes an extreme anachronistic license in having the statesman Pericles (c. 495–429 BCE) encounter Alexander the Great (d. 323). Pericles' celebrity may explain his presence here despite the historical distortion; but if Barbaro is suspected of modifying a different pairing in the sources, the combination of Xenocrates and the Cynic Diogenes (for whom 2.5.15 and n. 139) is suggestive: for the Cynic rebutting Alexander when the latter asked him to name anything he wanted, Cic. *Tusc.* 5.92, V. Max. 4.3 ext. 4a, and cf. D. L. 6.38, Plut. *Mor.* 331f-332c.

[110] For the legendary gourmet extravagance of the Roman general and statesman L. Licinius Lucullus (c. 117–57/6 BCE) see, e.g., Plut. *Luc.* 40-1.

[111] Surely Menedemus of Eretria (c. 339–265 BCE), founder of the Eretrian school of philosophy (see D. L. 2.125-44), not the third-century BCE Cynic Menedemus (for whom D. L. 6.102). Barbaro builds on Menedemus' reputation for austerity: frugal in hosting his own symposia (cf. D. L. 2.139-40, Ath. *Deipno.* 2 55d, 10 419e-420c), Menedemus allegedly reacted to his host's extravagance at one dinner party by lapsing into silence and reproachfully eating only olives (D. L. 2.129).

[112] Cf. 1.1.2 and n. 11.

[113] See n. 104 above.

servitute, putentque sui se iuris esse universos, eos vero praesertim qui nunquam fuere alieni, quales esse debent ii qui a nobis instituuntur. **31** Hos[114] enim pueros et innocentes [**66v**] fuisse semper oportuit quos vacare omni aegritudine volumus, sed ea nunc maxime quae ad luxum et gulam pertinet:[115] id autem facillime assequentur, si primum hoc egerint ne cibi et potus amore capiantur. Ab hac pravitate quemadmodum esset cavendum et a quibus satis dictum arbitror.

32 Quoniam vero, ut diximus, non solus est gustus ex sensibus quo elabamur, tactus etiam a foeditate[116] revocandus est et in continentia retinendus; iccirco enim delitias gustus a caelibe nostro dimovimus, ne ad perniciem tactus illecebris, ad quas istinc proximus saltus est, traheretur. Verum et propria quaedam sunt quae praecipi possunt in ea quam circa tactum fieri velim cautione. **33** Haec et dinumerare et digerere quam brevissime non erit inutile, ut quom de iis plene fuerit pertractatum, a quibus cavendum erit, proxime ad ea veniamus quae [**67r**] remedia esse adhibenda videbuntur. Prius enim, ut dictum est, a contrariis abstinere oportet quam utilia admovere: quare antiquiorem cavendi quam ictum inferendi curam fuisse semper apud gladiatoriae artis magistros invenimus. Sed propositum prosequamur.

34 Ante omnia igitur praecavendum erit ne mulierum conventus frequentet is qui, ita ut volumus, extra coniugium est victurus. Nam et hoc consilium haud importune dari solet iis, qui in coniugio versari pudice volunt; sed ad nos magis ut nostrum et materiae, quam sumpsimus, proprium pertinere visum est, ideoque est a nobis liberius usurpatum, si modo usurpari potest id quod nostro iure repetitur. **35** Nunc ad rem coguntur mulieres trifariam maxime: aut enim quom ludi publici celebrantur, aut quom festis solemnibusque diebus in unum coeunt locum, aut quom intra privatos parietes ad convi[**67v**]via propinquorum aut nuptias convocantur. Cum iis

---

[114] *Nos* MS, corrected to *Hos* in the right margin.
[115] *-inent* MS, Br., but see p. 5 above.
[116] *etiam a foeditate etiam* MS.

from slavery, and hold that they are all without exception their own master, but especially those who never did give up their self-ownership – the sort those taught by me ought to be. **31** For these boys whom we want to be free of all sickness, and free in particular now of that relating to self-indulgent appetite – it's always been necessary for them also to be of blameless character. They will most easily attain that goal if they first take steps not to be captivated by a love of food and drink. I think enough has been said about how this perversity is to be guarded against, and what things are to be guarded against.

32 Since, however, as I've said,[117] taste isn't the only one of the senses that causes us to slip, touch is also to be rescued from shamefulness and held fast in self-control; for I've put the allurements of taste out of our celibate's reach precisely to prevent him from being drawn to ruin by the charms of touch – charms that are the very next step from there. But there are also certain specific pieces of advice that can be given among the precautions I'd want to be taken about touch. **33** It won't be pointless both to enumerate and organize this advice as briefly as possible, so that when a full treatment has been given of the dangers to be guarded against, we come right away to the remedies that we'll see must be applied to them.[118] For, as has been said,[119] it's essential to steer clear of what is harmful before beneficial measures are to be applied: hence we find in teachers of gladiatorial skill that concern for defensive action always preceded that for inflicting a blow.[120] But let's pursue the matter at hand.

34 Above all, therefore, precautions will have to be taken to ensure that one who's destined to live outside marriage (just as we want) doesn't attend gatherings of females. For this advice is also conventionally given – not inappropriately – to those who want to live respectably in marriage; but it seemed more pertinent to us, as belonging in our domain, and of special relevance to the topic I've broached, and for that reason I've taken it over quite freely – if in fact something I claim by right can be 'taken over.' **35** Nowadays, for the matter at issue, women are brought together in three ways above all: when public festivals are held; when they congregate in one place on holidays or religious days; or within private houses, when they're summoned together to their relatives' banquets or weddings. Associating with them is always harmful, but most harmful when we drink and dine

---

[117] 3.5.9.
[118] 3.6.
[119] 3.5.1-6.
[120] For this wary approach cf. the 'old adage' (*vetus proverbium*) reported of gladiators by Sen. *Ep.* 22.1, 'that they plan their fight in the ring; as they intently watch, something in the adversary's glance, some movement of his hand, even some slight bending of his body, gives a warning' (tr. Gummere 1917: 149; further, Dunkle 2013: 41).

mala semper consuetudo est, pessima vero quom una bibimus et comessamur.[121] **36** Circunstat enim intus et extra calor, et tum maxime concitatio mentis oboritur quum nullus vacat sua voluptate sensus, nullus est sine titillatione, sed propemodum extra se quisque positus et conculcatus. Simul enim et multiplicibus et mollissimis dapibus vescimur, et dulciolae potionis, quam forte elegantis formae mulier porrigit, succum absorbemus. **37** Aures cytharedi cantibus mulcent, nares culinae sagacissimus nidor inungit, oculorum flexus, quocunque volvamur, ridentium exultantiumque foeminarum vultus excipiunt, lasciviunt omnes corporis partes, luxuriant in recessu spirituli: firmitas omnis atque constantia crebro quatitur ariete, tormen[68r]tisque per loca sua dispositis magno ardore impugnatur, et, quod periculo unumquemque propiorem facit, parum tunc aut nihil resisti potest. **38** Nulla enim expectari amplius subsidia possunt, fugato imperatore, quae, velut ex occulto praetorianae cohortes solent, subeuntia praelium et pugnam instaurent. Iacent enim sine ratione, ut dictum est, sensus, quanvisque desit tactus, non deest tamen tangendi cupiditas. **39** Nam sensus illius ea natura est ut caeteris sensibus facile obtemperet: his enim famulatur, hos sequitur, tantumque abest ut peccet quantum ut nequeat. Si lignorum struem ad pyram advehi iusseris, igni non admoto, ardebit profecto non ante quam faces immittantur: ignis vero eiusdem est ubique potestatis tantumque non urit quantum non habet quod absumat. Hac vero delitiarum omnium facie verecun[68v]dia omnis perit, pudor et decus et virtus, ut peregrinae quaedam res et ignotae, posthabentur, licentiam vero nobis facimus delinquendi veniamque nobis ipsis tacite dilargimur.

---

[121] *-amus* MS.

together. **36** Why? Because there's heat all around inside and out,[122] and there's a rise in mental excitement, especially at the moment when none of the senses is without its own pleasurable gratification, none without titillation, but each is placed almost outside itself and trampled upon. For in company we eat the daintiest meals of many courses, and we swallow down draughts of the delightful drink that's perhaps held out to us by a woman of delicate beauty. **37** Lyre players soothe our ears with their music, the keenest smell from the kitchen anoints our noses, the faces of joyously laughing women meet the shifting gaze of our eyes wherever we turn, all parts of the body are playfully unrestrained, and little stirrings of spirit run riot deep inside us. All resolute steadfastness is repeatedly shaken by a battering ram, and because missile engines are distributed throughout its domain, it's assailed by a great passion, and – what brings each and everyone closer to danger – the capacity for resistance is at that point inadequate or non-existent. **38** For when the general is put to flight, no relieving forces can be hoped for any more to enter the battle (just as the praetorian cohorts usually do from a hidden position)[123] and start the fight afresh. For the senses languish without reason, as has been said,[124] and though touch is lacking, there's nevertheless no lack of the desire for touching. **39** For the nature of that sensory mode is such that it easily submits to the other senses: it's subservient to them, it follows their lead, and it's only as far from acting improperly as it is incapable of doing so. If you order a pile of logs to be transported to a pyre without fire being applied to it, it certainly won't burn until it's set alight; but fire is unquestionably of the same capacity in all circumstances, and it only fails to have a burning effect to the extent that it has nothing for it to consume. Certainly, all sense of shame is undone by this outward appearance[125] of all the sensual pleasures; self-respect, dignity, and moral excellence recede in importance, as if certain alien and unknown qualities; but we make for ourselves our freedom to do wrong, and we quietly lavish[126] forgiveness on ourselves.

---

[122] In advance of the melodramatic language of siege warfare in 3.5.37, the 'soft' siege begins with the enveloping 'heat all around' (*Circunstat* ... *calor*) and the pleasurable sensory bombardment that Barbaro then textually activates through (i) the synesthetic engagement of taste, hearing, smell, and sight in 3.5.36-7, (ii) the soothing alliterative effect esp. of sonorous *c*, *m*, *s*, and *v* in the Latin, and (iii) the massing of highly sensuous descriptors (e.g., *titillatione*, *mollissimis*, *dulciolae*, *mulcent*, etc.) that cumulatively intensify the intoxicating atmospherics of the scene.

[123] The Praetorian Guards originated in the Roman Republic as a small escort protecting an army commander, and in 27 BCE were formalized by Augustus into a permanent imperial protection force; already on the Republican battlefield they acted as a final reserve, as in the defeat of the rebel Catiline in 62 BCE (Sall. *Cat.* 60.5).

[124] 3.5.9-10.

[125] Wordplay neatly seals the analogy: as fire (*faces*, lit. 'firebrands') burns wood, so the alluring appeal (*facie*) of sensual pleasure 'incinerates' self-respect, etc.

[126] *dilargimur* is here emphatic in terminal position: self-pardons are as freely given as the self-indulgences that prompt them in 3.5.36-7.

40 'Peccabitur, at humana res est et tolerabilis: poenitebit postea; inserviendum voluptati aliquantum, relaxandus quandoque animus, praesentibus parumper fruendum est bonis. Corneos esse aut saxeos non decet homines. Non effundar neque efferar nimium.'

41 Sed dum revoco spiritum, dum solor conclusos ignes, dum triste et anxium cor aliqua voluptate reficio, interim illi expulsa continentia male perduntur, quodque accidisse plurimis scio, qui annos multos sine labe consumpserunt, una hora partam prope victoriam ultro in hostium manibus turpissime relinquunt, longe nautis imprudentiores qui, quum ditissimi facti sunt, rursus se suaque omnia periculis sub[**69r**]iiciunt maris: quo fit ut plerunque procellis irruentibus rerum praetiosissimarum iacturam faciant.

42 In hoc tamen laudandi sunt qui, ne vitam amittant, tam claram supelectilem aspernentur: plus enim et maius quiddam est virtus quam illi puncto temporis tot laboribus partam demoliuntur. Puerilis sane res est et nullius veniae capax, nulla digna miseratione si quem, ut in proverbio est, nobis ipsi scientes dolorem aut damnum inurimus; quemadmodum mulorum potui, qui in Boetia et Thessalia generantur, nullus opem suam solet adhibere, quia puros et limpidos nacti fontes pedibus inculcantes aquarum claritatem exturbant et potu, quem sibi ipsis sic fecerunt, gaudent esculento. **43** Nisi forte eius pictoris

40 'Sins will be committed, but it's a human reality, and one that can be put up with. Regret will come afterwards. There has to be some submission to pleasure, the mind has to unwind now and again, and the good things that are in our grasp should be enjoyed for a bit. It's not fitting for humans to be hard as horn or rigid as rock. I won't be drained or carried away to excess.'[127]

41 But while *I* summon back my spirits, while *I* assuage the fires that have been shut away, and while *I* restore by some pleasure a heart that's sad and gloomy, *they* in the meantime are badly impaired by the banishment of their self-control; and – a phenomenon I know has happened to a great many people who've spent many years without a stain – in a single hour they most shamefully abandon, of their own accord, to the hands of their enemies a victory that's almost been achieved. They're far more misguided than sailors who, when they've become very wealthy, once again subject themselves and all that's theirs to the dangers of the sea; hence very often, as the storms rush in, they throw overboard their most valuable possessions. **42** In this matter, however, those are to be praised who, to avoid forfeiting their lives, spurn such gleaming paraphernalia: for something more and greater is the moral excellence that's been accomplished by so much hard work, and which those [unfortunates] destroy in a mere blink of an eye. Truly, it's a childish circumstance that can't be at all excused and deserves no pity if, as the saying goes, we ourselves knowingly brand ourselves with any pain or loss – just as in the case of mules bred in Boe[o]tia and Thessaly, no one usually brings his own help to bear to aid their drinking because, when they come across clean and translucent springs, they trample all over them and upset with their hooves the clearness of the waters, and they're pleased with the palatable drink that they've prepared for themselves in this way.[128] **43** Unless, perhaps,

---

[127] This is the first step in a sequence of argument (Q.: 'Why not permit some concession to sensuous pleasure?' A.: 'Any such concession may reverse the spiritual/moral progress already made') that finds striking precedents in the Stoic tradition. So, e.g., in denying that an emotion such as grief should be allowed some outlet (*Ep.* 116.2), Seneca warns of the dangers of a serious relapse in those lacking the fully perfected wisdom of the sage; for such philosophical progressives as *always* on slippery ground (*in lubrico*), cf. *Ep.* 71.28, 75.10 with Roskam 2005, esp. 76–84.

[128] With a touch of sarcasm in 'palatable' (*esculento*). Cf. Arist. *Hist. an.* 8.8 595b31-596a2: 'For drinking, the cattle look for clean water, but the horses do as camels also do: the camel prefers its drink muddy and thick, and does not drink river water before stirring it up' (tr. Balme 1991: 125). If Barbaro is seen to adapt this passage, why the shift to 'mules bred in Boeotia and Thessaly'? The mules sullying the waters they drink are analogically aligned with the transgressors (incl. those drinkers of 'sullied' intoxicants in 3.5.19) who bring their own defilement upon themselves. Those transgressors are themselves insentient 'mules' (for *mulus* of human foolishness cf. Catul. 83.3), with Boeotia a byword for stupidity (LSJ Βοιωτός), Thessaly for gluttonous self-indulgence (see Bakola 2005, esp. 611–12).

aut fictoris ingenium laudemus, qui tabulam vigiliis et sudore multo diligentissime elaboratam aut incisam magna opera in aes for[**69v**]mulam, ira percitus, laceraverit aut everterit, sive aedes quis magnificentissime fabricatas, dolore aliquo succensus, solo aequaverit. Quo quid vanius?

44 Sed quid disputo? aut quid ago? Nonne confessum est gravissimum esse id in homine praesertim coelibe futurum? Malum esse vitium arbitrari debent qui se hoc pacto instituendos praebent, et nos esse hoc manifestum et ambiguum nemini volumus; alioqui non eam curam suscepissemus. **45** Si quis enim volet ediscere vitiumne sit in ea re labi, a philosophis petat: nos ut principium hoc esse dicimus in libris nostris: esse vitia suapte natura detestanda, quemadmodum et virtutes propter se expetendas, quae boni viri et eius maxime, quem[129] fingimus, vitam beatissimam reddant. **46** Quare mathematicorum exemplo hoc nobis concedi volumus: ii[130] enim postulatis quibus[**70r**]dam confessisque principiis scientiam totam absolvunt: alioqui non hisceremus, nisi esset parata foelicitas quaedam, quam assequi nemo posset nisi qui abunde honestate et moribus esset insignitus. Supervacuum enim et ociosum esset praecepta tam multa ad bene vivendum excogitasse, nisi et uti possemus iis et capere etiam aliquam utilitatem liceret.

47 Fugiendus est itaque huiuscemodi coetus mulierum curandumque, ut dicere Caesar est solitus, ut non solum a crimine sed etiam a criminum suspitione vacemus; quanquam nondum id est quod volumus: suspitionem enim et dedecus, quae in populi sunt posita potestate, timere coelibem nolo. **48** Nam neque subiectus est cuiquam, neque ullo pacto consentaneum est ut is, qui populi favorem sit semel aspernatus, iuditium eiusdem pertimescat;

---

[129] *quae* MS.
[130] *iis* MS.

we're to praise the mentality of the painter or sculptor who, in a fit of anger, mutilates or ruins a picture that's been most carefully labored over with wakeful attention and a good deal of sweat, or a pretty shape that's been engraved into bronze with great effort; or if someone, because inflamed by some kind of anguish, levels to the ground a house built with the utmost lavishness. What could be more futile than that? **44** But why do I argue the point? Or plead my case? Surely it's an acknowledged fact that *that*[131] is going to be extremely troublesome in a celibate person in particular. Those who offer themselves for this kind of training must consider it a bad vice, and I want this to be clear, and doubtful to no one; otherwise I wouldn't have taken up that concern. **45** For whoever wants to learn thoroughly *whether* it's a vice to go wrong in this matter should ask the philosophers. I say that this stands as a guiding principle in my books: that vices are to be loathed because of their intrinsic nature, just as virtuous qualities, too, are to be coveted on their own account, because they render most blessed the existence of the good man, and especially of the person I'm shaping. **46** Hence, on the model of mathematicians, I want to be granted this concession; for they complete their entire system of knowledge after positing and granting certain first principles.[132] I'd otherwise not be opening my mouth, unless a certain happiness had been presupposed that no one could attain without being amply distinguished by his integrity of character. For it would be redundant and idle to have devised so many precepts for living well, if we couldn't put them to use and weren't allowed also to derive some advantage from them.

47 And so a female gathering of this sort is to be avoided, and care must be taken (as Caesar was in the habit of saying) that we be free not only of wrongdoing but also of the suspicion of wrongdoing[133] – though that's not yet what I'm after; for I don't want the celibate to be afraid of suspicion and infamy, which reside in the power of the multitude. **48** For he's subservient to no one, and on no terms is it fitting that he, the sort who's rejected popular favour once and for all, should fear the judgment of that same body. Nor can

---

[131] Not controlling the senses.
[132] For this distinction in 3.5.45-6 between philosophy 'building everything on its own ground' and mathematical reliance on first principles cf. notably Sen. *Ep.* 88.27-8.
[133] So Julius Caesar after divorcing his second wife, Pompeia, even though at the trial of P. Clodius Pulcher in 61 BCE Caesar denied all knowledge of any affair (Clodius was charged with trespassing during the Bona Dea festival disguised as a women – an incident linked to an attempted assignation with Pompeia); cf. Plut. *Caes.* 10.5-7, Suet. *Iul.* 74.2. A side effect of this allusion to Caesar and, by extension, to Clodius' ill-fated act of trespass on the all-female Bona Dea festival is that Barbaro wittily underscores his prohibition on attending female gatherings.

neque quicquam esse tam praeposterum [70v] potest quam ut is, qui honores divitiasque et reliqua, quae putantur in vita pretiosa, veluti minora et infra se posita, floci fecit, cogitare de iis vel minimum debeat. **49** Neque superesse ei tantum ocii est necesse, ut quemadmodum neque in Dionysium Platoni maledicendi fuit, fragilium rerum et caducarum curam ullam gerat. Nam et eorum, qui privatum ocium, non ad honestiorem aliquam praestantioremque vitam sed ad degendum sine molestia, negociis publicis anteferunt, nominatim laudes circunferuntur, quia honores ultro videntur aspernari. **50** Qua propter, ut ait Cicero, non siletur illud potentissimi regis anapaestum, qui senem laudavit et fortunatum esse dixit quia inglorius et ignobilis esset ad supremum diem perventurus. Quamobrem cavendum erit potius non ne ignominiam subeamus, sed ut non solum culpa careamus, sed ne nos culpae [71r] periculis obiectemus. **51** Quanvis enim non peccet is qui est in periculo sua sponte constitutus si nihil mali agat, ob hoc ipsum tamen peccat, quom peccandi sibi ipsi copiam facit. Nam etsi[134] moechus non sit qui domum alienam et lectum ingressus noctu neminem violavit, videtur tamen ob id deliquisse quia se discrimini tam manifesto imprudentissime obiectarit.

52 'At virtuti et constantiae fidendum fuit et temperantiae nostrae periculum aliquod faciendum.'

---

[134] *etsi* MS; *et si* Br.

there be anything as absurd as that a man who doesn't care a straw about public honours, wealth, and all the other things that are thought valuable in life, as being of lesser worth and set beneath him[135] – that such a person should think about such things even for the merest moment. **49** And it's essential that he doesn't have so much free time left over that he pays any serious attention to matters of fleeting impermanence, just as Plato had no time for badmouthing Dionysius.[136] Again, they too are widely praised by name because they're seen of their own accord to reject public honours – they who seek private tranquility over public occupations not for some nobler and more distinguished existence, but so as to live untroubled. **50** Therefore, as Cicero says, the well-known anapests of that most powerful king aren't passed over in silence – the king who praised an old man and called him blessed for being destined to reach his very last day in undistinguished obscurity.[137] Hence, rather, we shall have to be on our guard not against submitting to disgrace, but that we're not only free of wrongdoing but don't expose ourselves to the dangers of wrongdoing. **51** For although a person who stands in danger of his own accord doesn't sin if he does nothing bad, he nevertheless sins because of the very fact that he creates for himself the opportunity to sin. For though a man who entered someone else's house and bed at night without sexually violating anyone may not be an adulterer,[138] he nevertheless seems to have committed an offence precisely because he exposed himself with extreme rashness to so clear a danger.

52 'But there had to be trust in our moral goodness and strength of purpose, and some trial made of our self-control.'

---

[135] The celibate strikingly resembles the Stoic sage in his scorn for such indifferents as honours, wealth, etc. (so, e.g., Sen. *Ep.* 59.14, 76.30-1, 81.28, 94.8).

[136] Dionysius I, tyrant of Syracuse (*c.* 430–367 BCE). Cf. D. L. 3.21: 'Dionysius himself could not rest easy [after taking offence during Plato's first visit to Sicily in 388–387 BCE and ordering that he be sold into slavery]. On learning what had happened [Plato was eventually ransomed and restored to Athens], he wrote asking Plato not to speak ill of him. And Plato wrote back that he had no leisure to think about Dionysius' (tr. Mensch 2018: 144).

[137] In *non siletur . . . perventurus*, an almost verbatim rendering of Cicero's paraphrase at *Tusc.* 3.57 (itself probably via an intermediary Latin version: cf. Jocelyn 1969: 322) of Agamemnon's words to his elderly attendant early in Euripides' *Iphigenia in Aulis* (16-19): faced with the horror of having to sacrifice his daughter Iphigenia to the goddess Artemis to enable the Greeks to set sail for Troy, Agamemnon can but envy the old man's lowly obscurity and freedom from the burdens of high command.

[138] Perhaps with a backward glance at the scandal on which Julius Caesar remained silent in 3.5.47 and n. 133: for P. Clodius Pulcher infiltrating Caesar's abode for an assignation with Pompeia during the Bona Dea festival, Plut. *Caes.* 10.1-5.

53 Concedo dum hominem esse te neges, dum carere sensibus velis, dum sis demum talis qualis sperari non debet. Natare scimus et longos maris tractus sub aqua rependo incluso ferre spiritu et sustentare: quis erit vas ne nos pontus absorbeat fluctibus repente perturbatis, ne ex adverso polypus aut monstrificum aliquid ex occulto, quorum est refertissimum mare, inopinantes ludentesque rapiat et conculcet? [71v] quis spondere rursum audebit ne imbibito frigore membrisque rigentibus et torpore contractis in profundum exanimes rapiamur?

54 Audendum tamen est aliquid, sed eo usque procedendum unde statim ad temeritatem proxime non dilabamur: genus enim temeritatis est maximum experiri velle quae aut non prosint, aut noceant statim, aut nocere mox possint. Iis vero praesertim cavendum est ne experiri velint, ad quos experimenta non pertinent. **55** Nam si foret cum foeminis quispiam aut ut custos, ut Galli, aut ut latitans, quemadmodum de Achille praedicant fabulae, versaturus, hortarer profecto periculum aliquod continentiae suae facerent ut quemadmodum ii qui praelium inituri praeludiis exercentur, ita illi quandoque ad ferendas assuescerent cupiditates.

56 Eos vero, quibuscum nihil esse [72r] foeminis volumus, insanos putarem si ad id se componerent quod ad se minime pertineret: nam ut corporis fortitudinem ad perferendum facilius bellum laboribus ullis stultum est exercere iis qui non sunt in aciem descensuri, aves quoque neque natare pullos docent, neque pisces suos volare, sed utrisque generibus earum rerum est diligens cura quas ad suam rem facere natura cognoscunt, ita quor mulierum conventus frequentet is, qui non sit mulieres cogniturus, plane non video causam. Immo, ut mihi quidem videtur, ei qui est a mulierum consuetudine revocandus assuescendum est potius ut nunquam cum mulieribus diversetur.

53 I agree, provided that you deny you're human, that you want to be free of the senses, and that, ultimately, you're of a sort we mustn't hope to find. We know how to swim and, by moving along slowly with our breath held in, to endure and withstand long stretches of the sea underwater: what guarantee will there be that the sea won't engulf us with a sudden disturbance of its waves, or that an octopus[139] right in front of us, or some monster from its hiding place (the sea is absolutely crammed with such creatures), won't unexpectedly snatch and crush us with casual sportiveness? Who besides will dare to pledge that we won't be carried off lifeless into the deep after drinking in the cold, our limbs stiff and crippled with paralysis?

54 Still, some boldness is necessary, but we should only advance to a point from which we don't immediately slip away into rashness with our very next step; for the greatest form of rashness is to want to try out things that either aren't good for us or are immediately harmful or could soon do harm. Certainly, those above all to whom experimental exercises aren't suited should take care not to want to put things to the test. **55** For if someone were going to interact with women either as their protector (like the Galli)[140] or as a lurking presence (as myths declare of Achilles),[141] I'd undoubtedly encourage them to put their self-control to some test so that, just as combatants who are set to enter battle are given practice in training beforehand, so they get used to sometimes withstanding desires.

56 Certainly, as for those we want to have no involvement with women, I'd think them mad if they prepared themselves for what's of minimal relevance to them. For it's foolish for those not destined to enter the battle-line to enhance by any exertions their strength of body to endure war more easily, and birds too don't teach their chicks to swim, nor fish their young to fly, but each of the two species pays careful attention to the things they recognize as naturally compatible with their own circumstances. Accordingly, I simply see no reason why the man who's going to have no familiarity with women would attend female gatherings. Indeed, as I for my part see it, one who has to be summoned back from consorting with women should rather get used to *never* lingering as a guest with women.

---

[139] For no animal as 'more savage in killing a man in the water', Plin. *NH* 9.91; but for *polypus* figuratively of a grasping human (Barbaro's celibate as if endangered by a female predator?) cf. Plaut. *Aul.* 198 ('I know those octopuses: as soon as they've touched something, they hold on to it'; tr. de Melo 2011: 279).

[140] Eunuch priests, female in attire, of the Phrygian mother-goddess Cybele and her consort Attis.

[141] To thwart the prophecy of Achilles' death at Troy, Thetis, his mother, sought to hide him away in female disguise among the daughters of Lycomedes, king of Scyros. The story is famously treated in Statius' unfinished Latin epic *Achilleid* (late first-century CE).

57 Sed et quum rebus sacris et spectaculis oportet interesse, plurimum refert quid e regione, quid a latere, quid [**72v**] in arena fieri videamus. Non solum enim praecavendum ei est ne a mulieribus irretiatur, verumetiam ne detur ocasio aliqua delinquendi. Nam quid differt utrum hoc vel illo capiamur hamo? Suspensis et mersis una mors obvenit, et fluctus et laquei aeque a nobis extimescendi sunt.

58 Abesse itaque caelibes nostri ab iis locis velint, quos vitae quam delegerunt et moribus alioqui et honestati contrarios esse sciant. Catonem imitentur, qui tametsi rebus publicis maxime inserviret, indignum tamen esse viro frugi et bono cive arbitrabatur velle spectaculis omnibus interesse, semelque is tantum in theatrum ad floralia quom esset non ultro perductus, statim revertisse dicitur. **59** Quem morem si Thales Milesius, tametsi in reliquis habitus sapiens, hoc uno saltem imprudentior visus, servare et sequi voluisset, non eo mortis genere [**73r**] infoelicissimo scilicet et indignissimo exanimatus fuisset: is enim quom ludis gymnicis[142] abstinere non posset aestu et siti periit. **60** At mirum est nihil si labuntur etiam sapientes: nam et ab anicula repraehensum eundem philosophum perhibent accusatumque quod, quom syderalis disciplinae diligentissimus haberetur, caeli cursus et motus attentius semel inspiciendo observandoque, in foveam imprudens concidisset. Hoc enim statim viso, foemina anus miraculum putans esse: 'Quor,' inquit, 'o Thale, sublimia tantum callere voluisti, si quae ante oculos et pedes posita sunt videre non debebas?'

---

[142] *hymn-* MS, but *gymn-* (Br.'s conjecture, 113 n. 1) is more apposite; see my n. 148 ad loc.

57 But even when religious rituals or public shows have to be attended, it very much matters what we see happening directly opposite us, what to the side, and what in the arena.¹⁴³ For he should be on his guard not just against being ensnared by women, but also that no opportunity at all is offered for wrongdoing. For what difference does it make whether we're caught by this hook or that? To the hanged and the drowned death comes one and the same, and waves and nooses are to be equally feared by us.

58 And so our celibates should wish to keep their distance from those places that they know to be harmful to the life they've chosen and, besides, to moral character and respectability.¹⁴⁴ Let them imitate Cato who, though he was especially devoted to public affairs, nevertheless thought it unworthy of a man of sober character and a good citizen to want to attend all kinds of public shows; when just on one occasion – not of his own accord – he was induced to go to the theater for the festival of Flora, he's said to have gone back home right away.¹⁴⁵ **59** Thales of Miletus, though regarded as a sage in all other ways,¹⁴⁶ seemed rather foolish at least in this one respect: if he'd wanted to observe and follow this mode of conduct,¹⁴⁷ he wouldn't have died by that form of death that's evidently most unfortunate and unbecoming; for since he was unable to stay away from a gymnastics festival, he passed away through heat and thirst.¹⁴⁸ **60** But it's no wonder if even sages slip up: for they say that that same philosopher was also rebuked by an old woman and censured because, when on one occasion he was watching and monitoring the paths and movements of the heavens too intently (for he was regarded as a most careful student of astral science),¹⁴⁹ he'd foolishly fallen into a pit. As soon as she saw this, the old lady thought it a strange thing, and said: 'Why, Thales, did you want to know only what's up there if you had not to see what lay before your eyes and feet?'¹⁵⁰

---

¹⁴³ '[I]n the arena' perhaps also in the extended sense that the celibate is himself a quasi-combatant melodramatically engaged in a life-and-death struggle here, and seeking not to be ensnared by his female opponent (*ne a mulieribus irretiatur* below; cf. *OLD retiarius*, of a gladiator equipped with a weighted net and trident).

¹⁴⁴ Suggestively a reversal of Ovid's tactic in his *Art of love* (*Ars amatoria*) of identifying those Roman haunts in which the lover can pursue his erotic chase (see esp. 1.41-262).

¹⁴⁵ For Cato see 3.3.2 and n. 37. Founded in 238 BCE, the games in honour of the goddess Flora (*ludi Florales*) were made annual from 173 onwards (28 April-3 May under the Empire); they included mime-farces that were notoriously licentious. Rather than interfere with the crowd's wish for the actresses to perform naked onstage, the austere Cato walked out when he attended in 55 BCE (so V. Max. 2.10.8; cf. Sen. *Ep.* 97.8, Mart. 1 pref.).

¹⁴⁶ See 2.2.5-7 and n. 18.

¹⁴⁷ I.e., absenting himself as Cato did.

¹⁴⁸ Cf. D. L. 1.39, albeit Barbaro hints more strongly that Thales was the victim of his own voyeuristic captivation at the festival.

¹⁴⁹ See 2.2.7 and n. 21.

¹⁵⁰ For the anecdote cf. Pl. *Tht.* 174a, D. L. 1.34.

61 Quo exemplo admoneri possumus diligentiam esse in rebus omnibus adhibendam vitamque et opus debere semper cum moribus consentire, praecipuumque[151] illud in mente habere atque animo prudentiam atque consilium esse in rebus [73v] humanis certissima propemodum consuevisse: quorum ope universi, praesertim vero coelibes, tutissimi esse et constantissimi possint. **62** Ita demum eveniat ut quemadmodum a vulgi opinionibus et multorum consuetudine secesserunt, ita ea quae caeteri faciunt indigna arbitrentur quae ipsi aggrediantur. Qua in re simile illud est Alexandri Macedonum regis factum, quod imitari et admirari quantum res sua patiatur debebunt ii qui praestare reliquis volent. Is quom oblatas pacis, et quidem honestissimae, conditiones a Dario magno animo repudiavisset, Parmenonem quendam audivit dicentem: 'Equidem quae Persarum rex obtulit si Alexander essem accepissem!', 'At ego,' respondit, 'si Parmeno fuissem minime recusassem.' **63** Noverat enim egregius imperator nihil esse posse tam [74r] magnum quod suae gloriae et virtuti par esset; quae vero aliis ampla et honorifica videbantur, longe minora sese existimabat, neque non turpe poterat iudicare, si quod ex multis quilibet, unus perpaucorum effecisset. Debet enim excellentis ingenii vir hoc unum sibi potissimum cavere, ne ea quae sequi vulgus libenter solet probare ullo pacto videatur.

64 Sed excrescit nescio quo modo mirum in modum oratio: excresceret etiam magis si expatiari pro animi sententia vellem. Quod fieri a nobis hoc loco praesertim minus est laudabile, ne dum contra voluptatem disputamus, voluptati dicendi inservire videamur.

65 Sed, ut antequam ad remedia veniamus ea funditus quae impediunt capitulatim strictimque evellantur, adiicienda alia quaedam sunt quae nocere poterunt caste victuris, [74v] nisi se illi accurate tueantur. Diximus a cibi potusque intemperantia et ab iis, quae maxime venerem agunt, abstinendum

---

[151] *-uumque* MS; *-uum* Br.

61 We can be reminded by this example that close attention has to be applied in all circumstances, and that life and work must always be in compliance with good behaviour; and reminded to bear this point above all in mind and soul – that thoughtful deliberation is usually just about the most dependable commodity in human affairs, and that by its help all without exception, but celibates above all, can be very safe from harm and most resolute of purpose. **62** Accordingly, it may eventually happen that, just as they've distanced themselves from the views of the crowd and from the ways of the many, so they think that the actions of everyone else are not worth undertaking themselves. Similar in this matter is the well-known exploit of Alexander, king of the Macedonians; those who'll want to stand out from the rest will have to emulate and revere that exploit insofar as their own circumstances allow. When he'd grandly rejected the peace-terms offered by Darius (a peace that was in fact very respectable), he heard a certain Parmen[i]o saying: 'For my part, if I were Alexander, I'd have accepted the terms the Persian king offered!' 'But I,' he replied, 'wouldn't in the least have refused them if I'd been Parmen[i]o.'[152] **63** For that outstanding general knew that nothing could be so great as to match his own distinction and courage. Certainly, things that seemed grand and great to other people he regarded as far beneath himself, and he couldn't but consider it shameful if he – a singular exception even among the very few – had done what anyone of the many could have done. For a man of outstanding natural ability should look out for himself on this one point above all – that he not be seen in any way to think well of what the masses usually chase after with gusto.

64 But my discourse is somehow growing larger, and surprisingly so; and it would grow still more if I cared to elaborate according to my heart's desire. It wouldn't be very commendable for me to do that, especially at this point, for fear that, while arguing against pleasure, I give the impression of being in thrall to the pleasure of speaking.

65 But, so that the obstacles to progress are completely eradicated with summary swiftness before I come to remedies, certain other dangers are to be added that could harm those destined for the pure life unless the latter carefully protect themselves. I've said that it's necessary to refrain from excess in food and drink,[153] and from the things that most bring on sexual feeling.[154]

---

[152] For Darius III of Persia, see 2.5.9 and n. 117; Parmenio (c. 400–330 BCE) served as a general under Philip II of Macedon and then as Alexander's second-in-command during the conquest of Persia. For Alexander's famous quip cf. Diod. Sic. 17.54.4-5, V. Max. 6.4 ext. 3, Curt. 4.11.14-15, Arr. *Anab.* 2.25.2-3, Plut. *Alex.* 29.4.
[153] 3.5.17-31.
[154] 3.5.32-9.

esse; nunc de dormitione primum, qua plerique inconsiderate utuntur, pauca disseremus: neque enim singula minutatim in praeceptis his prosequemur. Sed ea dumtaxat tantumque attingemus, ex quibus prudentissimus coelebs abunde ex se colligat et secernat quid ad conservandam corporis et animi puritatem utile sit aut noxium.

66 Verum igitur capita et principaliora, si diligenter inspexeris, videbis a nobis fuisse consignata: nam reliqua, quae ad virtutes animi adipiscendas pertinebant, quia et aliorum intererat, duximus relinquenda. Ut enim diversae res sunt, ita et diversi opifices requiruntur: sed et in eadem re diversum et multiplex offitium quaeri potest. Nam et in plerisque [**75r**] artibus, et in medicina praesertim, alius est febribus doloribusque auxiliator, alius vulneribus ulceribusque adhibendus, ut ii quidem, quom opus sit, potione aut cibatu opem ferant aegroto, illi vero aut ustione aut incisione succurrant. **67** De moribus quoque varius esse tractatus potest, ut sint quidem non nulli qui oratorem instituant, alii qui regem effingant, plerique qui civem instruant, non desint qui de re uxoria abunde pertractent, et id, quod prope reliquum videbatur, suus coelibatui locus destinetur:[155] in quo quemadmodum prope omnia, quae in universis exiguntur, ita illud maxime virtutis specimen sibi proprium vendicavit, ut venerem nullam et labem sola ea vita cognosceret. **68** Quod ut assequi posse sperarent ii, qui id vivendi genus comprobabunt, tria caveri inprimis oportere diximus: cibi et potus [**75v**] ingluviem, mulierum et luxum libidinemque incitantium ocasionem, postremum vero, quod reliquum est, dormiendi indiscretam rationem.

---

[155] *-aretur* MS printed by Br., but see p. 5 above.

Now I shall first say a few words about sleep, which most people experience without due consideration; for[156] I won't pursue every single matter in detail in these directives. But I'll touch, up to a point and no more, on the properties from which the shrewdest celibate may fully infer for himself, and tell apart, what's useful or harmful for preserving the chasteness of body and mind.

66 But you'll therefore see, if you look carefully, that [only] the main points and more important features have been signposted by me; for I thought that all the remaining factors relating to the acquisition of noble qualities of mind had to be left aside, because they fell under the purview of others as well.[157] For just as circumstances differ, so also different practitioners are needed; but even in one and the same matter, a form of service can be required that's varied and many-sided. For instance, as in many areas of skill, also in medicine in particular one kind of helper is to be employed for feverish aches and pains, and another for wounds and sores, to the effect that, when need arises, some bring the patient aid with food and drink, while others help through either cautery or the surgical knife. **67** In matters of behavioural training as well, there can be a variety of treatments, to the effect that there are some advisers to instruct the orator, others to shape a monarch, many to teach the citizenry, and quite a few to examine issues relating to marriage in full detail; and (that area that seemed almost left behind) celibacy is set to receive its own allotted place.[158] Therein, just as celibacy claims almost all the qualities that are demanded in all [other areas of behavioural training] without exception, so it claims as its own special feature above all that token of virtue – that that way of life alone would know no sexual activity and no attendant stain. **68** So that those who will commend that form of existence may hope to be able to attain it, I've stated that three things have to be guarded against above all: greed for food and drink;[159] encounters with women and the catalysts that stir lustful indulgence;[160] but finally – the topic that remains – a random sleep-schedule.[161]

---

[156] Explaining why only 'a few words about sleep.'
[157] I.e., in capturing main points only, Barbaro concedes the need for the specialist knowledge of others in matters of detail; the medical analogy later in 3.5.66 creates the illusion that he himself, in his 'treatment' of the celibate, belongs to a community of expert practitioners.
[158] Barbaro not only implicitly elevates his *De coelibatu* here to the company of specialist treatises such as, e.g., Cicero's *De oratore*, *De officiis*, etc.; through the titular echo of his grandfather Francesco's *De re uxoria*, he also sets his treatise directly in counterpoise to that classic work (cf. Vol. 1 Intro. pp. 17, 20).
[159] 3.5.17-31.
[160] 3.5.32-9.
[161] Cf. 3.5.65.

69 Tria item sunt quae nocere in dormiendo possint: primum est si multum, secundum si crebro, tertio si imprudenter somnum capiamus. Ei enim qui multum dormit non solum sensus resolvuntur, sed etiam animus atque mens omnis hebescit: neque solum eos qui se ad ocium contulerunt nimius affligit somnus, verumetiam iis nocet plurimum quorum est vita in negocio constituta. **70** Aufert enim dexteritatem illam, immo strenuitatem, torporemque atque pigritiam per totum corpus inducit: quo fit ut et sermone cessantes et incessu languentes atque in agendo tardi et imbecilli ore vultuque etiam residente[162] videantur. Tantae demum sunt cum somno nobis [**76r**] inimicitiae, ut praeter id quod intelligentiam nostram, quae solum vigilantibus impartitur, obtruncat quodammodo atque intercidit, difficile etiam collectu sit utri plus animaene an corporis sanitati[163] vigorique detrahatur. **71** Et a me dubitatum est an servare tractatum hunc in eam partem oportuisset, in qua de iis, quae contemplationi adversantur, plenissime ad rem nostram exequeremur. Verum, quia et ad pudicitiam conservandam plurimum referebat quantum quis dormitaret, visum est faciendam esse super ea re hoc loco maxime mentionem, quoniam enim nihil est tam infestum ingenio quam somni intemperantia. **72** Quo fit ut nihil cum corpore male affecto virile animus promat, sed a sua decidens potestate sublimia deserat, haereat imis et rerum abiectarum sordescat speculatu: facillimum, [**76v**] ratione nulla prohibente neque mente curis ullis detenta, in scelus, id quod detestamur, erumpere.

73 Idem solet accidere iis qui crebro accubant, perinde ac nocte ad luxum modica expatiandique voluptatem adiicientes etiam diem et soli tenebras

---

[162] *-dente* MS printed by Br.; *residentes* (Br. 115 n. 2) is plausible but unnecessary.
[163] *-tate* MS.

69 Similarly, three factors have the capacity to do harm in sleeping.[164] The first is if we take a lot of sleep; the second, if we sleep often; the third, if we sleep ill advisedly. For in the case of one who sleeps a lot, it's not just that his faculties of perception are allowed to relax, but also that his entire mind and intellect are blunted;[165] nor does excessive sleep impair only those who've devoted themselves to leisure, but it also very much harms those whose existence is founded on being busy. **70** For it does away with that particular adroitness, or rather briskness, and it brings on a sluggish state of indolence throughout the entire body; hence they seem hesitant in speech and enfeebled of step, slow and weak in action, and also with a subdued facial expression. In sum, so harmful are our dealings with sleep that – beyond the fact that it butchers (so to speak) and shreds our intelligence, which is bestowed only on the wakeful – it's also hard to infer which of the two suffers the greater loss, the healthy vitality of the spirit or of the body. **71** I've also entertained doubts as to whether my treatment of this topic should have been saved for the section in which I'd elaborate most fully for my purposes on what stands opposed to contemplation.[166] However, because the amount one would sleep also had a very great bearing on preserving sexual purity, it seemed that reference had to be made to the matter at this point in particular; for nothing is as harmful to the intelligence as an over-indulgence in sleep. **72** Hence the mind produces nothing manly with a body that's badly impaired, but it falls away from its own position of strength; it abandons the heights to cling to the depths and becomes soiled by observing the basest matters. It's very easy, when no faculty of reason applies restraint and the mind has no responsibilities to hold it, to burst out into villainy – a circumstance I abhor.

73 The same thing usually happens to those who often lie in bed, as if – because the night gives only brief scope for indulgence and for the pleasure of nocturnal revels[167] – they also add on the day and pour darkness on

---

[164] Barbaro replicates (in a different order) the tripartite division applied to food and drink at 3.5.17; hence the special force of *item* ('similarly').

[165] A familiar characterization: already in *Laws* 7 Plato prescribes sleeping only as much as is necessary for health, as sleep connotes intellectual dullness (808b-c); in *Republic* 9 the healthy sleep-state is characterized by reason (*to logistikon*) remaining vigilant in its control of appetite (*to epithūmētikon*) and of passionate spirit (*to thūmoeides*; 571d-572a) – an extension of the idea that, in the world of particulars that are alienated from the truth of the Forms, life itself is a form of sleepwalk (cf. 7 534c-d; further, Wohl 2020: 136–42). But Barbaro's graphic picturing in 3.5.69-70 of the effects of sleep-induced sluggishness approaches a Sallustian (cf. *Cat.* 2.8, 13.3) and Senecan (cf. *Ep.* 55.5, 77.6, 88.41) pitch of condemnation. Contrast the ever-vigilant Seneca's scant sleep at *Ep.* 8.1, 83.6; but for measured sleep as necessary for refreshment, *Dial.* 9.17.5-6.

[166] Cf. 4.2.70.

[167] *expatiandi* lit. 'spreading out' in bed, but also with the fig. implication of 'wandering from the (right) course', 'going beyond normal bounds'.

offundentes. Qui usus, si Homeri tempore extitisset, liceret utique arbitrari illustrissimum vatem, quom versum illum effingeret... quo vir sapientissimus admonebat ne tota nox somno transigeretur, fuisse diem pro nocte dicturum, ut quod verbum ille ... dixit esset ... potius, aut idem significans aliud prolaturus.

74 Ast et alius quidam mos animo aeque ac corpori pernitiosus, quo non nulli se post cibum e vestigio in strata recipiunt gravatumque coenaticis epulis caput actutum deponunt in lectulo. Hoc a medicis [77r] petant, quae suae cervicis parentes sunt: apud has nihil est maiore diligentia dignum quam pastum lacte aut proximo cibo infantem puerumve cubitum ferre. 75 Exuritur enim, non coquitur prandium quom geminatus ex vi somni praeproperi calor, aestuantibus adhuc epulis, in materiam missam incenditur. Hinc exanguis ille in facie pallor, ille livens in oculis tumor, foedus oris alitus, crassa totius corporis habitudo subsequitur: omnia ad lassitudinem prona fiunt,[168] et, qui proximus est, ad libidinem faciunt gradum. Somnia vero terribilia atque confusa obveniunt, ut etiam si moderate cibum ceperimus

---

[168] *fiunt* MS; *sunt* Br.

sunlight.[169] If this practice had arisen in Homer's time, you could doubtless imagine that that most distinguished poet, when he was devising that well-known verse ... in which the wisest of men urged against the entirety of the night being spent in sleep,[170] was going to say 'day' instead of 'night' – to the effect that the word he[171] uttered as [all night] he was rather going to produce as [all day], or some other word that meant the same.

74 But there's also a certain other practice that's equally harmful to mind and body: a good number take themselves off to bed directly after eating; they at once lay down upon their pillow a head that's heavy with a large dinner. They ought instead to follow the example of midwives who are mothers in their own right:[172] for them, nothing is to be more carefully avoided than putting to bed an infant or young child who has just drunk milk or recently eaten. **75** For a meal is scorched, not digested, when the banquet still seethes within and the heat redoubled from the force of very hurried sleep is set aflame upon the fuel that's been dispatched.[173] Hence that anemic paleness of complexion follows, that discoloured swelling on the eyes, the mouth's foul breath, and the heavy bearing of the entire body. Everything becomes disposed to languor and takes a step – the very next step – towards carnal desire. Moreover, frightening and jumbled dreams present themselves,

---

[169] In Stoic terms, a perversion of living in accordance with nature, memorably condemned by Seneca in *Ep.* 122. For the importance from an ancient medical perspective of following a cycle of wakefulness by day, sleep by night, cf. the Hippocratic *Progn.* 10 (2.134 Littré) and then Gal. *In Hipp. Prog. comment.* 2.11 (18B.128-9 Kühn).

[170] Space is left in the MS after *effingeret* to accommodate *Il.* 10.159 ὄρσεο, Τυδέος υἱέ· τί πάννυχον ὕπνον ἀωτεῖς; (Nestor speaks, Barbaro's 'wisest of men'): 'Son of Tydeus [sc. Diomedes], rouse yourself! Why do you doze in sleep/ all through the night?' Space is then left below first for the Greek word πάννυχον (lit. 'all night') and then for its opposite, perhaps (Branca 1969: 116 n. 4) πανημέριον ('all day') – itself a Homeric word, but not an exact metrical equivalent for Homer's πάννυχον in *Il.* 10.159.

[171] Nestor.

[172] Cited by Branca 1969: 14 n. 3 as an example of Barbaro's occasional recourse in *De coelibatu* to common/spoken diction, *suae cervicis* amounting to 'di propria testa.'

[173] Barbaro portrays an excessive inflammation that impairs the relationship between moderate appetite, digestion, and sleep as theorized by the ancients. Aristotle for one posits that sleep arises when the exhalation (*anathūmiasis*) from ingested food enters the veins and moves upwards in the body, ultimately reaching the brain, where it is cooled off; when the brain makes this cooled substance flow back down to the heart, sleep is prompted by the sudden concentration of the substance about the heart, which is the seat of the primary sense organ (*De somn.* 3 456b17-34, 457b1-458a10 with Everson 2007, esp. 511–15; *Part. an.* 2.7 653a11-20); for Galen, too, connecting the process of digestion to sleep but with modification of the Aristotelian apparatus, see Van der Eijk and Hulskamp 2010: 66–74. As for Aristotle and Galen, fullness of the head has for Barbaro an important role in inducing sleep (3.5.74 'they at once ... dinner'); but the theorization of that fullness (as in *De somn.* 3 456b17-457a21) gives way to his far more melodramatic focus in 3.5.75 on the gruesome spectacle (with suggestive classical precedents, e.g., Pers. 3.88-106, Sen. *Q. Nat.* 4b.13.5-11) of the off-kilter, sleep-addled degenerate.

ipsa illa festinatio somni capiundi pro crapula nobis sit: quae efficiens et ipsa est terribilium somniorum. **76** Leguntur Socratis verba in libris iis, quos de republica Plato scripsit, sapientiae et doctrinae plenissima, et a Cicerone in latinum ex[77v]pressa, quum dormientibus, inquit, ea pars animi, quae mentis et rationis est particeps, sopita languescat, illa autem, in qua feritas quaedam est et agrestis immanitas, quom immoderato sit obstupefacta potu atque pastu, exultare eam in somno immoderateque iactari. **77** Itaque huic visa omnia obiiciuntur intellectu vacua et ratione, ut aut cum matre corpus misceri videatur, aut quovis alio homine vel deo, saepe[174] belua,[175] atque etiam trucidare aliquem atque impie cruentari multaque facere impure ac tetre cum impudentia et temeritate. **78** Quare contra evenit, ut idem inquit apud Platonem Socrates, ut qui salubri et moderato cultu atque victu sese quieti tradiderit, ea parte animi, quae mentis est et consilii capax, agitata et erecta saturataque honestarum rerum cogitatione, eaque parte animae, quae alitur [78r] voluptate, neque inopia afflictata neque satietate nimium roborata (quorum utrunque praestringere aciem mentis solet sive deest naturae quippiam sive abundet et effluat), illa etiam tertia parte animae, in qua irae subsistit ardor, sedata atque restricta, compressis temerariis duabus iis partibus, tertia illa pars rationis et mentis eluceat seque vegetam acremque praebeat ad somniandum. Ei tunc visa quietis occurrunt tranquilla atque veracia.

---

[174] *deo saepe* Br.; *sive* is conjectured for *saepe* by Br. 117 n. 1, but see p. 5 above.
[175] *bael-* MS.

so that even if we've eaten modestly, that very act of hurrying to go to sleep causes us a form of intoxication – which is itself also a cause of frightening dreams. **76** Very full of wise learning are the words of Socrates that can be read in the books Plato wrote *On the republic*,[176] and which were rendered into Latin by Cicero:[177] when we go to sleep, he says, the part of the soul that participates in rational thought[178] is subdued and lies at rest; but as for the part in which there's a certain savagery and an uncouth wildness, when it's befuddled by an excess of food and drink, [he says that] it runs riot in sleep and is tossed about in unrestrained excitement. **77** Accordingly, all the visions that are presented to this sleeper are devoid of thought and reason, so that he dreams that he's engaged in intercourse with his mother or with some other human being or god, and frequently with a wild beast;[179] and even to be killing someone and impiously staining himself with blood;[180] and to be doing many vile and abominable things with shameful recklessness. **78** Hence, on the other hand, it happens (as that same Socrates says in Plato) that when a person whose habits of living and eating are healthily restrained surrenders himself to sleep, that part of the soul that's capable of intelligent reasoning is eager and alert, and sated with reflection on respectable matters,[181] and that part of his spirit that's nurtured by pleasure[182] is neither distressed by abstinence nor overly invigorated by being glutted (as a rule, each of these alternatives blunts the mind's sharpness, whether one's nature is deprived of something or it's abundantly supplied to excess); and when that third part of his being in which the heat of anger is lodged[183] is becalmed and subdued, those two thoughtless parts are suppressed and that third part of reasoned intelligence shines forth, presenting itself as lively and energetic for dreaming. Then his dreams in sleep are peaceful and truthful.

---

[176] 9 571c-572a.

[177] *Div.* 1.60-1, reproduced by Barbaro with minor modifications in 3.5.76-8.

[178] The thinking part (*to logistikon*), as opposed to the 'spirited' (*to thūmoeides*) and the 'appetitive' (*to epithūmētikon*) portions of the tripartite Platonic soul (cf. *Resp.* 4 439d-441a, 441e-442b, and see also 3.5.69 n. 165, 4.2.39 n. 136, and 4.2.56 n. 179); the 'appetitive' rages in 'but ... excitement' below.

[179] For incestuous dreams of sex acts with one's mother discussed at length see Artem. *Oneir.* 1.79 (Hammond 2020: 63-6) with Harris-McCoy 2012: 460-5; sex with gods, 1.80.3 (Hammond 67-8); with a wild beast, 1.80.5 (Hammond 68).

[180] For dreams of murder and suicide see Artem. *Oneir.* 2.49-51, 4.59.1 (Hammond 2020: 125, 200); if, beyond or instead of suicide, cannibalism is implicated in 'and impiously ... blood' (so Wardle 2006: 260), cf. Artem. 1.70.2, 3.23 (Hammond 53, 146-7).

[181] Barbaro departs significantly from his Ciceronian source-text, modifying the latter's *saturataque bonarum cogitationum epulis* (1.61: 'sated with *a feast* of good thoughts'; the dining metaphor is itself Platonic, *Resp.* 9 571d), possibly to avoid replicating *epulis* after its literal use (with the pejorative connotation of excess) in 3.5.74.

[182] The 'appetitive' part: n. 178 above.

[183] The 'spirited' part: n. 178 above.

79 Plura dicerem nisi vererer ne suum sibi munus superstitiosa quorundam medicorum impudentia reddi vellet. Quod tamen nunc tam libenter ego faciam, quam si opus in nostro processu fiet: non timide ea omnia usurpabo quae ad rem facere videbuntur. Scio addi quam plurima potuisse non solum in cibi potusque et fugiendorum spectaculorum observatio[78v]ne et earum rerum omnium quae venerem concitant; de vestitu etiam dici plurima consuevisse et horum similibus, verum et in hac ipsa dormiendi ratione, ut si supino aut in latus, aut alio quodammodo quiescendum esset; quod plurimum tamen, quo pacto fiat, referre perspicuum est. **80** Sed quoniam hoc non modo alterius operae[184] videbatur esse, verumetiam[185] quia ad subtiliorem quandam diligentiam pertinebat, satis fecisse sum arbitratus si generaliora quaedam capita et communiora contra veneris impetum prima fronte collocata obiectassem.[186] Sed et haec, tametsi medicorum erant, non tamen ut medicus sum persequutus: verum haec intuli ut ea quae, si caveantur, ut est declaratum, honestam facere vitam possint, sin minus reddere inhonestam.

81 Verum et alia ratio fuit ut haec a nobis tractarentur: si enim adverteris [79r] animum diligenter, ea dumtaxat a nobis †dum†[187] ... decursa cognosces, in quibus laborare aetas nostra plurimum videbatur. Quis enim, per deum, est quoi ciborum omnis generis condimenta saporesque aut ignoti sint, aut inexperti? Quis nunc est omnium, aut ubi gentium quispiam, qui ulla libidinis foeditate non sit respersus? Quota eorum pars est qui ad nullam virtutis imaginem, ad nullam decori spetiem non sint intenti? **82** Quo fit ut, dum aeque conviviis et scortis indulgent, somno vinoque immersi et delitiis omnibus obruti turpiter iaceamus. Proh tempora! proh mores! Frigide reprehendo[188] et quidem recte fortasse. Non enim hoc est propositum prius,

---

[184] Br.'s compelling restoration (118 n. 1) for MS *opere*.
[185] *verumetiam* MS; *verum etiam* Br.
[186] *-assem* Br. 118 n. 2; MS *-assent* (*capita* misconstrued as nom. subj.?).
[187] †*dum*† Wi.; see p. 5 above.
[188] *Frigidae reprae-* MS.

79 I would say more were I not afraid that the wrong-headed effrontery of certain doctors would want their own function to be restored to themselves. I shall nevertheless now do this[189] as gladly as I will if the [same] need arises in the future progress of my work: I shall unflinchingly claim possession of all that will seem relevant to the matter at hand. I know that any number of things could have been added not only in my review of food and drink and the avoidance of public shows and all the things that stir sexual feeling (I know that a very great deal is usually said about clothing as well, and about like matters), but also in this very assessment of sleeping, to the effect of [discussing] if you should sleep on your back or on your side or in some other way. It's nevertheless clear that how sleep is achieved matters a very great deal. **80** But since this [focus on sleep] not only seemed to belong to a separate enterprise, but also because it lent itself to a more detailed sort of examination, I thought I'd done enough if I'd set out and brought to the fore some general and fairly familiar arguments against the assault of sexual feeling. But these points, too, though they belonged in the medical domain, I nevertheless didn't pursue as a doctor. Rather, I introduced them as the sort of phenomena that, if guarded against (as has been shown), could make life respectable, and if otherwise, could bring it into disrepute.

81 But there was also another reason for my treatment of these matters: for if you pay close attention, you'll recognize that I only went so far as to cover areas in which our own age appeared to be very much troubled. For who is there, by God, who either doesn't know or hasn't tried the seasonings and flavors of foods of every kind?[190] Who now is there of all people, or where on earth is anyone to be found, who isn't besmirched by any foulness of lustful appetite? How few are there of those who pay attention to any appearance of virtue or any semblance of decency? **82** Hence, while they give themselves up equally to feasts and whoring, we[191] shamefully lie buried in sleep and wine and overwhelmed by every kind of indulgence. Shame on the age and its ways! I offer my rebuke without enthusiasm, though perhaps with good reason; for this is no a priori assertion, but something I've now to some degree

---

[189] I.e., infringe upon areas in which others are more expert.
[190] In colourful climax to his condemnation in 3.5 of over-indulgence in lust-inciting food and drink, Barbaro rises to a pitch of time-honoured outrage at such behaviour (cf., e.g., Sall. *Cat.* 10-13, Sen. *Ep.* 78.23-4, 95.15-29, 110.12-13, etc.) that is inflected with a markedly Ciceronian accent in 3.5.82 'Shame … ways!' (cf. *o tempora, o mores!* at, e.g., *Cat.* 1.2, *Verr.* 2.4.55; for the rhetorical figure of such contrived emotion, Quint. *Inst.* 9.2.26).
[191] The abrupt shift from the third- to the first-person plural here allows Barbaro's readership no scope for complacent exceptionality: we are *all* dramatically implicated in the common disease.

sed id quod parte aliqua iam praestituimus, quo fieri scilicet pacto oporteret ut caelebs esse quis posset. Nunc ad reliqua transeamus.

[6] [79v] De iis quae adhibenda sunt ad pudicitiam in coelibatu conservandam remedia.

6.1 Dicta sunt itaque prope omnia et memorata quae suae integritatis custodibus nocere posse viderentur; quae ut magna sunt et nostrae foelicitatis inimica, ita natura factum et provisum est ut ea quae obessent declinare in nostra esset positum potestate.

2 Nunc vero postquam cavere didicimus, adhibere remedia doceamus (haec enim erat altera pars) quorum[192] ope fieri posse videbatur ut se quis inviolatum et incorruptum in vita servaret: facilior autem haec traditio nobis erit postquam adversa pepulimus. Quis enim, vel imperitissimus, nesciat si mihi ab humettis sit interdictum siccantia conductura, aut si calefacientia evitanda uti refrigerantibus oportere? **3** A cibo igitur et potu quomodo abstinendum [80r] esse dixerimus, ciborum vero alios tumefacientes, alios fervefacientes, ut ea quae a medicis observantur: reliquum esse videtur ut cibis et tepefacientibus et residere cogentibus vescatur is qui declinare statuit voluptates; in quo tamen ea cura est adhibenda ut pro sua quisque natura cibis utatur conducentibus et, si fieri tuto possit, etiam non ingratis.

---

[192] *quarum* MS, Br., but *-orum* is required by *remedia* as antecedent.

demonstrated[193] – namely, on what basis it would be reasonable to expect that someone could be celibate. Let's now pass on to the matters that remain.

[6] On the treatments to be applied to preserve sexual purity in celibacy.

6.1 And so almost everything has been stated and spoken of that seemed capable of causing harm to the protectors of their own moral uprightness. Just as these things pose a great risk of injury to our happiness, so nature brought it about and saw to it that we had it in our power to shun what would harm us.

2 Now, however, after we've learnt to take precautions, let's demonstrate how to apply the treatments (for this was the second part [of my agenda])[194] that seemed able to help someone keep himself unharmed and undefiled in life; and passing on this knowledge will be easier for me now that I've dispelled their harmful opposites. For who wouldn't know – even a complete ignoramus – that if I was warned against accumulations of phlegmy moisture, drying agents would be expedient, or that cooling agents have to be deployed if the causes of high temperatures are to be avoided?[195] **3** We should say, therefore, that food and drink are to be treated with restraint in whatever way;[196] and that without doubt, in the case of foods, some cause bloating and others induce fevers,[197] in line with the observations made by doctors. It remains, it seems, for one who decides to shun pleasures to eat foods that both induce a moderate warmth and compel a loss of intensity. In this matter, however, pains are to be taken to ensure that everyone according to his own nature consumes foods that bring advantage, and – if it can happen safely – are also not unpleasant.

---

[193] An important shift of strategy in light of 3.5.46: after relying there on 'certain first principles' of argument (i.e., vices are to be loathed because of their intrinsic nature, 3.5.45), Barbaro now moves from a priori assumption to *the apparently demonstrated fact* in the later part of 3.5 that vice is so rampant as to commend, even necessitate, the celibate life.

[194] See 3.5.33.

[195] For such basic (self-)knowledge see, e.g., Cels. *Med.* 1.3.13: 'But above all things everyone should be acquainted with the nature of his own body, for . . . some [are] hot, others more frigid; some moist, others dry' (tr. Spencer 1935: 57; cf. 1.3.27-9 for basic techniques of rendering the body heated, cooled, humid, and dried).

[196] For *quomodo* so construed (equivalent to *quocumque modo*) cf. LS p. 1519 *quomodo* III. The extreme alternative is to infer interrogative 'how' (so Branca 1969: 13) and an indirect question taking an infinitive, not the usual subjunctive; on this phenomenon, occasionally found in Late Latin but exceptional here in *De coelibatu*, see Pinkster 2021: 106.

[197] Cf. 3.5.17-18.

4 Neque enim quorundam accedo sententiae, qui ita inviolabili lege astringendos homines putant ut vix impetrare panem et aquam possit quisquam. Quod quidem [Chrysippus][198] philosophus non obscurus dicitur voluisse; cuius forte sententiae auctorem Euripidem sequutus videtur. Eius fuisse illa verba creduntur ... et reliqua. [**80v**] Hoc est: 'quid opus est mortalibus praeterquam duobus iis, cereris et aquae muneribus, quae et adsunt et ad alendum nos abunde sufficiunt?' **5** Verum is, dum paucis egere vitam hominis putat, in severam quandam descendit tenuitatem, quando et hoc illum fefellit quod, cum famem et calefactionis exsiccationisque appetitionem esse, sitim contra refrigerationis humetationisque, collegisset,[199] sufficere ad victum arbitrabatur si exurienti panis, qui calidae et siccae naturae videretur, et aqua sitienti, quae frigidae et humettae, succurreret.

6 Ego vero pluris facio eorum sententiam qui mitius cum humani generis fragilitate agendum putant. Nam, ut omittam etiam plurimum interesse quantum quis ferat et quoius roboris sit, nosse naturas praeterea et qualitates maximum in quaque re momentum habere neque singulorum corporum varie[**81r**]tates tractari uno modo posse, extimare etiam aequum est hominem, ut animantium reliquarum et fruticum unumquodque, quae materia fluxa, ut Plato dicit, et labili constant, tanto magis egere alimento quanto laboriosius degit. **7** Laboriosum autem voco non qui agriculturae aut baiulationi addictus in continuo corporis ex<er>citu[200] et motu versetur:

---

[198] A blank space is left after *quidem* in the MS; for Chrysippus, Br. 119 n. 1.
[199] *esse sitim contra ... humetationisque collegisset* Br.
[200] See pp. 5–6 above.

4 For[201] I don't agree with the opinion of certain thinkers who believe that humans are to be bound by a law so unbreakable that anyone at all should barely be able to succeed in his request for bread and water. This, at all events, is what the philosopher [Chrysippus][202] of no humble reputation reportedly aimed at, seemingly following Euripides, the originator – it so happens – of this viewpoint. The following are thought to have been his words . . . and so on. That is: 'What need do mortals have beyond these two things, the gifts of bread and water, which are both at hand and amply sufficient to feed us?' 5 However, while he thought that human life has few needs, he lowered himself to a type of harsh austerity; for he also made the mistake that, since he'd inferred that hunger was a natural desire for warmth and dryness, and that thirst, on the other hand, was a desire for coolness and moisture,[203] he considered that it was enough for living if bread (because it seemed naturally hot and dry) relieved hunger, and water (because naturally cold and wet) relieved thirst.

6 I, however, esteem more highly the opinion of those who think that the frailty of the human race should be handled more gently. For – to pass over the fact that it also makes a very big difference how large a burden someone is shouldering and how strong he is, that it's additionally of the greatest importance in each particular circumstance to know a person's essential qualities of character, and that the differing states of individual bodies can't be treated in just one way – it's reasonable as well to reckon that a human (like every single one of all the other animals and plants that consist, as Plato says, of a fleeting and perishable substance) needs an amount of sustenance proportionate to the toils of his existence.[204] 7 I call hardworking not the sort who's wholly given over to farming or ferrying goods and is in a state of constant bodily exertion and

---

[201] Elaboration of the case for taking at least some moderate pleasure in food.
[202] The missing referent is surely Chrysippus of Soli (c. 280–207 BCE), the third head of the Stoic school, given the association drawn with Euripides immediately below; for Gellius reports (6.16.6-7; cf. Plut. Mor. 1043e, 1044b) the frugal Chrysippus' deep engagement with the Euripidean verses (fr. 892N²) that are presupposed in the two-and-three-quarter lines left blank in the MS after *creduntur*, and which Barbaro summarizes later in 3.6.4 ('What need . . . to feed us?').
[203] Already a familiar idea before Chrysippus, as in, e.g., Arist. *De an.* 2.3 414b12-14: 'Hunger and thirst are desire, the former for what is dry and hot, the latter for what is cold and wet; flavour is a kind of seasoning of these' (tr. Hett 1957: 81).
[204] The Platonic allusion is surely (Branca 1969: 120 on §6) to *Tim.* 77a-c, on the basic needs of the newly created mortal being: 'Since man's life is spent in "fire and air" – i.e., he is exposed to sun and wind – he suffers the wasting of his powers by the action of both, and to make good this waste he needs aliment. To meet this need, the gods created vegetation at the same time as man. The vegetables are alive and are therefore properly to be called ζῷα [/zōa], but they have only the kind of life which belongs to the ἐπιθυμητικόν [/epithūmētikon] in ourselves, appetition [cf. n. 178 above] and a sense of pleasure and pain' (Taylor 1928: 540; see further now Schroeder 2021, esp. 340–1). For the gender of *animantium* here see 2.4.17 n. 99.

hunc enim et pinguibus et rusticanis et, quibus maxime Homerus censuit, cervinis carnibus et bovillis nutriri praestabit; at eum laboriosum intelligi volo quem graeci [θεωρητικόν²⁰⁵] circa mentis agitationem et veri investigationem posuerunt. **8** Eum lautioribus et quasi politioribus vesci cibis oportebit, ut levior ille pastus quom sit, prope concoctus in stomacho recipiatur, mox in caeteras corporis partes egestus, suam de se portionem in reliqua membra trans[**81v**]missurus abradat sine labore et difficultate. Praeter id enim²⁰⁶ quod imbecilli sunt stomachi qui dant operam litteris, adiiciendum est illud quod nostri coelibes²⁰⁷ sine ulla remissione sunt in eo studiorum genere versaturi: quapropter indulgentiores esse sibi ipsis illos oportebit quam reliquos.

9 Non tamen laxanda est habena tantum ut ea quae pro mediocritate a nobis conceduntur in delitias exeant et excessus. Scio enim eam fuisse consuetudinem apud plurimas nationes, ut ea quae a legum latoribus, aut parum consideratis aut minime ea timentibus quae accidere potuissent, bona fide essent licentius instituta, in luxum protinus et apertam laxationem effluerent. **10** Novi etiam eum esse mortalitatis morem ut ita nunquam suis limitibus sit contenta, ut semper avare id quod [**82r**] deest inquirat. Neque sum nescius, quum sapientes id plurimi praevidissent, circa mores instituendos severiores esse voluisse, quemadmodum Antisthenem accepimus, qui, quom solvi plurimum voluptate animos hominum usu percepisset, voluptates omnis fugiendas esse dictitavit. **11** Ego vero quom esse aliquam nobis cum voluptate consortionem volo, non id facio ut probare

---

[205] Proposed by Br. 120 n. 2 to fill the blank in the MS.
[206] *id, enim,* Br.
[207] *col-* MS.

movement; for it will be better for this type to be fed on fatty, peasant meats and (what Homer recommended most of all) venison and beef.[208] But by hardworking, the type I want to be understood is that which the Greeks have categorized as [*theōrētikon*] in terms of mental activity and the investigation of truth.[209] **8** This type will necessarily have to feed on finer and, so to speak, more cultivated fare so that, since that food is lighter, it's received in the stomach in a nearly digested state; then, when it's carried off to the other parts of the body, it easily and without effort shaves off a portion of its own self so as to pass it on to the remaining parts. For beyond the fact that constitutions that are devoted to literary study are delicate, the point must be added that our celibates are set to engage in that branch of study without any let-up; hence they will necessarily be more lenient to themselves than will all others.

9 The rein isn't to be slackened to such an extent, however, that the concessions made by us to facilitate a middle course develop into excessive self-indulgence.[210] For I know that for very many peoples it's been customary for the measures that had been rather loosely set in place in good faith by legislators who were either insufficiently circumspect or not in the least afraid of what had the potential to happen – it's been customary for these measures to melt away at once into soft living and an obvious slackening of standards. **10** I also know that it's the way of mortals never to be satisfied with their own limitations, in such a way that they always greedily seek after what they lack. Nor am I unaware (since the point had already been seen by a great many sages) of the past enthusiasm about setting in place a stricter code of behaviour, just as we hear of Antisthenes: since he'd gleaned from his experience of people that their minds were very much undone by pleasure, he repeatedly asserted that all pleasures were to be avoided.[211] **11** However, while I want us to have some association with pleasure, I don't mean to give the impression

---

[208] Venison notably at *Od.* 10.156-84, but the eating of domestic cattle, sheep, etc., is far more common in Homer, roasting the norm, and beef a prestige item (cf. Ath. *Deipno.* 1 9a). Its consumption implied wealth as well as the nourishing of heroic strength and courage (cf. Pl. *Resp.* 3 404b-c, and see Sherratt 2004, esp. 304–6, with Bakker 2013: 49–52); in Athenaeus, Homer's concern for propriety is said to explain why his heroes eat only meat and prepare it themselves (1 18a-b). This focus on meat intriguingly modifies Barbaro's apparent reference in 3.6.6 to proto-human reliance on a vegetable diet alone (see n. 204 above).

[209] For the hardworking contemplative as therefore engaged in the 'active' life cf. 1.4.14 and n. 74 and see Vol. 1 Intro. pp. 18–19, 21, 23–4.

[210] In an appealing fusion of theme and presentational technique, Barbaro's reflections on balance and proportion in 3.6.9-14 themselves exhibit a judicious restraint before he formally prioritizes the golden mean for the celibate in 3.6.15.

[211] A close associate of Socrates, Antisthenes of Athens (*c.* 445–365 BCE) acquired a reputation for austere self-sufficiency (so, e.g., D. L. 6.3: 'He often said, "I would rather go mad than feel pleasure"'; tr. Mensch 2018: 261) – an asceticism so rigid that he was later regarded as the founder of the Cynic school (cf. D. L. 6.2).

voluptates omnis videar, sed modum adhiberi oportere ut et in caeteris rebus omnibus et temperamentum assentio. Quod etiam Aristoteli maxime placet, cuius etiam illa sententia est vera esse oportere omnia quae philosophus docet, neque addendum neque detrahendum esse aliquid veritati, etiam si danda concedendaque essent ea quae male quis aut interpretari [**82v**] aut ad usum licentiorem accommodare[212] posset; quemadmodum neque illud est committendum etiam ne, quamvis plus arroget sibi quam iubeatur aut imperetur aegrotus, vera et conducibilia praecipiantur.

12 Minus tamen peccant qui totam auferunt voluptatem, ut ego quidem arbitror, quam qui nullam excipiunt. Nam et in hac edendi bibendique[213] observatione fuere etiam non nulli qui, quemadmodum in vitiis contingit omnibus, ubi media virtute a Peripateticis constituta utrinque peccatum[214] collocatur, ne inane et vacuum iaceret alterum extimum, concedere ausi sunt comessare potare quantum et quae animus cuique ferret nulla esse lege prohibenda. **13** Quod ut manifeste, non dico falsum est, sed turpissimum et quod Epicureum[215] totum sapiat, ita non est a nobis hoc loco refellendum, [**83r**] sicut neque illud quoque quod aliquibus visum est, literis etiam proditum. Hi, quum mediocritatem sese tueri initio operis faterentur, quandoque tamen plus iusto comedendum et bibendum putant: quo statim nomine suae videntur ipsimet sententiae repugnare. **14** Qui enim fieri potest

---

[212] *accomm-* MS; *accom-* Br.
[213] *bib-* MS; *bid-* Br.
[214] *perc-* MS.
[215] *Epic-* MS; *epic-* Br.

of commending all pleasures, but I agree that some limit and restraint ought to be applied to them, as in all other matters as well. This position is very much favoured by Aristotle as well. He too is of the opinion that all that a philosopher teaches has to be true, and that nothing at all should be added to or taken away from the truth, even if points were to be offered and concessions made that someone could wrongly interpret or adapt to a rather presumptuous purpose[216] – just as that mistake too is not to be made, of preventing true and helpful recommendations from being made, even though the ailing patient makes more assumptions for himself than he's told or enjoined to do.

12 Those who do away with pleasure in its entirety, however, are less mistaken, at least in my view, than those who exclude no pleasure. For even in this matter of keeping a watchful eye on eating and drinking, there've also been some[217] who – as happens in all moral failings when virtue is established by the Peripatetics as the mean, and transgression is located on either side of it[218] – [there've been some who,] to prevent the one extreme or the other from being left void and irrelevant, venture to allow that eating and drinking what the mind of each could bear in whatever quantity should be forbidden by no rule. **13** While this is clearly, I don't say false, but most disgraceful, and the sort of thing that smacks entirely of Epicureanism,[219] at the same time it's not to be refuted by me at this point, any more than that position as well that has appealed to some and has even been passed down in writing. These thinkers suppose that, although they profess as a starting-point for their work to uphold the mean, sometimes one should nevertheless eat and drink what's more than the right amount; on this account they themselves seem automatically to go against their own viewpoint.[220] **14** For how can it happen

---

[216] Cf. *EN* 1.6 1096a13-17 (in setting out to examine the notion of a universal Good, Aristotle rejects the Platonic Form of the Good): '... the Forms have been introduced by friends of our own. Yet it would perhaps be thought to be better, indeed to be our duty, for the sake of maintaining the truth even to destroy what touches us closely, especially as we are philosophers or lovers of wisdom; for, while both are dear, piety requires us to honour truth above our friends' (tr. Ross 1980: 7-8).

[217] Esp. the Cyrenaics; a likely glance back to Aristippus at 3.5.14.

[218] For the Peripatetics, 1.2.6 and n. 30. For the Aristotelian mean, *EN* 2.2 1104a11-27, 2.6-9 1106a24-1109b26 with the concise overview in Young 1988, esp. 522-5; in a nutshell, virtues such as temperance and courage 'are destroyed by excess and defect, and preserved by the mean' (2.2 1104a25-7; tr. Ross 1980: 31).

[219] Here with a strong pejorative emphasis, as if Barbaro merges the Epicurean and Cyrenaic (cf. n. 217) positions; but for the Epicurean hedonistic calculus see 3.5.8 and n. 64.

[220] A likely allusion to the difference between fixed and relative interpretations of the mean, as observed by Aristotle at *EN* 2.6 1106a26-b7: the arithmetical mean between two and ten is six; but if ten pounds is too much to eat, two too little, the mean of six pounds may yet be insufficient for a prime athlete like Milo, far excessive for an athletic beginner. Barbaro appears to round on this slippage between 'the mean of the thing' and 'that relative to us' down to 3.6.14 '... a medium state?' – but then to countenance the relative interpretation in 'Unless ... of this sort' (strenuous jobs justify 'excessive' food consumption beyond a theoretical mean).

ut mediocre sit quicquam quod iusto plus sit? Nisi forte ei homini plus iusto comedendum arbitrantur, qui sit aut in republica aut in navigatione aut vitae huiuscemodi genere aliquo versaturus; aut certe plus iusto id intelligi voluerunt ne semper homines de valitudine sua, aeque ac si aegroti essent, cogitarent. Quod ego ita sensisse[221] illos autumo neque quicquam errasse.

15 In coelibe autem nihil quod iusto plus sit concedemus, sed mediocritatem illam auream requiremus, quam viri sapi[**83v**]entissimi rerum humanarum regulam statuerunt. Hanc quivis adipiscetur celerrime, si non quod aequo plus sit sed quod in aequo et iusto sit positum sequi voluerit. **16** Hoc pacto neque malum erit quod est in mediocritate collocatum, ut Cicero prave interdum (per lusum fortasse) videtur interpretari, neque rursum semper atque omnino summum id quod in medio virtus est, quemadmodum nostri temporis quidam, quem modestiae gratia non nomino, in ea praesertim re, in qua errare visus est viris doctis omnibus, libris exscriptum[222] reliquit. **17** Quae quom ita sint, ne longius discedamus, nostram, hoc est, doctissimorum hominum esse sententiam iterum sciat coelebs: cibo potuque abstinendum quum sit, mediocriter utrisque et pro sua maxime quemque natura uti oportere.

---

[221] *-tisse* MS.
[222] *excript-* MS.

that anything that's more than justified constitutes a medium state? Unless perhaps they think that what's more than the right amount is to be consumed by a person who's set to be involved in public service, in sailing the seas, or in some branch of existence of this sort; or they doubtless wanted that concept of the-more-than-justified to be grasped so that people wouldn't always think about their own state of health just as if they were ill.[223] I reckon that they thought in this way, and were not at all deluded.

15 But in the celibate's case I shall allow nothing that's more than the right amount, but will look for that famous golden mean[224] that the wisest minds have established as an ordaining principle of human affairs. Anyone will very quickly grasp this principle, if he'll want to pursue not what is beyond reasonable, but what is based in the reasonable and the fair. **16** On these terms there will be nothing bad that's located in the mean, as Cicero sometimes seems perversely to understand (perhaps in jest);[225] nor, again, always and altogether supreme is that quality of virtue in the mean – as a certain author of our own time (whom I refrain from naming for propriety's sake) left noted down in his books, especially on that topic in which he seemed to all learned men to be in error.[226] **17** Since this is so,[227] and to avoid digressing any longer, let the celibate once again know my opinion – that is, the opinion of the most learned people: since food and drink have to be treated with restraint, each person must avail himself of both things with moderation, and above all in accordance with his own nature.

---

[223] I.e., they would view their health as a relative condition, albeit the Peripatetics did not recognize the mean in a bad state; i.e., there can be extreme sickness or a minor ailment, but no mean between them that is good (cf. Arist. *EN* 2.6 1107a.8-17).

[224] A conspicuous echo of Hor. *Carm.* 2.10.5 *auream ... mediocritatem*, itself with strong Aristotelian overtones (Nisbet and Hubbard 1978: 160–1 ad loc.).

[225] Barbaro vindicates the Aristotelian mean on two fronts, first by effortlessly, even snidely ('perhaps in jest'), turning on Stoic intransigence at *Tusc.* 3.22: to the Stoics, the Peripatetic theory of the mean as applied to the emotions, allowing for 'moderate states (*mediocritates*) either of disturbances or of diseases in the soul,' is unacceptable; for 'every evil, even a moderate one, is an evil; but our object is that there should be no evil at all in the wise man' (tr. King 1945: 253).

[226] Barbaro's second vindication of the Aristotelian mean, this time discrediting an alternative view by implicating it 'in error.' The unnamed author is plausibly (Branca 1969: 122 on §16) Lorenzo Valla, the allusion to his *De voluptate/On pleasure* (cf. 1.3.3 and n. 37); first appearing in 1431, the work was revised as *De vero falsoque bono* (*On the true and false good*, 1433) and later renamed *De vero bono* (*On the true good*) in a third bout of revision in 1444–9 (see on this evolution Lorch 1970: xv-lvii). What is the greatest ethical good? Over three books the question is debated from the Epicurean, Stoic, and Christian viewpoints, with Epicurean hedonism giving way to the shaping in Book 3 of a Christian form of morality based on pleasure. Along the way in Book 3 Valla's Christian spokesperson, the humanist Franciscan Antonio da Rho (*c.* 1398–1450/3), attacks the Aristotelian view of virtue as a mean between vicious extremes (see esp. 3.4.3-31; tr. Hieatt and Lorch 1977: 237–51). Barbaro resorts to sarcasm in 'nor, again ... in the mean,' as if endorsing a position that he in fact steadfastly rejects.

[227] I.e., Barbaro's commitment to the Aristotelian mean as stated in 3.6.15.

18 Quae vero[228] ... **[85r]** ad radices Olympi montis sedens in caute[229] camerata philosophabatur ... quoque simulata valitudine in Asclepianum concessit ibique deambulabat. Neque id quidem morbi causa fecit, sed quod scholas eo in loco constituendas putaret, quo soli confluerent disciplinae appetentes.

19 Fabulae quoque idem nobis in Orpheo ostendere voluerunt. Is enim, quom poetari securius et cum Musis expeditius vivere decrevisset, inaccessam

---

[228] F. 84 is missing: see n. 230 below and Vol. 1 Intro. p. 6.
[229] *incaute* MS, Br.

18 But as for what[230] ... sitting at the foot of Mt. Olympus on an arched crag, he applied himself to philosophy[231] ... [Crantor] also,[232] feigning sickness, retired to the temple of Asclepius, where he proceeded to walk about.[233] He didn't in fact do this because of illness, but because he thought philosophical schools should be set up in a place to which only those eager for training would flock.

19 Myths also aimed to demonstrate the same point to us in the case of Orpheus.[234] For since he'd decided to indulge his poetry with a greater peace

---

[230] The complex sequence of argument in 3.6.18-48 is impaired at its beginning by the vandalism that excised f. 84 from the MS (see Vol. 1 Intro. p. 6); Branca 1952: 85 and 1969: 11 conjectures that f. 84 contained a miniature illustration of Mt. Olympus to accompany Barbaro's allusion to the mountain in 3.6.18. The first of the three modes of self-distancing from society that Barbaro surveys in §§18-24 is therefore sadly truncated: **A** (§§18-20): to live in isolation from the city; **B** (§§21-2): to remain in the city, but with avoidance of public places and gatherings; **C** (§§23-4): to remain in the city, but with permanent excuse-making to avoid company and distraction from one's work. Then (§25) review of which of these three modes is best, beginning with **A** (§§25-39): those prone to wrongdoing should stay away from the city (§25), but it takes strength of mind to separate oneself from the pleasurable (esp. erotic) stimuli that the city offers (§26). Little is to be expected of one lacking that strength (§27), even though such weakness is not beyond treatment (§28); for no mind is so vitiated at birth that it cannot be rehabilitated by therapeutic means (§§29-30). Despite differentials of natural ability or personal affliction, human reason allows everyone at least to aspire to celibacy (§31), but the celibate *does* require an exceptional steadfastness of life-long devotion (§§32-3); hence weaker natures should not be encouraged in this direction (§34), as natural aptitudes should be heeded (§§35-6). Weaker temperaments are therefore better off away from the city, but so too are the hardier types who would find philosophical immersion safer or more conducive elsewhere (§37), Anaxagoras being a case in point (§38); and so those two types should keep a distance from the city (§39). After this intricate extrapolation of **A**, Barbaro progresses to **B** in §§40-1 and to **C** in §§42-6 before his crowning focus in §47 on insulating the celibate from all exposure to vice; in terms of the review initiated in §25 ('which of these three modes of behaviour is the best'), **A** resoundingly carries the day.

[231] The subject of *philosophabatur* is lost with f. 84 if the blank after the verb presupposes instead the subject (Crantor?) of *concessit* and *deambulabat* below. The person to whom *philosophabatur* refers is presumably no less historical than Crantor, given 3.6.19 'Myths also ...'

[232] The Academic philosopher Crantor of Soli (*c*. 335-275 BCE) offers a good fit for what follows; for his retirement to the Asclepieion of Athens, D. L. 4.24.

[233] With a philosophical nuance after D. L. 4.24 *peripatei* ('he walked about while discoursing'; tr. Mensch 2018: 191); see LSJ περιπατέω 2, and cf. 1.2.6 and n. 30 on the Peripatetics.

[234] The main myth of this legendary singer – his tragic failure to recover his departed wife Eurydice from the Underworld (cf. Virg. G. 4.453-527, Ov. Met. 10.1-85, 11.1-66) – is carefully edited in Barbaro's retelling here so that the focus falls on Orpheus' antisocial misogyny and, in consequence, his death at the hands of the Maenads (miscast in the MS as *Menades*), or the scorned devotees of Dionysus (cf. *Met*. 11.7: 'Look, look! Here's the one who rejects us!'); after the loss of Eurydice, he thus resembles an extreme celibate, even a celibate martyr.

prius Rhodopaei Thracii montis rupem perpetuo inhabitasse fertur: quo circa[235] et mulieres odio habuisse et sacra solemnia atque pompas neglexisse, ne suae diligentiae aliquid anteponeret, per fictionem quandam et exemplum est traditus; signum etiam subdiderunt quod dilaniatum articulatim decerptumque muliebri furore in proximum fluvium Menades proiecerunt.

20 Porro ex [85v] iis palam esse debet videri urbanos coetus animi laedere et labefactare constantiam posse: vacationem vero et sedes minime negotiosas eiusdem tueri et roborare firmitatem.

21 Alter[236] modus ab hoc, quem supra enarravi, proximus suos etiam habuit fautores. Is autem eorum erat qui, quom se in urbe continerent,[237] non tamen publicos adibant locos, sed aut domi claudebantur, aut soli in adversam a foro[238] urbis partem exercitationis gratia obambulabant, aut ut Stoici porticum Peripateticique et philosophorum plurimi Achademias incolebant. 22 Quare Theophrastus eiusque quam plurimi successores[239] locum quendam philosophari volentibus communem testamento reliquerunt, et, quod de Platonis vico vulgatum est, mercari is agrum voluit et publico studiosorum hominum usui condonare. Frequen[86r]tabunt hos illi locos in quibus excolere animum et exercere corpus commode poterunt, qui urbanam consuetudinem anteponent.

---

[235] *quo circa* MS; *quocirca* Br. (so too Br. *contra* MS at 4.2.11, 15, 35, but *quo circa* with MS at 3.6.31, 45, 4.2.45).
[236] *lter* MS, rubricated *A* yet to be added (cf. Br. 123 n. 1).
[237] *-entur* MS.
[238] *a foro* MS in left margin.
[239] *success-* Br. for MS *succuss-*; *succurs-* ('helpers') is also suggested by Br. 123 n. 3, but better *success-* in the context of inheritance (see my n. 242 below).

of mind and to be more disencumbered in his life with the Muses, he allegedly settled permanently on a previously inaccessible crag of Mt. Rhodope in Thrace. In consequence, he was said – through a kind of fiction as an example – both to have viewed women with hatred and to have disregarded religious observances and festivals so as not to give precedence to anything over his own devotion [to poetry]; the stories also fraudulently introduced a warning-sign[240] because, in their female frenzy, the Maenads tore him apart limb-by-limb and threw his mutilated form into the nearest river.

20 In turn, it should appear obvious from these cases that forms of social intercourse in the city can harm and destabilize firmness of mind; but that freedom [from such involvements], and dwelling-places that have very little to do with the busy life, can protect and reinforce that robustness of mind.

21 The second method [of self-distancing from society], very close to the one I mentioned above, has also had its supporters. This was the method of those who, though they remained in the city, nevertheless didn't go to public places but would either be confined at home or in the habit of walking on their own, for the sake of exercise, to a part of the city in an opposite direction from the forum; or [they avoided public places] just as the Stoics used to frequent the porch, and the Peripatetics and a great many philosophers the Academies.[241] **22** Hence Theophrastus and as many of his successors as possible left by will a certain shared place for those wanting to practice philosophy;[242] and – the story commonly told about Plato's home district – he wanted to buy a piece of land and give it for the shared use of those dedicated to learning.[243] These places will be heavily visited by those who will prefer the habit of city life, and will be able suitably to cultivate the mind and exercise the body in them.

---

[240] Against adopting the celibate life.
[241] Stoicism took its name from the 'painted porch' (Gk. *stoa poikilē*) in the Athenian agora where the school first congregated under Zeno (for whom 2.5.13 and n. 129). For the Peripatetics 1.2.6 and n. 30; for the Platonic Academy, 2.2.4 and n. 16, but plural 'Academies' here loosely embraces the different schools at Athens.
[242] For Theophrastus, 1.2.1 and n. 24; see D. L. 5.52-3 for the bequest of his estate in Stagira to Callinus, his books to Neleus, and '[t]he garden and walkway and all the houses adjoining the garden ... to any of the friends listed below who wish to philosophize there together' (tr. Mensch 2018: 240).
[243] D. L. 3.20 asserts that Anniceris of Cyrene bought Plato 'the small garden that is in the Academy,' possibly identifiable with the second of the two estates mentioned in Plato's will (D. L. 3.42); this appears to have been a private property where Plato associated with his disciples while the main business of the school was conducted in the public park that was the Academy proper (further, Dillon 2003: 2–11).

23 Tertius est modus eorum qui et in urbe quidem et intra moenia continentur; sed quom aut amicus, ut fit, aut affinis aut hospes eripere illos a studiis velint, aut aegritudinem simulant, aut balneum et coenam excusant, aut tale aliquid omnino semper causantur quominus ab opere abducantur suo. Demosthenem vero oratorem accepimus dimidium capitis, parte altera cum capillis relicta, velut ad calvitium abrasisse sibi, cavernamque effossa humo manufactam integris mensibus incoluisse.

24 Solebat avus meus (ne domesticis etiam exemplis carere videamur) imperare famulis ut domi esse se negarent omnibus, quos ornatiore cultu [**86v**] aut accuratiore vestitos conspexissent, ea scilicet ratione, ne, si non patuisset aditus, qui huiuscemodi hominibus ut mollibus effeminatisque negabatur, succensendi ocasionem praeberet iis, quos minime hunc in modum laedi posse arbitrabatur. Nunc vero etiam infimus quisque, quom est occupatus, scit negare se non[244] esse domi, ut efficiat id quod in manibus habet.

25 Trium horum qui mos sit optimus et qui maxime coelibi nostro approbandus breviter aperiemus. Abesse ab urbe semper ii debent, qui, quum fragiliore ingenio sint et ad culpam protinus inclinato, periculo proximi videntur, si urbem incolant, in qua vel invitis pleraque libidinem cientia possunt occurrere, quae debiliorem animum de statu prope deiiciant. **26** Quamquam nescio an fieri queat ut is solitudines et deserta ferat, qui minutulas animi affectiones et [**87r**] parvas titillationum motiunculas tolerare non sciat, nisi forte credendum est eos muros tormentis omnibus contra staturos, qui parvo ariete conquassentur, aut eam nivem solis ardorem perpessuram, quae admota ignis modici favilla liquescat. Qua propter nos supra diximus fortem et robustum animum esse illius oportere, qui se a voluptatibus praesertim veneris sit sequestraturus. **27** Quod si nondum est quispiam assequutus, ut grandi iam aetate, quae, quia neque iuventae calore neque frigore senectutis infestatur, tutissima esse solet, abstinere et resistere

---

[244] As pleonastic negator, Pinkster 2015: 730 8.48 (cf. 4.2.53).

23 The third method belongs to those who indeed remain in the city and its walls; but when (as tends to happen) a friend, relative, or guest wants to snatch them away from their studies, they either feign sickness or plead in excuse a bath and a dinner, or they always in all circumstances give some such reason so that they're not taken away from their work. Moreover, we're told that the orator Demosthenes shaved half his head, as if to the point of baldness, but left the other half with hair, and that he lived for entire months in an excavated hollow underground.[245]

24 My grandfather[246] – let me show that I can draw examples from my own family as well – used to instruct his servants to say to every visitor whom they'd observed to be dressed rather elaborately or with excessive care that he wasn't at home. Why did he do this? Evidently to ensure that, if access to him hadn't been made available – access that was denied to people of this first sort as being soft and unmanly – he wouldn't give cause for anger to those he reckoned least capable of being offended in this way. Now, moreover, even everyone of the lowliest station, when he's preoccupied, knows to say that he's not at home so as to finish what he's engaged in.

25 I shall briefly explain which of these three modes of behaviour is the best, and which in particular is to be endorsed by our celibate. Those should always keep away from the city who, since their disposition is rather frail and prone to wrongdoing from the very first, seem very close to danger if they reside in the city; there, even against their will, a great many stimuli of sexual desire can come upon them of the sort to all but overthrow the weaker kind of mind. 26 Admittedly, I'm not sure it can happen that one who doesn't know how to put up with tiny predilections of feeling and small stirrings of ticklish arousal would endure the loneliness of solitude – unless, perhaps, we're to believe that the sort of walls that are shattered by a small battering ram will otherwise stand firm before all kinds of missile engine, or that snow that melts when the embers of a smallish fire are put near it will endure the sun's scorching heat. Hence I said above that one who's going to separate himself from the pleasures above all of love ought to have a strong and sturdy mind.[247] 27 If someone hasn't yet achieved this – to the effect that, at a now mature age which, because it's troubled neither by the heat of youth nor by the chill of old age, is usually on a very safe footing, he knows how to steer clear of and to withstand the nagging of vices – there will have to be no great

---

[245] For the anecdote (Demosthenes too ashamed to leave his lair), Plut. *Dem.* 7.3, *Mor.* 844d, and cf. Quint. *Inst.* 10.3.25.
[246] Presumably his paternal grandfather, Francesco.
[247] 'I said above': cf. 3.6.20, but Barbaro may mean a phase of argument that ended there after beginning in the now-lost f. 84.

vitiorum importunitati sciat, ab hoc neque sperare quicquam admirabile oportebit, neque perseveraturum existimare qui sit natura impotentissimus procreatus. **28** Sunt enim, ut in corporum habitudinibus, imbecillae quaedam naturae et malis omnibus [**87v**] atque morbis[248] expositae: ita et in animorum statu plerunque fit, ut primo impetu ab omni perturbatione ex innata fragilitate capiantur. Non eo tamen inficias quemadmodum et valitudinariorum plerosque ope medica aut casu plerunque incolumitatem assequutos fuisse, ita et debilissimas quorundam atque inhonestas appetitiones consuetudine aliqua et actione revocatas fieri posse, ut aut tollantur aut reprimantur; et ne ab eodem exemplo recedamus, biliosos quosdam expertum est natura ipsa factos cura circa id diligentiaque acri adhibita in meliorem tutioremque habitum transitum fecisse; idem fieri in animo posse concesserim, alioqui non esset in nobis ea virtus, qua bona possemus eligere, mala declinare. **29** Quod nemo tantum negare debet quam is qui eam curam quam nos profitetur et ge[**88r**]rit. Veruntamen solent non nulli dubitare ut, si vera sit prorsus ea similitudo, quae cum corporis habitu et animi facta est, quom frequenter[249] accidat, ut ita quisquam ab ipsa protinus genitura sit morbo aliquo vehementer implicitus, ut nullis sanari medicamentis, nulla iuvari arte possit, num accidere quoque par sit interdum, ut tam pravo animo nascatur ullus qui singulis perturbationum motibus ita sit opportunus, ut nulla corrigi ratione,

---

[248] *moribus* MS.
[249] *-ar* MS, but corrective *e* added above *a*.

expectation of anything worth admiring in such a person, and no thought that one who was naturally lacking all self-control as a fact of birth will go on to be resolute of purpose.

28 For just as in the case of bodily conditions, certain weak natures are liable to all sorts of troubles and ailments, so it often happens in the case of their mental condition as well that, because of an inborn frailty, at the first onset they are seized by all possible disturbance. Yet I don't deny that – just as a great many invalids, too, have often found safety through medical help or by chance – so even the most feeble and disreputable impulses of certain people can become checked by some process of habituation and active intervention so that they are either removed or suppressed. And, to persist with the same illustration, experience tells us that certain people who were made full of bile[250] by nature herself have managed the transition to a better, more secure condition through the careful and vigilant attention that was brought to bear on it. I'd grant that the same can happen in the case of the mind; otherwise, we wouldn't have within us that quality of excellence that enables us to choose the good and deflect the bad.[251] **29** No one should deny this[252] as much as the person who professes and pursues the same concern as I do. But even so, a fair number habitually harbor doubts to this effect: if the similarity that's been drawn between body-state and mind-state is straightforwardly true, since it often happens that someone has been so grievously gripped by some disease right from the very moment of birth that he can't be cured by any medicines or helped by any professional skill, wouldn't it sometimes also be reasonable for this to happen – that any given person is born with a mind so vitiated, a person so prone to every single stirring of strong emotion, that he can be straightened out by no appeal to reason and remedied by no kind of

---

[250] Yellow or black bile, two of the four bodily humours (see 2.6.21 and n. 177).
[251] See conveniently Gill 2006: 200-2 on the complex philosophical background to the issues raised here. Already in *Tim.* 86b-90d Plato connects illnesses of the psyche and moral faults (e.g., sexual incontinence) to bodily/constitutional defect, sometimes in combination with poor education; but the focus in response should fall on therapy and promoting better health, not on censure, as the individual is not responsible for the failings in body/mind (cf. *Tim.* 86d: 'for no one does wrong voluntarily'). In development of such ideas, and in a partial movement away from the kind of blamelessness posited in Plato's *Timaeus*, humans are in Stoic and Epicurean thought responsible rational agents who are capable of responding positively to therapy and education, and can therefore change their behaviours accordingly. This general picture is complicated by later contributions (so, notably, Galen: Gill 201); but the stress on rational agency and responsibility importantly informs Barbaro's own rehearsal of the point in 'otherwise,... the bad.'
[252] I.e., that impairment of the mind as well as of the body *can* in fact be ameliorated by appropriate therapies.

nullo emendari consilio possit. **30** Quod quum falsissimum sit, necesse est ut non sit ex toto simillima animi et corporis valitudo; quare neque cogendi sumus unquam ut ullum esse hominem fateamur qui non sit ea cum reliquis potestate donatus, qua et sequi quae bona sunt et fugere quae mala possit; alioqui esse non hominem eum hominem oporteret, qui [**88v**] homo quum sit ab hominis fuisset ratione deiectus.

31 Concedendum tamen est referre quantis sit quisque muneribus natura insignitus aut contra incommodis afflictatus: inter haec autem esse neminem qui sit prorsus communi illa animi potestate rationeque spoliatus. Quo circa negare non possumus adversissima etiam ingenia aspirare posse ad coelibatum, sed id quidem sine periculo et difficultate fieri non posse arbitrantur omnes. **32** Nihil enim est, quod stabiliorem animum requirat, quam eius studium, quod tunc dici absolutum poterit, quom vita erit absoluta: coelibatus autem nostri ea natura est, ut non ante sit quispiam coelebs nominandus, quam vita sit functus. Nam si exacta etiam priore aetate innocenter atque caste semel tantum deliquerit quisquam, operam omnem laboresque nequiquam[253] videbitur [**89r**] perdidisse. **33** Ut enim ea, quae ad bellum summo studio et diligentia sunt comparata, nisi victoria, quae finis erat, subsequuta sit, evanescant oportet, ita et eorum in quae animus ingenti labore prius incubuit, nisi ad quod tendit in eo constanter perseveret, cassam et vanam fuisse solicitudinem est necesse.

34 Quamobrem hortari amice[254] debemus eos, qui molles et delicati sunt, omnino vero ad huiuscemodi studium minus accommodati, ne contra

---

[253] -*quicquam* MS.
[254] -*ae* MS.

counsel?[255] **30** Since this is very misguided, soundness of mind and soundness of body are necessarily not very alike at all. Hence we're never to be forced to admit that there's any human who isn't endowed with the capacity (along with his other capacities) that enables him both to pursue the good and to avoid the bad; otherwise, that human would necessarily not be human, because, though human by existence, he'd have been an outcast from human reason.[256]

31 It nevertheless has to be granted that the extent of the gifts that naturally mark out each individual makes a difference – or, by contrast, the extent of the troubles that afflict him; but that between these opposites, there's no one who is altogether stripped of that rational capacity of the mind that is shared by all. Hence I can't deny that even the most contrary temperaments are capable of aspiring to celibacy; but everyone thinks that that at any rate can't happen without risk and difficulty. **32** For there's nothing that needs a greater constancy of mind than devotion to celibacy – a devotion that could be called complete only when life will be complete. Such is the character of my notion of celibacy that no one is to be termed a celibate before he's died.[257] For if someone commits a wrong only once, even after spending his prior existence in blameless purity,[258] he'll be seen to have wasted all his effort and hard work to no purpose. **33** For just as the preparations that are made for war with the utmost energy and carefulness necessarily come to nothing unless the goal of victory follows, so also, unless the mind resolutely persists towards the goal of its striving, the pains it has taken over those matters to which it earlier devoted itself with vast effort inevitably prove to have been futile and empty.

34 For that reason we must encourage in a friendly manner those who are weak and tender – in all respects, in fact, not very suited to this sort of pursuit – not to want to strive against nature, and not to start on the journey that they

---

[255] A good example of Latin syntactical style carrying much of the burden of argument, as the complex analogy worked here is more rhetorically alluring than logically compelling, and therefore easily dismissed in 3.6.30 'Since this is very misguided': the symmetry between two units, the first featuring the ailing body (*quom ... accidat, ut ... ut nullis sanari medicamentis, nulla iuvari arte possit*) and the second the ailing mind (*num accidere ... par sit ..., ut ... ut nulla corrigi ratione, nullo emendari consilio possit*), creates the illusion of an exact correlation that is belied by the (mere) extrapolation of an inference ('wouldn't it ... happen ...?') from a hypothetical premise ('if the similarity ...').

[256] See 1.1.2 and n. 11.

[257] Adaptation of the famous maxim (allegedly Solon to Croesus) 'Count no man happy until he is dead'; cf. Hdt. 1.32.7, 86.3, Arist. *EE* 2.1 1219b6-7, *EN* 1.10 1100a10-11, Cic. *Fin.* 3.76.

[258] Cf. for this scenario 3.5.41.

naturam niti velint, neve iter id incohent,[259] quod ut peragant sibi esse difficillimum sciunt. Neque enim ad unam rem omnes apti sunt natura rerum varietati consulente: ergo neque sequi aliud debent quam id ad quod natum esse se quisque non ignorabit. **35** Quod si impetrare a non nullis liceret, qui se observationibus quibusdam nulla habita ratione ingenii [**89v**] sui inconsiderate et temerarie per imprudentiam alligant, non essent illae miserrimae[260] miseriarum varietates, quibus maxime affici eos videmus, qui sanctimoniae leges subierunt; neque ullum esset in civitate felicius institutum, quam ut in coeteris artificiis officiisque atque muneribus, ita praeviderent potissimum magistratus, ne cives ulli diversum vivendi genus eligerent, quam id ad quod apti natura viderentur. **36** Quam rem ut esse discretu difficillimam in promptu est omnibus iudicare, ita utilissimam fore rebus humanis opem et ad communem omnium foelicitatem accommodatam nemo esse debet qui addubitet.

37 Sed expatiandi longius in hac re quandoque opportunius dabitur tempus. Nunc egressi in tantum materiam sumus, ut ostenderemus non probari a nobis eius ingenium [**90r**] qui tanta debilitate sit ut manere in urbe non possit circa labem et vitium. Quod si is esset quispiam ut manere quidem in urbe posset, sed tutius quietiusque extra urbem se philosophaturum putaret, improbare non possem sed et summopere laudarem, quando praesertim videri nequit quod opus urbe sit ei qui se a negotiis urbis abduxit. **38** Anaxagoras nanque, tametsi summa vir integritate et continentia esset et haberetur, patrimonium tamen reliquit omne seque, rei et publicae et privatae negligens, ex urbe profectus, ad speculandam naturae potestatem contulit. **39** Quae quum ita sint, manifestum est duo esse hominum genera

---

[259] -*ant* MS, but corrective *e* added above *a*.
[260] *ille miserrime* MS.

know to be very difficult for themselves to accomplish.²⁶¹ For not everyone is suited to one and the same thing, since nature pays attention to the diversity of things. Therefore, they mustn't go in pursuit of something other than that to which each individual will be well aware he was born. **35** If it were possible to secure this much from some people who, through thoughtlessness, attach themselves with ill-advised rashness to certain practices without taking account of their own natural disposition, there wouldn't be those thoroughly miserable vicissitudes of wretchedness that we see to be especially hurtful to those who've submitted to the laws of moral purity. Nor would any ordinance in the state have a happier outcome than that, as in all the other skilled occupations and official posts and commissions, so the magistrates would ensure above all that no citizens opted for a mode of existence different from that to which they seemed naturally suited.²⁶² **36** While it's easy for everyone to consider this matter very hard to decide, at the same time no one should doubt that it would be a resource of very great benefit to human affairs and well fitted for the shared prosperity of all.

37 But a more suitable occasion will be granted sometime for speaking at greater length on this matter. For now I've gone beyond my topic to such an extent to show that I don't commend the temperament of one so frail that he can't remain in the city in close proximity to ruinous vice. But if someone were the sort who could indeed persist in the city, but thought it safer and more restful for him to engage in philosophy outside the city, I couldn't voice any disapproval but would even praise him most highly, especially since it's impossible to see what need of the city there would be to one who's distanced himself from the city's busy dealings. **38** For indeed Anaxagoras, though a man of the utmost uprightness and self-restraint, and regarded as such, nevertheless abandoned his entire estate and, with no concern either for the commonwealth or his own wealth, he departed from the city and devoted himself to contemplating nature's power.²⁶³ **39** That being so, it's clear that

---

[261] Given Barbaro's broader recourse in *De coelibatu* to Cicero's *De officiis* (see Vol. 1 Intro. pp. 18–19), his focus in 3.6.34-6 on the importance of heeding one's individual nature is perhaps shaped by Cicero's coverage of the second of the four 'roles' (*personae*, derived from Panaetius, for whom Vol. 1 Intro. p. 19) that should inform appropriate action: (i) our universal nature (1.100-6); (ii) our natural disposition as individuals (1.107-14); (iii) our circumstances (1.115); and (iv) our choices in terms of career and the kind of life we want (1.115-21).

[262] The implication is that, by being allowed to 'serve' in conformity with his individual nature, Barbaro's celibate receives the state's sanction for his vocation.

[263] For Anaxagoras, 2.5.12 and n. 126; for the anecdote, D. L. 2.6-7, and cf. Plut. *Mor.* 831f.

qui abesse ab urbe velint: unum eorum qui ita sunt imbecilles ut nulli cupiditati resistere valeant: hos ego mallem uxorem ducerent et opem aliquam suae [**90v**] debilitati quaererent; alterum est eorum qui, quanvis in urbe et extra urbem constantes et fortes sint, liberius tamen et minore cum molestia sese victuros arbitrantur, si ex oculis multitudinis abeant: hos ego ad coelibatum capescendum idoneos esse maxime assero.

40 Secundus erat, ut diximus, quorundam mos, qui se in urbe continent aut domi, publicosque non solum non adeunt locos, sed despecta amicorum propinquorumque omnium consuetudine, neminem neque timentes neque curantes si ex eo se aliqui oderint, secum semper aut cum iis maxime diversantur, quos sibi disciplinarum sotios asciverunt. **41** Quorum consilium si est propter ea commoda, quae afferre urbis vicinitas potest, probo; sin minus, mallem abessent ab iis locis in quibus nullum esse usum [**91r**] sui aperte intelligunt. Quantum enim ad pudicitiam conservandam spectat, nemo est qui dubitet: peccare facilius potest qui propior[264] est peccandi licentiae, quam qui procul.

42 Reliquus erat eorum modus, qui, quum a spectaculis conviviisque velint abesse, ne amicorum sodaliumve rogatu, quod fit, aliquo pacto a studiis divellantur, simulque, ne cuiuspiam animum laedant, cuius iram aut odium subeant, si assentire illius precibus nolint[265] aut obtemperare, causas quaerunt[266] multiplices, quibus ab huiuscemodi impedimentis sine invidia aut malivolentia liberentur. **43** Verum hos ad rem publicam administrandam promptiores fore, quam ad coelibatum putaverim, quippe qui vereri odium maxime videantur, quod ad civilem hominem et in turba versaturum pertinet. Is enim favorem multitudinis mereri studet et adver[**91v**]sam in se quuiusvis voluntatem quantum potest nititur reconciliare atque in gratiam redire cum inimicis. **44** Quo fit ut populares maxime et aeque tractabiles esse eos oporteat, qui rem publicam gerunt: contra esse alii debent illorum mores qui se minime implicant rebus urbanis. His neque ullius odium pertimescere, neque amorem quaerere aut suffragium, ut aiunt, ambire conveniet, sed in

---

[264] -*prior* MS.
[265] -*it* MS.
[266] *quer*- MS.

there are two kinds of people who want to keep a distance from the city.²⁶⁷ The one consists of those so weak-willed that they can't resist any desire; I would prefer them to marry and seek some succor for their own weakness. The other consists of those who, though they are unwavering and strong in the city and outside it, nevertheless think that they will live with greater freedom and less discomfort if they move out of sight of the crowd. I very much maintain that these are qualified to enter upon celibacy.

40 The second mode of behaviour, as I've said,²⁶⁸ characterized a certain number who remain in the city or at home, and not only avoid going to public places, but disdain associating with all their friends and relatives; they're not afraid of anyone and unconcerned if, as a result of that neglect, some dislike them. They always keep their own company, or that of those in particular whom they've admitted as partners in their own studies. **41** I commend their strategy if it's for the sake of the advantages that proximity to the city can bring; if not, I'd prefer them to keep a distance from those places in which they clearly understand that there's no benefit for themselves. For as far as regards preserving sexual purity, no one can be in any doubt: one who's closer to the unbridled opportunity to transgress is more easily able to transgress than one who's far way.

42 The remaining mode²⁶⁹ consisted of those who, though they want to stay away from shows and banquets, are afraid of being pulled away from their studies on any terms at the request (as happens) of friends or associates, and at the same time fear offending anyone whose anger or hatred they may suffer if they refuse to assent to or comply with his entreaties; they go looking for manifold reasons by which to find release from obstacles of this kind without resentment or ill-feeling. **43** But I'd have thought that such people would be more disposed to managing the affairs of state than to celibacy, inasmuch as they seem very much to go in fear of the dislike that applies to the political type who'll engage with the masses. For his sort is eager to earn the crowd's support, and strives insofar as he can to recover the goodwill of anyone who's turned against him, and to become reconciled with his enemies. **44** Hence those involved in public affairs have to be especially people-minded and consistently amenable; by contrast, the disposition of those who have very little involvement in civic matters is necessarily of a different order. It will suit this sort not to be terribly scared of anyone's antipathy, or to seek to be liked, or to go round canvassing (as they say) for a vote, but to focus

---

²⁶⁷ This in closure to the sequence of argument beginning in 3.6.25-7.
²⁶⁸ 3.6.21-2.
²⁶⁹ 3.6.23-4.

rem unam dumtaxat incumbere: illam unam, ob quam esse fortunatissimi possint. **45** Quo circa et Demosthenes et avus meus non se ad coelibem vitam componebant, sed ad eam, quam pluribus annis administravere, rem publicam capescendam. Necessarium enim est iis, qui vitam illam seligunt, curae id esse potissimum, ne, tametsi negotiis involvi multis et variis sit necesse, ita tamen negligens et effusa sit [**92r**] eorum consuetudo ut neque ad agendum utiles, neque ad contemplandum idonei fiant. **46** Nam et continentiae temperantiaeque et frugalitatis praecipua esse debet cura in re publica versaturis: habent enim et illi virtutes suas, quas si recte perfecteque fuerint consequuti, splendidissimi et clarissimi nominis fient. Neque, ut arbitror, id quidem immerito, utpote qui proximam coelibi dignitatem sortiri posse honestissime videantur.

47 Perfectiores vero praestantioresque erunt virtutes omnes in coelibe, ut in quo summa omnia et absolutissima requirantur. Quare et curam adhibere maiorem oportebit, ne vitio ulli eorum animus pateat, quorum haec una professio est, ut vitio careatur; sed, ut diximus, in ea re adhibeant maximam, quae maxime propria[270] illis est et peculiaris: in castitate scilicet conservanda et iis omnibus, quod sequens est, [**92v**] abigendis, quae aut obstare aut adversari huic virtuti videbuntur. **48** Quam rem, quemadmodum esset adipiscenda, in parte conati sumus ostendere. Sed reliqua tantum est una res, a qua ut cavere docuimus, ita etiam remedium aliquod pro nostri more instituti tentabimus admovere. Is enim ordo servatus a nobis est, ut posteaquam abhorrere a vitio et improbitate bonum esse est demonstratum, quo id fieri pacto possit statim subiiceretur.

---

[270] *propa* MS, *i* added above *pa*.

attention on just one thing – that one thing that can cause them to be very blessed. **45** For that reason both Demosthenes and my grandfather prepared themselves not for a celibate existence, but for engaging in the matters of state that they managed for many years.[271] For it's essential that, for those who choose the latter existence, it constitutes their absolutely primary concern, so that, although they are necessarily wrapped up in many different forms of business, their way of doing things nevertheless avoids being heedless and disorderly in such a way that they become neither fit for discharging their duties nor suited to contemplation. **46** Moreover, in those set for a public career there has to be a paramount concern both for self-control and for moderation and sober habits;[272] for they, too, have their own qualities of virtue, and if they'll have attained them with a proper completeness, they will achieve the greatest luster of famous reputation – and that by no means undeservedly, I think, seeing that they appear capable of obtaining with the greatest integrity a rank of distinction second only to the celibate.

47 However, all the qualities of virtue will be more complete and more pre-eminent in the celibate, as one in whom all the supreme elements of perfection may be looked for. Hence also greater attention will necessarily have to be paid to ensuring that there's no exposure to any vice for the minds of those whose sole calling is this – to be free of vice. But, as I've said,[273] they should pay their greatest attention in the matter that is most special and personal to them: namely, the preserving of chastity and, in consequence, the removal of all the obstacles that will be seen to get in the way of or act against this quality of virtue. **48** This object – how it's to be achieved – I've tried in part to demonstrate. But only one matter remains at issue, and just as I've shown how to guard against it,[274] so too I'll try to apply some remedy to it in keeping with the usual procedure of my instructional program.[275] For the thematic sequence I've observed means that, after my demonstration that it's good to recoil from sinful depravity, it would immediately follow to ask how that [remedial process] can come about.

---

[271] If the examples of Demosthenes and Francesco Barbaro appeared abruptly introduced in 3.6.23-4, their role in the larger schematic economy of 3.6 now becomes apparent. For Demosthenes' public career in overview, Karvounis 2019; for Francesco's, King 1986: 323–5 with 2015: 2–8.
[272] For these kindred virtues (in the Stoic tradition, synonymous with one of the four cardinal virtues, *sōphrosyne*/temperance) cf. Cic. *Off.* 3.96, 116, *Tusc.* 3.16, Sen. *Ep.* 115.3.
[273] Cf. 3.2.8, 3.5.6.
[274] I.e., the harmful effects of not sleeping properly (3.5.65-82).
[275] Cf. 3.5.33, 65 (dangers described, remedies then prescribed).

49 In ea itaque dormitione a qua cavendum diximus, trifariam peccari posse ostensum est, videlicet si multum, si crebro, si indiscrete dormiatur. Triplex igitur medicamentum pro natura uniuscuiusque est assignandum. Haec autem breviter libanda duabus de causis duximus. **50** Una est, quia, quum ea sit natura contrariorum ut si alterum sit plane deprehensum facillime utrunque cognoscatur, ne[**93r**]mo erit qui non intelligat, si neque multum neque crebro neque indiscrete sit dormiendum, adhibendam esse rationem et modum in quiescendo, ut et moderate et in tempore unumquodque fiat. **51** Altera est, quia, quum nihil sit apud medicos tam vulgare quam somni capiendi praeceptio, relinquendam esse maiorem illam diligentiam arbitrati sumus iis qui membratim ista discutiunt, ne affectatae ambitionis aut imprudentiae arguerer, si (quod evenire plurimum solet iis, qui aliena sibi libenter usurpant) multa potius et peregrina quam bona et ad rem nostram facientia ingessissem.

52 Sed ad rem veniamus. Inspiciendum est itaque primum, ut idem saepius repetatur, quae aut qualis[276] coelibis nostri sit, id quod non erit difficile iudicare, quum non ut caeteri, qui variis muneribus aut officiis obligantur, variam quoque valitudinem et multiplicem habi[**93v**]tum habere possunt, sed una sit natura propemodum omnium, qui coelibes esse voluerint. **53** Quare non inepte dicemus: tantum quantum bonam valitudinem et servet et augeat dormiendum esse. Aequa esse debet in reliquis omnibus observatio, ut scilicet pro congruente totiens atque eo tempore cubatum eatur, quotiens et quo suus cuiusque humorum, sic enim graeci vocant [ὑγρῶν κρᾶσιν[277]], complexus feret: ita fiet ut neque corpus incommodum neque ulla pars animi

---

[276] Br. 128 n. 1 conjectures *vita* or *natura* to complement *quae aut qualis*.
[277] Proposed by Br. 129 n. 1 to fill the blank in the MS; *graeci* also a slip for *latini* (Br. ibid.)?

49 Accordingly, in the matter of sleeping that I said had to be guarded against, it was shown that lapses could happen in three ways, namely by sleeping in large amounts, by sleeping frequently, and by sleeping irregularly.[278] Consequently, a threefold treatment is to be applied according to each individual's distinctive character. I've thought that this ought to be touched on only briefly for two reasons. **50** One is because, since it's the nature of opposites that, if one of them is clearly grasped, each of the two is very easily understood, no one could fail to see that, if you shouldn't sleep much or frequently or irregularly, system and limit are to be applied in the matter of rest,[279] so that each one [of those three aspects of sleep] happens with due temperance and at the right time. **51** The second is because, since nothing is as common among doctors as the injunction to get sleep, I've thought that greater attention in this area is to be left to those who investigate such matters in detail;[280] this to avoid being accused of pretentious ostentation or a lack of judgment, if (as is very much accustomed to happen to those who gladly claim for themselves what belongs to others) I'd kept saying a lot that was outlandish rather than well-grounded ideas that suited my topic.

52 But let's come to the point. Accordingly, close attention first has to be given to returning again and again to the same topic – what, or what quality of, [existence] characterizes our celibate. This matter will not be hard to decide, since – unlike all the rest who are tied up with different kinds of duties or tasks, and who can also have a variable state of health and a disposition with many sides – there is a single, unchanging temperament in almost all those wanting to be celibate. **53** Hence I'll declare suitably enough: we should sleep as much as both preserves and promotes good health. In all other respects there ought to be a steadiness of practice, to the effect, of course, that you go to bed in a consistent fashion as often as, and at the time when, each individual's own combination of the humours (for so the Greeks use the term [*hugrōn krāsin*]) will prompt it.[281] In this way neither the body

---

[278] Cf. 3.5.69.
[279] Already a basic precept in ancient medicine: see, e.g., the Hippocratic *Epid.* 6.6.2 (5.324 Littré), Gal. *De san. tuen.* 2.12 (6.158 Kühn) with Hulskamp 2008: 72-3, 97-9.
[280] In conclusion to Book 3, a less confrontational stance towards medical specialists than in 3.5.79.
[281] In Galenic theory the four fundamental qualities (hot, cold, wet, and dry) are related to the four bodily humours (for which 2.6.21 and n. 177) and form different 'balances' through mixture with each other; if the mixtures and the consequent body-state are not optimal, the calibration of rest and motion, sleep and waking, etc., is to be modified according to the individual case (see, e.g., *Ars med.* 24 [1.370-1 Kühn] with Hulskamp 2008: 98–104).

quicquam patiatur, sed et libido omnis resideat, et mentis potestas tota integra relinquatur. Sed haec, quia cum omnibus communia sunt praecepta, facilius assequi poterit unusquisque, tribusque his diligenter observatis sine labore et difficultate caetera transiget.

nor any part of the mind will suffer any unpleasantness, but all sexual desire will subside and mental power will be left entirely undiminished. But, because these injunctions are applicable to all, each and everyone will be able to grasp them rather easily, and if these three [scenarios[282]] are carefully watched, he will effortlessly accomplish all the rest[283] with no effort and trouble.

---

[282] I.e., sleeping too much at any one time, too often, or irregularly.
[283] I.e., the beneficial outcomes described in 'In this way ... undiminished' above.

Quae sit definitio contemplationis quaeque res subiectae sint speculari volentibus. Liber IIII

1.1 [94r] Diximus coelibis vitam duplici observatione fieri consummatam[1] posse: una erat ut a congressuum omni genere et luxus temperaret, reliqua ut contemplatione et cogitatione rerum maximarum detineretur: quibus id demum eveniret ut diis immortalibus proximus redderetur.[2] Primum quo assequerentur modo superiore libro monstravimus; nunc eam partem, quae restat, pro mediocritate nostra absolvemus.

2 Incipiendum itaque videtur a contemplationis et contemplatoris diffinitione, quae tractandarum rerum fundamentum erit, ut id de quo agitur aperte intelligatur. Contemplationi philosophorum plerique alii alia subiecerunt: verum haec omnium fuit opinio, ut quae quisque scivisset ea speculari hominem posse dictitarent.

---

[1] *consumm-* Br. for MS *consum-*, as at 3.2.6; cf. 2.1.2 and n. 2 and 4.2.56 and n. 178.
[2] *redd-* conjectured by Br. 131 n. 1 for the easy corruption in MS *redol-*.

On the definition of contemplation, and the topics in the purview of those wanting to engage in mental speculation. Book IIII.

1.1 I have said[3] that a celibate existence can be made complete by careful observance on two fronts: one was to refrain from every kind of physical union and self-indulgence; the other was to be occupied by contemplative reflection on the most important matters. The eventual outcome of these measures would be to be rendered the nearest thing to the immortal gods.[4] I demonstrated in the last book how they might achieve the first of these; I shall now complete the part that remains, to the best of my modest abilities.

2 Accordingly, we should begin, it seems, from the definition of contemplation and of the contemplative – a definition that will provide a basis for the subjects to be treated, so that the matter at issue is clearly understood.[5] Many different philosophers have made different things the object of contemplation; but the general belief of all was such that they repeatedly said that man was capable of reflecting on the knowledge that each had acquired.[6]

---

[3] Cf. 3.2.5, 8; 3.4.5.
[4] Cf. 2.3.9 and n. 54; in this climactic book, the divine analogy is taken up in 4.1.16, 20-1, 4.2.43-6, 49, 51, 53-4, 61, 88-90, 96.
[5] Cf. for this stress on definitional rigour 1.2.6 and n. 31; for the more abstract feel that seemingly elevates the treatise to a more ethereal plane in 4.1 see Intro. pp. 2–3.
[6] The term for 'reflecting' (*speculari*) is here importantly loaded in connotation. Barbaro's tracing of the philosophical tradition from the Pythagoreans to Socrates/Plato in 4.1.3-6 below is structurally similar to Aristotle's coverage of both in *Metaph*. 1.5-6 – part of Aristotle's larger review in that book of theories of causation, beginning with the distinction that he draws between 'knowledge from experience (*empeiria*),' i.e., knowledge of particulars, and 'knowledge from art (*technē*),' i.e., knowledge of universal principles; for the distinction cf. *Metaph*. 1.1 981a1-7, 12-30. Hence 'true' wisdom lies in the science investigating first principles and causes (*epistēmē theōrētikē*, 1.2 982b7-10); this is not a productive (*poiētikē*) but a speculative science (1.2 982b11-19), undertaken 'for the sake of knowledge, and not for any practical usefulness' (1.2 982b20-1; cf. n. 18 below). The Aristotelian distinction gives a special weight to Barbaro's *speculari*: the latter denotes the Aristotelian category of speculative, not productive, science.

3 Nam Pythagoras quidem, nihil nisi mathematica cognosci posse ratus, [**94v**] eorum esse dumtaxat contemplationem existimavit, tantumque haec illius sententia sive fortuna favente sive[7] hominis auctoritate invaluit, ut ad plurimam aetatem sine controversia et adversario perdurarit. Quo factum est ut magnae non solum, ut dixi, auctoritatis, sed etiam gloriae pythagoricum nomen esset, neque solum Pherecidem praeceptorem superasse credebatur, verumetiam effecisse ut nullus esse locus posset laudis comparandae iis qui post Pythagoram essent futuri, quippe quem posteritatis honorem longo retro tempore meruisse annalibus proditum sit. **4** Nam quom bello samnitico consultus Apollo Pythius sapientissimo graecorum statuam Romae dicari iussisset, senatus Pythagoram exculpi fecit atque in comitii cornibus collocavit. Tantus autem fuit in philosophum eum favor inclinatus, ut eruditi omnes rerum naturam et singulas pro[**95r**]pemodum disciplinas constare numeris faterentur. **5** Imitatus hunc etiam Plato mathematicis quidem proximam dedit dignitatem, divinarum autem rerum atque intellectilium capacitatem esse principem voluit, ex quibus tertium sciendi genus emanaret, quod, ut erat naturale, ita sensibus patentia atque ima omnia specularetur. **6** Socrates vero, pinguiore forsan ingenio aut potius religione motus, nihil sciri posse affectavit, quom inferna haec fluxu suo et mobilitate interire,

---

[7] *favente, sive* Br.

3 For instance, Pythagoras, because he thought that nothing could be known except mathematical ideas,[8] valued the study only of those, and, whether because of fortune's favour or the man's prestige, this view of his was so influential that it persisted for a very long span of time without being contested or opposed. Hence it came about that Pythagoras' name achieved a greatness not just of influence, as I've said, but also of fame; he was believed not only to have surpassed his teacher, Pherecydes,[9] but also to have ensured that there could be no scope for those coming after Pythagoras to achieve renown, inasmuch as it was transmitted in historical records that he'd earned the respect of future generations a long time in the past. 4 For instance, when the Pythian Apollo was consulted in the Samnite War and had instructed that a statue be dedicated at Rome to the wisest of the Greeks, the senate had a sculpture of Pythagoras made and placed it in the corner of the Place of Assembly.[10] Such was the favourable disposition towards that philosopher that all the learned accepted that the order of nature and almost every single branch of study were based on numbers. 5 Plato, too, emulated him, and bestowed on mathematics a standing that was second-best; he wanted the ability to comprehend divine concepts of a purely mental nature to be primary – concepts from which a third class of knowledge would be derived that was based in the physical world, and would accordingly observe all that was available to the senses in the lower world.[11] 6 Socrates, however, perhaps with a duller intellect or rather because he was stirred by religious scruple, pretended that nothing could be known,[12] since this lower order of things seemed to perish through their own transience and changeability, while the

---

[8] The parts of the Pythagorean philosophical system that can be confidently attributed to Pythagoras of Samos himself (c. 570–495 BCE) are not easily separated out. Hence Aristotle refers to 'the so-called Pythagoreans' (seemingly viewing Pythagoras as a legendary figure) in describing the primacy that they attributed to number as the essence of all things (*Metaph.* 1.5 985b23-986a21; cf. D. L. 8.11-12, 25, and see further Guthrie 1962: 212–51).

[9] For Pherecydes of Syros, 2.5.12 and n. 128; that he was Pythagoras' teacher (so, e.g., Cic. *Div.* 1.112, *Tusc.* 1.38, D. L. 1.119, 8.2) may well be more legend than reality (see Granger 2007: 137 and n. 8).

[10] Barbaro draws directly on Plin. *NH* 34.26, but cf. also Plut. *Num.* 8.10; the precise date of the statue's installation during the Samnite Wars (343–341, 326–304, 298–290 BCE) remains uncertain.

[11] For the Platonic theory of Forms, 1.4.21 and n. 87 with 3.5.69 n. 165, and see n. 15 below; for the intermediate status of the objects of mathematics between sensible particulars (*ta aisthēta*) and Forms (*ta eidē*), Arist. *Metaph.* 1.6 987b14-18, and cf. 1.5.7 and n. 101.

[12] With a touch of Socratic irony in 'a duller intellect,' the point extends to Socrates' own ironic claim to ignorance (for the received legend cf., e.g., Cic. *Ac.* 1.44, *Luc.* 74); 'stirred by religious scruple' because Socrates, declared wisest of all by the Delphic oracle (cf. 3.3.1 and n. 29), sought to reconcile the hallowed authority of the oracle with what he knew to be his lack of wisdom (cf. Pl. *Ap.* 21b-22e).

superna minime percipi ullius animo viderentur; sed unam tantum invexit morum et bene vivendi disciplinam, qua cuiusque offitia distinguebat: circa hanc totam esse hominibus contemplationem oportere dictitavit.[13] 7 Proxime Peripatetici succedentes subtilius omnia et verius etiam digesserunt: Aristoteles vero imprimis et Theophrastus triplicem sciendi modum seu [**95v**] genus diligentissime feruntur conquisivisse. Nam et sempiterna et nulli obnoxia corruptioni et ea item quae a mathematicis pertractantur, mundana demum haec et plena mutationis cognosci percipique mente hominis posse, esseque inter se ita distincta ut neque mathematicis opus esset ea philosophia, quam primam vocant, neque physici hominis ulla cognitio a formis illis Platonicis[14] dependeret, verissimis rationibus concluserunt. Quare et ea esse subiecta contemplari volentibus ut confiteantur consequens est.

---

[13] *dictitavit* MS; *dictavit* Br.
[14] *Plat-* MS; *plat-* Br.

higher order seemed to be beyond any perception by the human mind.[15] But he introduced only the one subject, concerning ethics and the good life, by which he separated out the duties of each person; he repeatedly said that for humankind philosophical contemplation should be centered entirely on this subject.[16] 7 Next came the Peripatetics, who classified everything with more nuance, and also more correctly. Certainly, Aristotle in particular and Theophrastus[17] are said to have very carefully sought out a mode or order of knowledge that has three elements. For they inferred by very sound processes of reasoning that the human mind can recognize and grasp that there are everlasting entities that are liable to no process of disintegration; next, there are the entities that are carefully studied by mathematicians; and, finally, these worldly phenomena that are full of changefulness.[18] And [they inferred that] these [three categories] differ among themselves in such a way that mathematicians have no need of that philosophy that they call 'primary,'[19] and no knowledge possessed by the natural scientist depends on those well-known Platonic Forms.[20] Hence it follows that philosophers[21] admit that those ideas as well[22] are in the purview of those wanting to engage in contemplation.

---

[15] Again (cf. nn. 6, 11 above) with illumination from Aristotle's *Metaphysics*, here at 1.6 987b1-10: 'And when Socrates, disregarding the physical universe and confining his study to moral questions, sought in this sphere for the universal and was the first to concentrate upon definition, Plato followed him and assumed that the problem of definition is concerned not with any sensible thing but with entities of another kind; for the reason that there can be no general definition of sensible things which are always changing. *These entities he called "Ideas," and held that all sensible things are named after them and in virtue of their relation to them*; for the plurality of things which bear the same name as the Forms exist by participation in them' (tr. Tredennick 1933: 43; my emphasis).

[16] Cf. 2.2.20 and n. 44.

[17] Cf. 1.2.1 and n. 24; 3.6.22 and n. 242.

[18] For this tripartite division see esp. Aristotle's comparison of natural science, mathematics, and theology in *Metaph.* 6.1. All intellectual activity (*dianoia*) is practical (*praktikē*), productive (*poiētikē*), or speculative (*theōrētikē*, 1025b25; cf. n. 6 above); since natural science, mathematics, and theology are forms of investigation for their own sake with no end beyond themselves, they are all speculative branches of study. But (i) while natural science investigates objects that have a principle of change within them such as (e.g.) growth or motion (1025b26-8; cf. Barbaro's 'and, finally, ... changefulness'), (ii) the objects of mathematical study (e.g., numbers and theories) are considered, at least in some branches of the discipline, as unchanging and separable from matter (1026a8-10; cf. Barbaro's 'next, there are ... mathematicians'); and (iii) 'theology' is set apart as the investigation of principles of causation that are separate from matter, unchanging, and eternal (hence 'divine,' 1026a15-18; cf. Barbaro's 'For they inferred ... disintegration'). 'Theology' is thus superior to the other speculative sciences (1026a22-3) – in effect, identifiable with the 'primary philosophy' of metaphysics (1026a15-16, 24, 29-32), in that the universal prime mover and causal principle are ultimately self-thinking thought, or god (12.7 1072b13-30).

[19] I.e., metaphysics (see n. 18 above).

[20] See 4.1.5-6 and nn. 11, 15 above.

[21] Philosophers in general, as in 4.1.2.

[22] The ideas of the Peripatetics as surveyed in 4.1.7.

8 Nos quoque, quoniam nobilitatur animus hominis hac sententia maxime, idem necesse est comprobemus. Aliorum vero opiniones non pertinet hoc loco ad nos refutare: utimur autem his, ut concessis et auctoritate maiorum confirmatis. Ex quo colligi potest eam esse contemplationem, cui, ut inquit Cicero, quasi [**96r**] materia quam tractet et in qua versetur, subiecta est veritas; seu contemplationem esse rerum earum omnium speculatum, quas capere nostra mens potest: neque enim dubitatur, si qua cognoscuntur, nulla vi alia fieri posse id quam ea quae mentis et animae est. Haec una est quae laborat, una quae cogitat, una quae invenit, una quae se ipsam iuvat et nutrit. **9** Nam sensibus etiam agentibus nihil, nihilominus illa [munus[23]] exercet suum, ut videri possit cogitandi, contemplandi, intelligendique vim, non sensum, ut Democritus et Leucippus delirantur, sed aut animam ipsam esse aut animae aliquam partem et praerogativam[24]; quae, si Aristoteli acutissime deprehendenti credimus, praesentissima actione (quid enim aliud est illius [ἐνέργεια[25]]?) ita operetur, ut in ea parte animae, quam [ὑλικὸν νοῦν] seu [παθητικόν] vocat, rerum omnium imagines facillime imprimantur.

10 Sed [**96v**] quid rem arduam sum aggressus? Evenire vulgo experimur ut nullis sensibus agitatis plerique tantum intenti sint contemplando, ut

---

[23] Proposed by Br. 133 n. 1 to fill the blank in the MS.
[24] *prerog-* MS.
[25] Here and below, Br.'s proposals (133 nn. 3–5) to fill the blanks in the MS.

8 Since the human mind is ennobled by this way of thinking above all,[26] I too necessarily commend this same practice. At this point, however, it's no concern of mine to disprove the views of others; but I avail myself of them, as views granted and made stronger by our forebears' weight of influence. Hence we can infer that contemplation is that whose object, as Cicero says, is truth – the material, as it were, that contemplation handles and treats;[27] or that contemplation is the observation of all those things that our mind can grasp – for there's no doubt that, if any knowledge is acquired, that can't happen by any force other than that of mind and soul. This is the sole force that exerts itself, the sole force that reflects, the sole force that discovers, the sole force that helps and nurtures its own self. **9** For even when the senses do nothing, that force nevertheless performs its [function], so that it's possible to imagine that the power of thought, contemplation, and understanding is no sensory capacity, as Democritus and Leucippus madly assert,[28] but either the soul itself or some part and privileged aspect of it. If we believe Aristotle's very sharp-witted insights, this aspect of soul functions with the greatest immediacy of action (for what else is its [activity]?) in such a way that representations of all things are very easily impressed on that part of the soul that he calls [the material intellect] or [the acted upon].[29]

10 But why did I start on a difficult topic? We find it commonly happens that, with no stirring of the senses, a good many people are so focused on contemplation that they are left half-dead and lifeless. Take, for instance,

---

[26] Contemplation itself, regardless of the particular school.
[27] In *cui... veritas* ('that whose object... treats'), a direct rendering of *Off.* 1.16 (on truth as fundamental to the first of the four primary Stoic/Panaetian virtues, wisdom).
[28] In the early atomist system of Democritus of Abdera (b. 460/57 BCE) and Leucippus of (probably) Miletus (*fl. c.* 440), thought is a form of sensation caused when the soul atoms are affected by atomic complexes penetrating from without: cf. Arist. *De an.* 1.2 404a27-31, 405a8-13, *Metaph.* 4.5 1009b12-17 with Guthrie 1965: 451-4.
[29] Barbaro here distils Aristotle's treatment of the nature of thought in two stages in *De an.* 3.4-5, with the active intellect distinguished from the passive, receptive aspect of soul: (i) On the analogy of perception that functions by a sensory capacity being acted on by a sensible form, thinking 'must be either a process in which the soul is acted upon by what is thinkable, or something else of a similar kind. This part, then, must... be receptive of the form of an object, i.e., must be potentially the same as its object, although not identical with it: as the sensitive is to the sensible, so must mind be to the thinkable' (3.4 429a14-18; tr. Hett 1957: 165); (ii) The intellect is a capacity that has no real existence until it thinks (3.4 429a22-4), and (a critical distinction introduced in 3.5) it is both passive and active: whereas the passive intellect 'becomes all things,' the active 'makes all things; this is a kind of positive state like light; for in a sense light makes potential into actual colours. Mind in this sense is separable, impassive and unmixed, since it is essentially an activity [*energeia*]; for the agent is always superior to the patient, and the originating cause to the matter' (3.5 430a14-19; tr. Hett 171).

semimortui et sine ulla vita relinquantur. Nam et illud, quod de Hermotimo[30] Clazomenio sua sibi effinxit antiquitas, animam illius relicto corpore errare solitam vagamque a longinquo multa nuntiare, quae nisi a praesentibus[31] nosci non possent, nihil significari aliud existimandum est, quam ita occupatam esse in cogitando animam alicuius, ut evolare a corpore iudicari possit. **11** Verumtamen non est id omnino fabulosum, quippe quod nostra etate in muliere Philippa, Nicolai cognomento Boni Senatoris et patricii, accidisse nemo sit qui ignoret, tanta cum omnium admiratione, ut cum relictum illius corpus sensibus sequestratis immoto et rigenti membrorum flexu exangue et inanitum staret, mox [**97r**] anima redeunte reviviscere videretur. **12** Inesse nobis illam animi vim vel impiissimi faterentur, ex qua, quemadmodum quum adesset vivere et actitare possemus, ita quum abesset extincti propemodum fieremus. Hanc itaque nacta potestatem anima sola est quae contemplatur, sola quae corporeorum et incorporeorum intellectum habet.

13 Verum ut videre videor, adhuc <non> satis[32] est declaratum quid sit contemplatio, nisi finem aliquem statuamus, cuius gratia nostrae mentis virtus omnis opera sua exerceat.[33] Nam qui honoris aut lucri aut voluptatis causa scire rerum naturam studet, hic a toto munere contemplandi cadit. Ut enim eum, qui virtutis haberi studiosus vult, necesse est ut nihil ea[34] putet

---

[30] *-tino* MS.
[31] *pres-* MS.
[32] *adhuc satis* MS, but *non* required to offset *nisi* below.
[33] *-ent* MS, but corrective *a* added above *n*.
[34] *ei* MS.

Hermotimus of Clazomenae,[35] and what his contemporaries in antiquity imagined about him – that his soul habitually left his body and roamed abroad, and that on its wanderings it would report from afar much that could only be known by eye-witnesses. We have to believe that this can only mean that someone's soul is so engrossed in thinking that it could be considered as flying away from the body. **11** However, this is by no means altogether the stuff of fiction, inasmuch as in our own times in the case of Philippa, wife of the patrician senator Nicholas Bon,[36] everyone knows that this happened, to the great astonishment of all: when her body was left abandoned by the removal of her sensory capacities and it stood pale and drained,[37] with her limbs unbending in their motionless stiffness, her breathing returned soon after and she was seen to come back to life. **12** Even the most irreligious of people would concede that we have in us that particular force of mind that has this effect: just as, when it's present, we'd be capable of being lively and active, so, when it's absent, we'd become virtually dead. Accordingly, since it has acquired this capacity, only the soul engages in contemplation; only the soul has an understanding of material *and* immaterial entities.

13 As I seem to realize, however, it has not yet been adequately shown what contemplation is, unless I identify some end for the sake of which all our excellence of mind applies its efforts.[38] For the person who is eager for knowledge of the natural order for the purpose of winning esteem or gain or pleasure lapses from the entire function of contemplation; for just as one who wants to be regarded as a committed student of virtue ought to think nothing

---

[35] A shadowy and possibly legendary (sixth-century BCE?) seer: see Plin. *NH* 7.174, quoted almost verbatim in 'that his soul ... eye-witnesses' below (further, Beagon 2005: 393). Given the structural similarities between 4.1.3-6 and Arist. *Metaph.* 1.5-6 (see nn. 6, 11, 15 above), it is suggestive that Hermotimus too figures in *Metaphysics* 1 (as a precursor of the Anaxagorean theory of Mind: 1.3 984b18-20). After Pythagoras is mentioned in 4.1.3-4, Barbaro's allusion to Hermotimus here is perhaps playfully complicated by the tradition that Hermotimus was a pre-incarnation of Pythagoras (cf. D. L. 8.5).

[36] The Bon family was one of those admitted to the Venetian Patriciate before the Serrata ('closing') of the Great Council in 1297 defined the ruling class of the nobility – a pedigree that enhances the striking effect of Philippa's example.

[37] With an elegant play in *inanitum* on *inanimum* ('lifeless').

[38] In advance of directly invoking Aristotle in 4.1.18-21, Barbaro in 4.1.13-17 connects virtue, contemplation, and proximity to the divine in ways that anticipate his appropriation below of a parallel tendency in the *Nicomachean ethics*. But the Aristotelian stress on the contemplative attaining the divine is realigned in a Christianizing direction by Barbaro, who portrays the celibate as ordained from birth to fulfill his potential – even his obligation – 'to be as close as possible to God the maker' (4.1.16; cf. 4.1.22). Further appropriation of the language of Stoicism also aligns the virtuous celibate with the Stoic sage (see n. 43 below).

virtute praestantius, ita qui contemplari volet necesse est ut nihil ei studio anteponat. **14** Quis nesciat caduca haec omnia atque mortalia, fortunas, honores, [**97v**] bonam valitudinem, ita expetenda esse, ut virtutem, quae finis est, facilius assequamur? contra virtutem assequi iccirco non esse expetendum, ut aut divites, aut robusti, aut gloriosi et honorati fiamus? reverti enim id esset a fine, non ad finem tendere, essetque omnino praeposterus rerum ordo: qui error ubique est pessimus. **15** Quare si voluptati validitative[39] studens quisque totam contemplandi rationem aeque praeverterit, non erit amplius contemplator; aut si tueri se nomine ipso, quod non ut nos facimus ita videatur arctatum, pertinaciter volet, non poterit tamen effugere quin fateatur non esse eum profecto quem quaerimus.[40] **16** Neque enim de verbo, sed de re disputatur. Non ergo in aliud tendant abiectum et infra se positum quaerentes finem, sed propter hoc scire velint, ut sciant, ut quam proximi sint opifici Deo, ut id demum prae[**98r**]stent ad quod nati esse videbuntur. **17** Natus autem homo est praeclarum animal et excellens maxime mediumque, ut inquit Plato, et tertium divinae opus architecturae, intelligibilis exemplar animae, et rerum sensilium princeps et caput, ut quum tam perpetua et sempiterna quam[41] mortalia atque fluxilia, hoc est inferna et terrena, cognosceret, tantarum rerum effectorem servatoremque admirabundus observabundusque imitaretur. Hunc esse terminum contemplandi, hunc finem ultimum atque postremum cognoscendi, in quo foelicitas cumulate[42] tota constaret sapientissimi viri voluerunt.

---

[39] *valitative* MS.
[40] *quer-* MS.
[41] *quam* MS; omitted by Br.
[42] *-atae* MS.

more outstanding than that quality of virtue,⁴³ so one who'll want to engage in contemplation will necessarily value nothing more highly than that devoted form of study. **14** Who doesn't know that all these fleeting and perishable commodities – wealth, high office, good health – are only to be desired in such a way that we more easily achieve virtue, which is our end?⁴⁴ That, by contrast, the acquisition of virtue is not to be desired for the purpose of our becoming rich, or strong, or distinguished and esteemed? For that would be to go backwards from the end, not to strive towards it, and the order of things would be altogether inverted – which is the worst deviation from the right path in any circumstances. **15** Hence, if every devotee of pleasure and bodily strength will apply himself to the same degree to the full process of contemplation, he will no more be a contemplative;⁴⁵ or, if he stubbornly wants to cloak himself in the very terminology [of the contemplative] on the grounds that it doesn't seem to be as narrowly defined as I'm making it, he will still be unable to avoid admitting that he's certainly not the person we're looking for. **16** For at issue here is not a matter of wording, but of substance. Let them therefore not strive in a different direction, seeking an undistinguished end that's set beneath them, but let them want to gain knowledge for this reason: to acquire understanding, to be as close as possible to God the maker,⁴⁶ and, in short, to fulfill the promise to which they will be deemed to have been born. **17** Man came into existence as a distinguished being and very much preeminent, and, as Plato says, an intermediate entity – the third product of the divine art of construction, a reproduction of the intelligible world-soul, and the ordaining head of the perceptible order of things, so that when he'd come to recognize permanent and everlasting entities as much as perishable and transitory ones (that is, lower order, terrestrial entities), he would imitate with awe and deference the originator and protector of so great a world-order.⁴⁷ The wisest men wanted *this* to be the limit of contemplation, *this* to be the furthest and final end of learning – the end that consists of complete blessedness in rich abundance.

---

⁴³ Adaptation of a staple Stoic idea towards Barbaro's Christianizing goal: cf., e.g., Cic. *Fin.* 3.45 ('if the Stoic definition of the End of Goods [*bonorum finis*] be accepted, it follows that all the value you set on bodily advantages must be absolutely eclipsed and annihilated by the brilliance and the majesty of virtue'; tr. Rackham 1931: 265), 4.15, 41.
⁴⁴ For this approach to (in Stoic terms) such indifferents as wealth, health, etc., cf. 2.5.4 n. 111 and 3.5.48 and n. 135.
⁴⁵ I.e., he cannot truly be a contemplative unless *wholly* and *exclusively* devoted to contemplation.
⁴⁶ For this proximity, 4.1.1 and n. 4.
⁴⁷ Man is 'the third product' in terms of the three-stage process of cosmic construction in Plato's *Timaeus*: (i) *the world* created by the Demiurge after the likeness of an everlasting original (the Living Creature in the world of the Forms, 30c-d), with the World-Soul set

18 Qua in re non est etiam sua laude fraudandus Aristoteles, cuius ea quoque sententia fuisse ex verbis illius, quae ex iis libris quos de moribus scripsit colliguntur, aperte demonstratur. **19** Si itaque, inquit, id nostra mens est quae, quum ad ducendum et [**98v**] imperandum nata esse videatur, praestantium rerum et divinarum curam habet et cogitationem, divina profecto quum sit res aut eorum quae nobis insunt divinissima, nimirum erit huius opus perfecta beatitudo, et paulo post, videtur, inquit, sapiens et contemplator operam suam non <nisi> propter[48] illam dumtaxat amaturus. Nihil enim est praeter contemplationem expectandum. **20** Item infra subiecit: mentis actio contemplativa quum sit, nullum habebit praeter se ipsam quem appetat finem. Item alio loco: contemplationem esse absolutam perfectamque operationem ex eo manifestum est, quod deos iccirco beatos dicimus et felices, quia semper contemplentur; hominem quoque hoc fine fieri felicissimum oportebit, quia Deo esse quam simillimus videatur. **21** Item alio loco: si enim dii curam gerunt rerum humanarum, gaudere illos optimo quoque et cognatissimo [**99r**] verisimillimum est; hoc esse mentem ipsam et mentis instructores non est ambiguum; quamobrem favent iis dii[49] et sibi carissimos et amicissimos esse volunt. Haec atque talia pluribus locis ab illo repetuntur, quibus aperte ostenditur eam esse contemplationis diffinitionem quam retro posuimus.

---

[48] *non propter* MS; but *nisi* required (Br. 135 n. 2) to reproduce Aristotle's exact emphasis in the Greek.
[49] *diis* MS.

18 In this matter, Aristotle, too, is not to be cheated out of his due praise: that way of thinking is also clearly shown to be his from the statements of his that are found in the books he wrote about ethics. **19** Accordingly, if it's our mind, he says,[50] that, since it seems to exist to guide and command us, gives close attention and thought to things noble and divine – since it is undoubtedly a divine entity, or the most divine of those elements within us, the activity of this [part of us] will evidently constitute complete happiness. And a little later, the contemplative sage, he says,[51] seems destined to love his own activity for no purpose except for its own sake; for nothing is to be aimed for except contemplation. **20** Likewise, he added below:[52] since the activity of the mind is contemplative, that activity will have no end to aim for except itself. Similarly elsewhere:[53] that contemplation is a complete and consummate activity is clear from the fact that we call the gods blessedly happy precisely because they always contemplate; man, too, will necessarily be rendered very blessed through this end, because he is seen to bear as close a resemblance as possible to God. **21** So in another passage:[54] if the gods have concern for human affairs, it's very likely that they rejoice in each [part of humankind] that is best and most akin to them. There's no doubt that this is the mind itself, and the mind's teachers; hence the gods are favourably disposed to them, and they want them to be very dear and well-inclined to themselves. These and other such points are derived from several passages of his, and they clearly show that that is the definition of contemplation that I posited above.[55]

---

in its midst (34b); (ii) the creation of *the heavenly gods* (fixed stars, planets, and earth in their spherical construct at 39e-40d; Plato turns briefly to the origin of the traditional gods of religion in 40d-e), to whom the Demiurge assigns the task (41b-c) of creating the remaining three kinds (after the gods) of living creature – the inhabitants of air, of water, and of earth; (iii) *man* is one of those three kinds, with plants (77a; cf. 3.6.6.and n. 204) and lower animals (91d-92c); woman is formed from man at 91a-d. Barbaro characterizes man as 'intermediate' in the sense that (i) in the *Timaeus* the human soul has implanted within it what was left of the ingredients originally used by the Demiurge to form the World-Soul, i.e., the blended natures of the Same, Other, and Being (37a-b); (ii) the human skull contains the brain and divine part of the soul (44d-e – the human equivalent of the spherical universal body containing the revolutions of the World-Soul); but (iii) the rest of the human body is a mere 'vehicle' to transport the head (44e, 69c) and is subject to change, decay, etc.; and so (iv) man is 'intermediate' in the balance between his divine component in (ii) above and his bodily limitations in (iii).

[50] *EN* 10.7 1177a13-17.
[51] *EN* 10.7 1177b1-2.
[52] *EN* 10.7 1177b19-20.
[53] *EN* 10.8 1178b7-9, 21-3.
[54] *EN* 10.8 1179a24-32.
[55] 4.1.8.

22 Nunc vero addendum est unum, quod sic rursus breviter concludemus. Contemplatio est ea mentis operatio qua de rebus omnibus, a Deo aut factis aut procreatis ad summam foelicitatis acquirendam, cogitare et potestatem Opificis admirari et venerari quis potest. Idem enim erit finis et foelicitas et Deus ita contemplanti, ut propter externam aliquam rem non contempletur: ita autem coniuncta sunt illa duo ut cogitatione potius quam re separari posse videantur. Hactenus quae diffiniendae contemplationis ratio sit diximus. Nunc ad reliqua ordine transitum [**99v**] faciamus.

23 Quoniam vero indiscusse et quodammodo generatim, ut aiunt, illa tractavimus, diligentiae nostrae consultum erit si distinctius omnia particulatimque tradita esse voluerimus: qua in re neque modum ullum excedemus, neque iactationi vel minimae[56] quidem ostentationi studebimus.

[2] Quarum disciplinarum esse studiosus debeat coelebs contemplator.

2.1 Divisere maiores nostri disciplinas in duo potissimum genera: unum earum ut esset quae ad corporis actionem pertinerent, alterum quae ad

---

[56] *-ime* MS; but *-imae* (Br. 136 n. 1) for neat agreement w. *ostentationi*.

22 For now, however, one point needs to be added which I'll briefly sum up again as follows. Contemplation is that activity of mind by which one can [i] reflect on all the things that are either done or engendered by God for the purpose of attaining the completion of happiness, and [ii] marvel at and revere the Maker's power. For to the contemplative both happiness and God will be the same end, such that he doesn't engage in contemplation because of any external factor; and those two are connected in such a way that they appear capable of being separated in thought rather than in fact. So far I've stated the rationale behind my defining of contemplation. Let's now make the transition in due order to the matters that remain.

23 Since, however, I've investigated those matters without close examination and in a somewhat generalizing manner, as it were, it will be in the interests of my own careful practice if I want everything to be laid out in a more precise and piecemeal fashion. In doing this, I shall neither go beyond any reasonable limit nor indulge any eagerness for boasting, or even for the least degree of showiness.

[2] The branches of learning to which the celibate contemplative should be devoted.[57]

2.1 Our forebears divided the branches of learning into two principal categories, one of those branches relating to physical activity, the other, to

---

[57] This section bears the hallmarks of the humanistic educational tendencies that spread widely across northern and north-central Italy in the fifteenth century (see Grendler 1989, esp. 111–41, with Kallendorf 2002: vii-xvi; on Venice in particular, Grendler 2013, esp. 677–84, with Ross 1976). Not least because of the rediscovery of important classical texts (cf. Vol. 1 Intro. pp. 9–10), the medieval curriculum gradually gave way to the *studia humanitatis* that were rooted in classical culture; those studies embraced (Kristeller 1961: 10) grammar, rhetoric, history, poetry, and moral philosophy through close consultation of the canonical Latin and, to a lesser degree, Greek authors. Barbaro's review of the celibate's curriculum in 4.2 is shaped partly (i) by the humanistic tradition of pedagogical treatises emblematized by Pier Paolo Vergerio's *De ingenuis moribus et liberalibus adulescentiae studiis/The character and studies befitting a free-born youth* of c. 1402–3 (see Kallendorf 2002 with McManamon 1996: 89–103, and cf. Vol. 1 Intro. p. 41 n. 130), and (ii) by the traditional collection and division of the liberal arts that extended back to antiquity and was famously formalized by Martianus Capella in his fifth-century CE allegorical encyclopedia, *De nuptiis Philologiae et Mercurii/On the marriage of Philology and Mercury*; the two categories were the *Trivium*, consisting of the linguistic branches of knowledge (grammar, rhetoric, and logic), and the *Quadrivium*, which focused on the mathematical branches (arithmetic, astronomy, geometry, and music; see further on the Capella tradition Hicks 2012). But this section also reflects the rise of the humanistic curriculum in fifteenth-century Venice in particular: at the beginning of the century Venice could claim many independent teachers who often set up their own schools,

animae. Pepulimus iam a coelibe omnis eas artis, quae negotiosae nuncupantur; reliquas tantum eas illi fecimus, quae praestantiores sunt proculdubio et sanctiores. Sed et in iis quoque exceptioni aliquis locus erit, quom et modus et tempus et finis requirantur: id fiet ex sequentibus, siquid [**100r**] deerit, manifestum.

2 Et primum quidem id sciat, non esse sibi grammaticae insudandum diu: id enim esse assequutus debet, dum puer fuerat. Nam officium illud non modo est illiberale, sed etiam turpe, in sene vero turpissimum. Huius curae admonere quempiam supervacuum erat, nisi ordinem sequi institutum oportuisset.

3 Geometriae, Musicae, Arithmeticae, et ei quam graeci [ὀπτικήν[58]] vocant, nos spectativam seu perspectivam, tantam dare operam velit, quanta animum assidua rerum sublimium indagine fatigatum parumper levet. Affert enim non solum voluptatem quandam varietas studiorum, verumetiam in huiuscemodi genere doctrinarum solet esse iccirco praecipua, quia sine labore ullo aut ambiguitate ad ea statim artificiose venitur, quae scire volebamus. **4** Sed et desyderari huiuscemodi cognitiones ob aliam causam

---

[58] Proposed by Br. 136 n. 2 to fill the blank in the MS.

mental activity.⁵⁹ I've already removed from the celibate all those forms of knowledge that are declared relevant to the busy life; I've designated for him only those remaining ones that are beyond question more preeminent and venerable.⁶⁰ But even among those as well there'll be some room for restriction, since a measured approach, time, and a sense of limit are needed.⁶¹ If anything will be wanting, that will become clear from the following.

2 In the first place, he should understand that he mustn't sweat for long over the study of grammar; for he ought to have acquired that as a boy. For that task is not only ungentlemanly but also shameful – in fact, in an old man, extremely shameful.⁶² Reminding anyone of this concern would have been superfluous, had I not been obliged to follow a prescribed order.

3 He should want to devote his attention to geometry, music, arithmetic, and what the Greeks call [*optikēn*], we the visual or optical art⁶³ – as much attention as may briefly relieve the mind wearied by the constant investigation of exalted matters. For a diversity of intellectual pursuits not only brings a certain pleasure, but there's also, in the category of branches of learning of this sort,⁶⁴ usually a special pleasure precisely because we immediately reach what we wanted to know, without any effort or uncertainty, through accomplishment in the given art. **4** But studies of this sort also tend to be

---

prominent among them Guarino Guarini (for whom Vol. 1 Intro. pp. 13, 14); Francesco Barbaro was one of his pupils. Already as early as around 1408 the Scuola di Rialto was established with public support, introducing to Venice the study of Aristotelian philosophy; but a still more emphatic endorsement of humanistic schooling as central to Venetian civic ideology came with the foundation in 1446 of the Scuola di San Marco (see Grendler 2013: 678–9). In this context Barbaro's review of the celibate's academic formation in 4.2 fully reflects the larger humanistic commitments of Venetian schooling in his own times; but he nevertheless recommends that the celibate be educated independently at home so that he is safely protected from social infection (cf. 2.3.21-7).

⁵⁹ In keeping with Barbaro's differentiation of the active and the contemplative lives (cf. 1.1.9-10; 1.3-4; 3.2.1-2).
⁶⁰ Cf. 1.4.13-19, 21-3.
⁶¹ I.e., the celibate cannot learn all subjects equally – a point taken up in 4.2.62.
⁶² Basic to the *Trivium*, grammar was naturally learnt at a young age (so already, e.g., Sen. *Ep.* 88.20), but cf. also Quint. *Inst.* 1.4.5 ('necessary for children and pleasurable for the old').
⁶³ Geometry, music, and arithmetic were staple features of the medieval *Quadrivium*, but optics, the science of seeing (already an Aristotelian preoccupation), emerged as a sub-specialism of the mathematical branch under the guiding influence of such eminences as Robert Grosseteste (*c.* 1169–1253), Albert the Great (*c.* 1200–80), and Roger Bacon (*c.* 1214/20–92); concisely, Lindberg and Tachau 2013. The medieval term for optics was (*ars*) *perspectiva*. If Barbaro here means *perspectivam* in the latter sense, the word gives an added technical nuance after *spectativam*, which itself recurs in 4.2.9 in reference to painting, engraving, etc.
⁶⁴ I.e., specifically the mathematical branches, not all those 'relating ... to mental activity' in 4.2.1.

solent, [**100v**] ut scilicet hac ope facilius enucleatiusque ea percipiantur, quae facere ad nostrum finem videbuntur. Nam pulcherrimam coeli machinam et lucentium stellarum immensitatem contemplari rite non prius licet, quam cognita sit earum rerum natura et magnitudo. **5** Id autem nescio an fieri possit sine Mathematicorum disciplina: nam, ut Platonem omittam, qui numeris tonisque et quantitate omnia propemodum demonstrabat, Aristotelem quoque videmus non posse quicquam de coeli et mundi natura plene tractare, nisi alienas mutuetur rationes. Pariter et Astrologiae non esse ignarum oportebit, quemadmodum neque alterius ullius, quae ad Mathematicos attineat, disciplinae. **6** Laudatur Xenocrates quod, quum quendam Geometriae et huiuscemodi artium ignarum frequentare ludum suum conspexisset: 'Abi,' inquit, 'bone vir, nam adminiculis philosophiae cares.' Ita tamen in his omnibus gerere se ipsum debet [**101r**] ut neque ad architecturae neque ad computationis tenuitatem descendat. Iudicare quoque et futura enuntiare palam nolit, sed id aut intra se aut inter amicissimos exercebit. **7** Non enim vacare illum amicorum consortio velim, ut suo loco dicemus; verum neque id quidam effuse ita faciet, ut nulli rei tantum studere

much desired for another reason – namely, so that by their help the knowledge that will seem conducive to our end-goal is more easily and precisely grasped.[65] For instance, you can't properly ponder the surpassingly beautiful heavenly apparatus and the vastness of the glittering stars before the nature and scale of these things are understood. **5** I doubt this can happen without mathematical training. For, to say nothing of Plato, who explained almost everything in terms of numbers and musical pitch and harmonic quantity,[66] I see that Aristotle, too, was unable to deal in any complete way with anything concerning the nature of the heavens and earth without borrowing the calculations made by others.[67] It will be equally necessary to have some knowledge of astral science,[68] just as of any other branch of learning that has a relevance to mathematics.[69] **6** Xenocrates is extolled because, when he'd noticed that a certain person who had no knowledge of geometry or studies of that sort was attending his school, he said: 'Off with you, sir; for you don't have the basic tools for philosophy!'[70] He must nevertheless conduct himself in all these areas in such a way that he avoids resorting to the rarified quality of either architecture or detailed accountancy.[71] He should also be reluctant openly to pronounce on and disclose the future, but he'll do so either for himself or within his innermost circle of friends. **7** For I wouldn't want him to be without any close connection with friends, as I shall say in the appropriate place;[72] but neither will someone do that[73] in so unrestrained a manner that he seems so greatly devoted to nothing else, but [he'll do so]

---

[65] Cf. already Arist. *Pol.* 8.3 1338a37-40: 'It is also clear that there are some useful things, too, in which the young must be educated, not only because they are useful (for example they must learn reading and writing), *but also because they are often the means to learning yet further subjects*' (tr. Sinclair 1981: 457; my emphasis).

[66] See, e.g., *Tim.* 31b-32c (elemental fire, air, water and earth fixed in ratio to each other, 'air being to water as fire to air, and water being to earth as air to water': tr. Bury 1929: 61), 35a-36d (the World-Soul divided into harmonic intervals), and 53c-57d (the geometry of the 'primary bodies' or particles constituting each of the four kinds of matter – fire, air, etc.) with Mueller 2005.

[67] For overview, Hussey 2002.

[68] The term *astrologia* can denote both astronomy and astrology: cf. *OLD* 1a, *DMLBS* 1a, b.

[69] Barbaro's limited endorsement of astrology in 4.2.6-8 reflects (i) the increased respectability of astrology that accompanied the reconciliation of the natural sciences/ Aristotelian rationalism and Christian theology; (ii) the medieval proliferation of medical astrology (see esp. 4.2.8); and (iii) the regular use of astrology in policy formation among Renaissance ruling elites (cf. Azzolini 2013, esp. 2–5). See in summary Carey 2010, esp. 891–4, with Azzolini and Mosley 2014.

[70] For Xenocrates, 2.5.11 and n. 124 (cf. also 3.5.16, 28); for the anecdote, D. L. 4.10.

[71] I.e., the narrower, more specialized application of the numerical sciences.

[72] 4.2.79-80.

[73] Engage in astrology.

videatur, sed aut voluptatis remissionisque alicuius gratia, aut ut naturae ordinem, qui ex superioribus illis corporibus maxime pendet, ex annua illa rerum atque ipsius mundi volutatione scire melius assuescat. **8** Sed et suae quoque valitudini consulere opportunius poterit, si ventura atque imminentia longe ante praeviderit. Id enim est illi non in secundis habendum, ne aegritudine ulla ab opere honestissimo abducatur, quippe qui, ut inquit Aristoteles, dignissimus sit qui diutissime vivat incolumis. Sed hoc locis suis accomodatius potest intelligi.

9 In ea vero, quam spec[**101v**]tativam diximus, quantum ad picturam caelaturamve et huiuscemodi artes pertinet, non magno studio versari velit, verum, ut saepius diximus, et hoc esse in omni disciplina caput et institutum debet: tantum hanc artem et reliquas omnis attingat, quantum facere ad suum finem animadvertet. Finis autem esse debet divinissimae rei cognitio summae foelicitati et voluptati coniuncta.

10 Eloquentiam vero frustra requiri in huiuscemodi homine video, quippe quae ad usum tantum rerum forensium et urbanarum sit reperta, nisi forte credere oportet gaudere etiam hac virtute deos, quibuscum sit coelebs assiduo

either for some degree of pleasure or relaxation, or to get used to a better understanding, on the basis of that yearly turning of the world and of the firmament itself, of nature's system, which depends above all on those more exalted bodies. **8** But he'll also be able to take thought more advantageously for his own health as well, if he foresees far in advance what's to come and is looming.[74] For avoiding being drawn away by any illness from a task of the greatest respectability – he shouldn't regard *that* as second best, inasmuch as he thoroughly deserves (as Aristotle says) to live for the longest time unimpaired.[75] But this point can be more appropriately understood in its own proper context.

9 He shouldn't want to involve himself very enthusiastically, however, in what I termed the visual art, insofar as it relates to painting or engraving and skilled pursuits of this sort.[76] But, as I've said rather often,[77] *this* has to be the main point and purpose in every branch of learning: he should concern himself with this art, as all others, only so far as he sees it to contribute to his end-goal. The end must be gaining knowledge of the most divine subject matter – knowledge closely connected with the greatest happiness and pleasure.[78]

10 I see no point, however, in looking for eloquence in a person of this sort, inasmuch as it was devised only for deployment in legal and civic affairs – unless, perhaps, we're to believe that this skill, too, gives joy to the gods, with whom the celibate is destined to be in constant dialogue.[79] The pleasure of

---

[74] Iatroastrology: see n. 69 (ii) above.

[75] Cf. *EN* 1.10 1101a14-16: 'Why then should we not say that he is happy who is active in accordance with complete virtue (*kat'aretēn teleian*) and is sufficiently equipped with external goods [e.g., good health], not for some chance period but throughout a complete life (*teleion bion*)?' (tr. Ross 1980: 22). The precise meaning of 'complete' (*teleios*) is complicated in this and other passages in *EN* 1.10 and elsewhere (cf. 1.7 1098a16-20, 10.7 1177b24-6) because of the different qualitative and durational connotations of *teleios* (i.e., 'absolute,' 'perfect' vs. 'to the end of life'): see Farwell 1995 with Lear 2015 and Emilsson 2015.

[76] The eye for aesthetic appreciation that Barbaro associates with *spectativam* here (cf. also 4.2.3 and n. 63) is similar to that which Aristotle associates with drawing (*hē graphikē technē*) in *Pol.* 8.3 – a branch of education that has utility (1338a17-19) but also nurtures an eye for the beauty of shape and figure (1338a40-b4). Vergerio, in *De ingen. mor.*, departs explicitly from Aristotle in offering a far more limited endorsement of drawing (*designativa* [*ars*], 41; tr. Kallendorf 2002: 49–51); whether or not directly influenced by Vergerio, Barbaro's own coolness towards 'the visual art' similarly modifies the Aristotelian position on *graphikē*.

[77] Cf. for this insistent stress on the *finis*/end 1.1.3-4, 1.2.7, 2.3.5, 4.1.22, 4.2.4.

[78] The linkage of knowledge, happiness, and pleasure in the divine here reaffirms 4.1.19-22.

[79] Barbaro departs here from a curricular staple of Venetian civic humanism: cf. Verg. *De ingen. mor.* 40 on eloquence as 'a distinct part of civics ...; through eloquence we can speak with weight and polish, which is the one skill that most effectively wins over the minds of the masses' (tr. Kallendorf 2002: 49). See further n. 89 below, and cf. Intro. p. 2.

loquuturus. Cuius rei voluptas ita cadere in Deum potest, quemadmodum in Endymionem[80] dormiendi: corporis enim utrunque munus est, sed et impium erit arbitrari capi Deum posse verborum ornatu, quod aegre in imperitissima etiam plebe im[**102r**]petratur. **11** Quo circa[81] admirari soleo quorundam sane importunissimam severitatem, qui siquid ab iis inornatum aut minus latinum verbum exciderit, qui se a rebus gerendis ad meliorem vitam transtulerunt, statim exclamant ineptos et barbaros homines et postremum indignos quorum consuetudine homines ulli delectentur. Neque vident quanta sit imprudentia requirere quicquam ab aliquo, quod ad illum pertinere nequaquam videatur. **12** Amare id quuius[82] finem aliquis aspernatur, nonne insaniae et furori simillimum est? Quis autem ignorat eloquentiae[83] usum spectare ad rerum publicarum administrationem, non ad solitariam atque lucifugam vitam? Iis, qui tam male sentiunt, necessarium est et propemodum consequens confiteri virginibus iis, quae se in religiosum obtrudunt locum, suendi nendique scientiam capescendam esse, neque ullum putare [**102v**] discrimen oportere inter coeteras mulieres et illas esse. **13** Quid quod et in iis artibus, quae sunt ad actionem institutae, aperte deprehendimus non esse ubique necessariam eloquendi facultatem?[84] Nam et in Senatu quoque atque conciliis non esset hac virtute opus omnino, si aequis legibus aut iudicibus uteremur. Quo apparet in republica bene instituta non esse eloquentiam expetendam, sed in ea duntaxat in quam odium, factiones, discordia,[85] dominatus, formido et affectiones reliquae irruperunt.

---

[80] *-ione* MS.
[81] *quo circa* MS; see p. 76 n. 235 on 3.6.19.
[82] *quuis* MS.
[83] *ael-* MS.
[84] *Quid? quod . . . -tatem* Br.
[85] *discordia* tentatively after Br. 138 n. 3; *miseri-* MS, but 'compassion' is hardly fitting here.

this commodity can fall to God in the same way as the pleasure of sleeping did to Endymion:[86] for each is a function of the body, but it will also be irreverent to imagine that God can be captivated by rhetorical embellishment – something scarcely accomplished even in the case of the very ignorant masses. **11** Hence I tend to marvel at the truly uncompromising harshness of certain people who, if an inelegant or not quite Latinate utterance slips out from those who've transported themselves from a life of business to a better existence,[87] immediately jeer at them as witless, uncivilized people, and ultimately unfit to give other people any enjoyment through conversation with them. Nor do they appreciate just how misguided it is to look for a quality in someone for whom it seemingly has no relevance at all. **12** To take pleasure in something when the fulfillment of it is treated with disdain by someone[88] – is that not very like raving madness? But who is unaware that the practice of eloquence bears on the management of state affairs, not on a solitary existence out of the public eye?[89] For those who think in so misguided a fashion, it's imperative – and just about logical – to grant that a knowledge of sewing and spinning is to be acquired by those maidens who close themselves off in hallowed quarters, and to imagine that there must be no difference between them and the rest of womankind.[90] **13** What of the fact that, even among those skills that were established for the active life, we clearly find that a capacity for eloquence is not essential in all circumstances? For even in the Senate, too, and in council assemblies, there would be no need whatsoever for this form of excellence if we had fair laws and judges. It's plain from this that in a well-established state eloquence is not to be sought after, but only in that which has been invaded by hatred, partisan divisions, strife, despotism, acute fear, and the other such stirrings of mind.[91]

---

[86] The goddess Selene's lover, put into an eternal sleep by Zeus; eloquence is no more refreshingly gratifying to God than sleep is to Endymion. Given Barbaro's evident recourse to Aristotle's *EN* 10.8 in 4.1.20-1, he may well have drawn the Endymion comparison from there (cf. 1178b19-20).

[87] Ironic, implying elevation to social heights where condescension reigns and rains down.

[88] I.e., to look for a purity of diction in one who scorns such finery.

[89] Markedly Ciceronian in phraseology (cf. Vol. 1 Intro. pp. 21, 29, 32 with 46 n. 213): for *rerum publicarum administrationem* cf. *De or.* 1.165, *Fin.* 4.68, 5.58, *Rep.* 1.35; rare *lucifugus* at *Fin.* 1.61. Given the contemplative-philosophical inclinations of the celibate, Barbaro touches lightly here (as perhaps in 4.2.10) on the tradition of philosophical antipathy towards the 'ruder Muses' of crowd-swaying eloquence (cf. Cic. *Brut.* 283, *Orat.* 13).

[90] But for ample evidence of such handiwork – and of its economic importance – in the medieval and early Renaissance convent see Strocchia 2009: 113–26 with Pearson 2001: 1385.

[91] Barbaro here adapts the familiar argument that eloquence most thrives in times of political instability, strife, and corruption, as at Rome in its periods of constitutional crisis (see esp. Tac. *Dial.* 36-41, and cf. [Long.] *Subl.* 44).

14 Consentiunt his illa a summis auctoribus in excusationem defensionemque eloquentiae accersita. 'Excolere,' inquiunt, 'figuris orationem aut exemplis stabilire aut quovis pacto illustrare, movere affectus, arte demum atque cuniculis contendere non oporteret, si boni darentur causarum cognitores.' 15 Quo circa[92] ad prohibendum potius malum videtur inventa dicendi ars, quam ad bo[103r]num aliquid afferendum excogitata. Frustra itaque inter bonos exerceretur,[93] quare neque hanc utique caelibes exercebunt: viri enim boni erunt et cum bonis semper versabuntur. Quamobrem, ut concludatur, non erit omnino in coelibe eloquentia[94] expectanda, verum ita loquetur ut natura doctus non arte videri eruditus possit. 16 Purus sit sermo, non excultus, non accersitus, non mobilis, sed gravis, sed constans: is demum unus, quo sponte naturae[95] donatus est; erit autem non incomptus aut rusticanus aut non paratus arte, sed benignitate naturae compositus. Nam verba confundere et sensum cogitationemque morari audientis et lapides, ut inquit Plautus, loqui, non erit in contemplatore ne accidat pertimescendum. 17 Id enim mala efficit corporis habitudo: eum vero, qui nostris victurus est legibus, vacare omni corporis vicio et tempe[103v]ratam habere naturam oportebit; quam rem, cum ex aliis quoque signis compluribus, tum vero maxime et ex tactus mollicie percipi posse Aristoteles tradidit. 18 Quod si

---

[92] *quo circa* MS; see p. 76 n. 235 on 3.6.19.
[93] *-eretur* MS; *-etur* Br.
[94] *ael-* MS.
[95] *mat-* MS. Br. prints *naturae* but proposes *-a* (139 n. 2); but for *sponte naturae* cf., e.g., Plin. NH 7.4, 9.160, 11.263, 14.53, 74, etc.

14 This is consistent with the arguments summoned in justification and defense of eloquence by the highest authorities. 'There would be no need,' they say, 'to adorn a speech with figured expression or to consolidate it with examples, or to embellish it by whatever means, to rouse the emotions, in short, to exert oneself with technical skill and hidden contrivances, if advocates of cases were assigned who were morally good.'[96] **15** Therefore the art of speaking seems devised for keeping wickedness in check rather than invented to confer some benefit. Accordingly, it would be a pointless exertion among good people, and for that reason celibates will doubtless not work on it either; for they will be morally good, and will always associate with the morally good. Hence (to bring the matter to a close) eloquence will in no circumstances have to be expected in the celibate, but he will speak in such a way that he can appear taught by nature and not trained in an artificial skill.[97] **16** His speech should be plain, not highly adorned, not forced, and not variable, but weighty and consistent – in short, that one form of speech that was conferred on him by nature's will; it will not be inelegant, rough-and-ready, or furnished with no artfulness, but well-ordered through nature's kind indulgence. For jumbling his words, impeding the listener's perception and thought-processes, and, as Plautus says, speaking stones[98] – there should be no fear that that will happen in the contemplative's case. **17** For that is caused by a poor bodily condition; but the person who's going to live by my rules will necessarily be free of all bodily shortcomings, and have a measured constitution[99] – a circumstance that, as Aristotle related, could be observed not just from several other indications besides, but especially also from the softness of touch.[100] **18** But if it were to transpire that he stammered or got his

---

[96] Cf. the interlocutory objection in Quint. *Inst.* 12.1.33, to the effect of: 'Why so much artful technicality in rhetorical training *unless* the power of eloquence is sometimes allowed to override the truth?' Quintilian parries this thrust (12.1.34-45), thereby upholding his position that the true orator must be virtuous (cf. 1 pref. 9, 2.16.11, 3.7.25, 12.1.31, 12.2.1, etc.) and that eloquence is intrinsically honourable and 'the most beautiful thing in the world' (1.12.16, 18; cf. 12.1.32). Barbaro departs from Quintilian in distancing his celibate *bonus vir* from what he here portrays as the morally compromised art of eloquence; but cf. nonetheless the familiar classical correlation between speech/style and character when he stresses the naturalness of the celibate's speech in 4.2.15-16 (see further n. 97 below, and cf. Vol. 1 Intro. pp. 32–3).
[97] Adaptation of the familiar correlation drawn between speech and character, style and lifestyle; see esp. Sen. *Ep.* 114.1 (after Cic. *Tusc.* 5.47), and cf. 40.2, 75.4-5, 115.1.
[98] Plaut. *Aul.* 152, the only extant classical example of the phrase.
[99] See 2.5 (the celibate's physical robustness) and 2.6.8 (his concomitant steadfastness and restraint).
[100] Cf. *De an.* 2.9 421a21-6: '... in touch [humankind] is much more discriminating than the other animals. This is why he is of all living creatures the most intelligent. Proof of this lies in the fact that among the human race men are well or poorly endowed with intelligence in proportion to their sense of touch, and no other sense; for men of hard skin and flesh are poorly, and men of soft flesh well endowed with intelligence' (tr. Hett 1957: 121).

eveniret ut is aut balbutiret aut difficulter et cum mora exprimeret,[101] quod[102] viris tametsi clarissimis scimus accidisse, sine impietate fieri non posset ut illi a contemplatu propter hanc unam rem tantum interdiceretur, eoque id esset stultius atque crudelius, quum animi solum mentisque praestantia,[103] non oris aut linguae suavitate, opus sit iis qui contemplari decreverunt. Quare hortamur etiam nos ut naviter contemplentur, talesque utinam sint quales optamus! **19** Quod si magna fuerit loquendi difficultas, concedemus aliquam esse quaerendam opem, aut ad tollendam oris asperitatem aut ad molliendam, quemadmodum curasse Demosthenem summum oratorem mo[**104r**]numentis est traditum. Hoc autem studium iccirco adhibeatur volo, ne aut ad exprimendas secum, ut plerunque fit, cogitationes aut ad communicandas cum iis, a quibus aut doceri aut iuvari poterit, et ad alia pleraque facilius atque illaboratius factitanda, quae possunt speculantibus evenire, impedimento sit exprimendarum rerum inscitia et difficultas. **20** Tantam autem operam det explicandae expoliendaeque sermonis fragositati, quantum ad prompte[104] contemplandum et ad ea quae istuc perducant sufficere arbitrabitur. Ex iis ergo, quae sumus praefati, aperte intelligi potest non esse habendam eloquentiae[105] rationem ei qui mentem solam exercet.

21 Poeticae quoque studium acre et multa praelectio oratorum et longa cum historicis consuetudo abhorrere videtur ab eo fine quem figimus. Ista autem semel est utile forsitan percurrisse, non quod prodesse multum [**104v**] possint, sed quod profectum aliquem creant ex sententiarum varietate, in ea praesertim aetate quae puerorum est. **22** Sed historiae minus trepide[106] sumi in manibus debent, quia hinc cognitio, quam ex caeteris maior, ab experimentis exemplisque ducitur: quo fit ut ad maiora quandoque illa nobis suppetant exque illis interdum, velut initiis, ad altiora veniatur. Sed neque poetas omnis neque oratores sicut neque historicos legisse velit: plerique enim ex iis libris, quos nostra iuventus in sinu gerit, ita impuri impudicique solent circumferri,

---

[101] Br. 139 n. 3 proposes that an object (e.g., *verba*) be supplied for *exprimeret*; but for intrans. *exprimo* cf. 4.2.34, *De off. leg.* 16.
[102] *-eret quod* Br.
[103] *pres-* MS.
[104] *-ae* MS.
[105] *ael-* MS.
[106] *-ae* MS.

words out with difficulty and haltingly (a plight that we know has happened to men of the highest distinction nevertheless), it couldn't but be an act of immorality for him to be debarred from contemplation because of this one thing only – and it would be that much more stupid and cruel, since those who've decided on the contemplative life need excellence of soul and mind alone, not sweetness of mouth or tongue. Hence I also encourage them to work hard at contemplation – and may they be such as we want them to be! **19** But if they face great difficulty in speaking, I'll grant that some help has to be sought either to remove or to soften any harshness of utterance, just as the historical record reports that Demosthenes, the supreme orator, treated it.[107] But I want this strenuous effort to be applied precisely to ensure that inexperience or difficulty in articulating ideas is no obstacle either to expressing one's thoughts to oneself (as often happens) or to sharing them with those by whom it's possible to be either taught or helped; and [no obstacle] to routinely doing, rather easily and without strain, the many other things that can happen to those engaged in contemplation. **20** Let him give as much effort to smoothing out and polishing any roughness of speech as he'll think adequate for engaging in contemplation without difficulty, and for the steps leading to that point. Therefore, from what I've mentioned earlier, it can be clearly understood that one preoccupied with employing his mind alone doesn't have to pay regard to eloquence.

21 The enthusiastic study of poetry, too, seems to be incompatible with the end-goal I've established, as is much recitation of the orators and prolonged engagement with historical writers. It's perhaps useful to have run through such texts once, not because they can bring much benefit, but because they yield some profit from their diverse ways of thinking, especially in the period belonging to boyhood.[108] **22** But historical works should be taken in hand with less anxiety, because, from demonstrated proofs and examples, a more important form of knowledge is derived from them than from the other [kinds of writing]; hence those features[109] sometimes lend us their support for greater undertakings, and from them, as if from a starting-point, we occasionally arrive at higher things. But there should be no desire to have read all the poets and orators, just as in the case of historical writers; for the majority of those books, which our young people hold dear, are usually so shamefully immoral as they do the rounds that they are not only not to be opened or read, but not

---

[107] Cf. Cic. *De or*. 1.260-1, Plut. *Dem*. 6.3-4, 11.1-2, D. L. 2.109; see also 3.6.23 and n. 245.

[108] For variations in the value attached to poetry, oratory, and history in the humanistic curriculum cf. Verg. *De ingen. mor*. 40-3 (tr. Kallendorf 2002: 49–53), Brun. *De stud. et litt*. 18-28 (tr. Kallendorf 109–23), Piccol. *De lib. educ*. 60-73 (tr. Kallendorf 207–25), and Guar. *De ord*. 22-8 (tr. Kallendorf 285–93).

[109] The 'demonstrated proofs and examples' above.

ut non modo non sint aperiendi aut legendi, sed ne nominandi quidem. **23** O sanctissimum institutum Senatus Populique romani et, nisi puderet sequi bonos mores, nostrae tempestatis aegritudini accommodatum! Decreto publico cremati sunt in foro libri quos [Petillius[110]] praetor sepulchro Numae Pompilii erutos adinvenit, ob unam [**105r**] causam tantum, quia severissimam disciplinam aut solvere aut mitiorem aliquanto reddere viderentur. **24** Nam Lacedaemonii suo iure poetas nocentiores expulerunt, quippe qui neque Timotheo pepercerint, quia laxare animos iuventutis dissolutior illa chordarum adiectio putabatur. Nunc vero confusae passim bibliothecae et scelestissimo quoque ex libris refertissimae omnibus patent, ubique exscribuntur, neque aliae in honore sunt quam quae nullo poetarum vacent. **25** Sed, age, quid de aliis loquimur? concedamus hos alios legere, mihi cura meorum sit. Hi nihil impurum non dico praelegent, sed ne manu quidem attrectabunt. Haec cum optimis quibusque nostra quoque sententia est: honestiores vero libros, et ex quorum numero non pauci sunt elegantiores, si volent, ea semper conditione percurrent, ut inde fructum aliquem capiant, qui ad supremum illum finem [**105v**] facilius adipiscendum conducere videatur.

26 Dialeticae vero (audacter promemus sententiam nostram) non sint vel in minimis rebus expertes, sed et acrem et continuam operam impendant est necesse eos qui cognitione rerum plurimarum atque ipsius veritatis delectantur. Quis enim alius est laboris nostri terminus quam intelligentia et veritas? Hanc autem facit ut assequamur maxime ea scientia, quae falsum a

---

[110] *Potilius* proposed by Br. 140 n. 4 to fill the blank in the MS, but *Petillius* is the more familiar form in the sources (cf. n. 111 below).

even to be mentioned by name. **23** O for that most venerable practice of the Roman senate and people – a practice well suited to the sickness of our times, were we not ashamed to follow good behaviour! By public decree there was a bonfire in the forum of the books that the praetor [Petillius] found unearthed from the tomb of Numa Pompilius; they were burnt for only one reason – because they seemed either to impair the strictest standards of orderly conduct, or to render them somewhat less harsh.¹¹¹ **24** Again, the Spartans took it upon themselves to banish poets of the more harmful kind, in that they showed Timotheus no leniency because the rather dissolute increase that he made to the number of lyre-strings was thought to slacken the minds of the young.¹¹² Now, however, libraries that are everywhere in turmoil and absolutely crammed with all the most scandalous of books lie open to all; written copies are being made all over the place; and the only libraries that are respected are those stocked with every single one of the poets. **25** But come, why speak of others? Let's allow that others read such books; let my concern be with my own charges. I don't just say they will recite nothing immoral, but they won't even lay a hand on such works. This is the view I too share with all those of the highest character: if they will in fact want books of a more respectable kind (and no few of that number are rather attractive), they will run through them always on the condition that they derive from them some benefit that seems advantageous for more easily achieving that ultimate end-goal of theirs.

26 As for dialectic,¹¹³ however (I'll boldly state my opinion), they shouldn't be ignorant of it even in the smallest matters, but those who take pleasure in acquiring knowledge of a great many subjects and of truth itself must apply themselves to it with a relentless and unremitting effort. For what is the end-goal of our work other than understanding and truth? What more than anything causes us to acquire such understanding and truth is the knowledge that distinguishes falsehood from truth; and what undoubtedly brings that

---

¹¹¹ In 181 BCE farmworkers digging on the Janiculum recovered two stone coffins, the one (by then empty) allegedly that of Numa, the legendary second king of Rome, the other containing his books. Half of those books were in Latin, dealing with pontifical law, the other half in Greek; the latter were philosophical in content, Pythagorean according to some sources. Q. Petillius, urban praetor in 181, found in those materials elements that undermined Roman religion; hence, after a complex sequence of events, he arranged for their public cremation. For the story, variously told but broadly consistent in its essentials, cf. Liv. 40.29.3-14, V. Max. 1.1.12, Plin. *NH* 13.84-7, Plut. *Num.* 22.4-5 with Willi 1998.

¹¹² For this anecdote of Timotheus of Miletus (*c.* 450–360 BCE), allegedly the leading musical innovator of his time, Cic. *Leg.* 2.39, Plin. *NH* 7.204 with Maas 1992, esp. 77–81.

¹¹³ Logic-based discourse, along with rhetoric and grammar a fixture of the medieval *Trivium* and embraced by the humanistic curriculum (cf. Piccol. *De lib. educ.* 38, 90; tr. Kallendorf 2002: 179, 247); for Barbaro's conventional stress below on dialectic as a means of distinguishing truth from falsehood cf., e.g., Cic. *Fin.* 3.72, *Luc.* 91, Sext. Emp. *Pyr.* 2.229.

vero diiudicat: id certe quod efficit ea disciplina, quam rationalem rationativamve nuncupamus. **27** Verum, ut in plerisque, male bonis uti coeptum est: nam et hanc ipsam Dialeticam, quum disputandi ars esset, non nulli in minutulas argutiunculas contraxerunt, quorum tamen studium aliquanto fortasse tolerabilius est, quia ad acuendum ingenium repertum esse videatur. Sed metus est, et iam in multis patent experimenta, ne fractus hoc [**106r**] usu animus in pertinaciam quandam illiberalitatemque consenescat; quare se abstineat quantum potest ab ista tenuitate non solum vir, sed etiam puer quum erit et adolescens. **28** Scire enim debemus in ostentationem et fastum[114] cessurum esse potius hoc disceptandi genus et ad superbiam altas radices immissurum. Nimirum piget improbare id studium, quo solemus interdum oblectari: sed aperienda fuere omnia quae sentiebamus. Neque enim esse ullum mendacem minus oportebat, quam qui de veritate cognoscenda erat praecepta traditurus. **29** Mitius tamen agere possumus, faterique afferre utilitatis aliquid posse huiuscemodi cavillationes atque fallacias iis qui non ad eum finem tendunt, quem in nostro coelibatu requirimus, sed iis qui aut in re publica versaturi sunt, aut aliud acturi quippiam quod ad negotiosam vitam attineat. Hos enim habere nomi[**106v**]nis aliquid in populo et auctoritatis opinionisque necesse est; quam scilicet ex illa vociferatione iactationeque digitorum atque totius corporis agitatione, quibus capi maxime vulgus solet, extemplo mereantur, neque vertendum illis vitio erit, si ad bonum aliquem finem honorati esse voluerint. **30** Is vero, qui neque gloriam quaerit neque fastum ullum sequitur, non sine magno dedecore in ea corona stabit, in qua sit eo pacto disputandum. Quare cavillari, tueri pertinaciter maledictum,[115] conviciis postremo agere, quae ex artis illius studio proficiscuntur omnia, indignum putaverit ea vita, quam selegit.

---

[114] *falsum* MS, corrected to *fastum*.
[115] *maledictum* MS; *male dictum* Br.

about is the training we call reasoning-based or logical. **27** But, as in so many things, forces for good have begun to be misapplied: yes, even this very dialectic, though it was a skilled technique of argument, has been reduced by a good number of its practitioners to tiny little hair-splitting details;[116] but their devoted pursuit of it is nevertheless perhaps somewhat more acceptable because it seems to have been devised for sharpening the intellect. But there's the fear (and with proofs already plainly visible in many cases) that the mind exhausted by being applied in this way wastes away[117] into a certain stubbornness and meanness of bearing; hence not only should a grown man refrain as much as possible from this rarified form of subtlety, but even when he's a boy and a young man. **28** For we have to understand that this type of argumentation is instead likely to give way to a conceited form of showiness, and to sink deep roots leading to arrogance. It's certainly regrettable to take to task the pursuit in which we're accustomed occasionally to find diversion; but the entirety of my thinking had to be revealed. Why? Because no one should less resort to lying than one who's going to deliver advice on mastering the truth. **29** I can nevertheless proceed more indulgently by granting that sophistic quibblings and trickeries of this sort can bring some advantage to those who aren't striving for the end that I look for in my vision of celibacy – but to those destined either for public life or for some other mode of activity that's connected with the busy life. For such people have to have a measure of renown among the general public, and of prestige and good reputation; and they may of course earn it right away from all that haranguing and finger-wagging and the excited motions of the entire body by which the crowd is usually most captivated, nor should it be treated as a fault in them if they want to win acclaim to some[118] good end. **30** But as for the person who neither seeks renown nor aims at any superior attitude, he'll incur great dishonour by standing in that judicial setting where he has to argue on these terms. Hence he'll think that to use quibbling sophistry, stubbornly to defend a slanderous statement, and ultimately to act with angry clamoring (all of them techniques arising from the devoted pursuit of that skill) – he will think it unworthy of the life he's chosen.

---

[116] For dialectic as a mode of compressed eloquence, eloquence a form of expanded dialectic, Cic. *Brut.* 309, *Fin.* 2.17, *Orat.* 113-14; but for dialectic's desiccating excesses long decried (damning diminutives here in *minutulas argutiunculas*), Sen. *Ep.* 45.5, 8-13, 48.4-12, 71.6, Quint. *Inst.* 12.2.10-14, Gell. 1.2.3-13.

[117] Lat. *consenescat* lit. 'grows old,' the mind as if exhausted and crushed (*OLD fractus* 2, 3) by dialectical finery that is itself 'broken' and jerky (cf. *OLD fractus* 1c). The old age implicit in *consenescat* is offset by the younger blood that prevails in 'hence ... a young man' below, with *illiberalitatem* also hinting at a distortion of the 'true' humanistic liberal arts.

[118] Faint praise (cf. *OLD aliqui*[1] 4b, 'in exprs. of qualified approval'); the *finis* of public life is starkly contrasted with the 'end' (*finem*) of the contemplative/celibate existence in 'those who ... celibacy' above.

31 Naturalem vero disciplinam, quam in duo genera intelligi volumus separatam, in divinarum scilicet et mortalium rerum cognitionem, tanto studio complectatur quanto fieri maximo potest: hinc enim proximus erit ad metam gradus et fini contiguus. Vereri enim et colere, [**107r**] admirari opificem Deum finem esse diximus foelicitatis: id autem tunc plane assequi possumus, quum opera illius ingentia usui nostro fabricata fuisse cognoscimus; id autem nobis praestat ea scientia, quae de natura, hoc est causis effectibusque rerum omnium, abunde pertractat. Hanc itaque, ut maxime peculiarem sibi, is vendicet qui contemplari volet. **32** Verum, quia naturae subiecta esse videtur medicina, dubitari potest utrum huic arti danda etiam aliqua opera sit, quam nos quaestionem tractare polliciti sumus. Non nulli, quum turpe et minime liberale in omnibus officium medendi videatur, turpissimum in coelibatu atque illiberalissimum putant, quom non modo indecentissimum sit attrectare et satagere, quorum usus venit munus id deligentibus, verumetiam indignissimum homine ingenuo inde esse videri possit, quod servire et ministrare vilissimis etiam corporibus sit ne[**107v**]cesse. **33** Ex his arbitrantur se fortiter collegisse medicinae non esse incumbendum,

31 As for the science of nature, however, which I want to be understood as divided into two classes, namely the investigation of matters pertaining to the gods and to mortals, he should embrace it with the greatest enthusiasm that can possibly be mustered; for the next step from here will be to our goal, with the end in reach. For I've said[119] that the zenith of happiness is to revere, worship, and go in awe of God the maker. We can clearly achieve as much at the moment when we recognize that His immense works have been contrived for our benefit.[120] What gives us that awareness is the branch of learning that occupies itself extensively with nature, that is, the causes and effects of all things. And so the person who will want to engage in contemplation should lay claim to this knowledge as of very special relevance to himself. **32** But, because medicine seems to be subordinate to nature, there's room for hesitation as to whether any serious effort is to be given to this area of knowledge as well – a problem that I promised to deal with.[121] Since the doctor's duty appears unseemly and by no means befitting a gentleman in all circumstances,[122] some think that it is most unseemly and ungentlemanly in celibacy: not only is it most unbecoming to handle and busy oneself about the things dealt with by those who choose that line of work, but it can also seem to be most unworthy of a gentleman because of the need to be at the service of and tend to even the basest of bodies.[123] **33** As a result, they have

---

[119] Cf. 4.1.16-22, esp. 22.
[120] That humankind was the beneficiary of an anthropocentric world-order was a central tenet of ancient Stoicism (see esp. Cic. *Nat. D.* 1.4, 2.133-67), but the idea was already present in earlier Greek thought (see Pease 1955-8: 2.949 on *Nat. D.* 2.154 *hominum causa* with Moore 2017: 47–52). But also implicated here is the Judeo-Christian anthropocentrism rooted in the creation of humans in God's image in Genesis 1 – a model that by one view shaped a medieval demythologizing of nature and informed Renaissance/early modern attitudes to the exploitation of nature for human benefit (for overview, Simkins 2014 with Moore, esp. 4–18).
[121] Cf. 3.6.37, in a context where Barbaro has previously countenanced the possibility of innate physical infirmity defying medical therapy (3.6.29; in 3.6.30 he takes a different view of recovery from mental infirmity); in at least this *physical* respect medicine is cast as 'subordinate to nature' at 4.2.32.
[122] Cf. Verg. *De ingen. mor.* 45: 'Medicine is a very fine thing to know about and very useful for bodily health, but its practice contains very little that is suitable for the noble mind' (tr. Kallendorf 2002: 55). Beyond the unedifying physical aspects that Barbaro identifies, Vergerio seemingly 'disliked the demand for money and concomitant lack of moral sensibilities among practicing physicians in his day' (McManamon 1996: 96).
[123] This distaste is partly in keeping with the disdain for the body shown by the sage whose soul is corporeally imprisoned (cf. 2.5.6), his physical health important only insofar as it aids his calling to contemplation (2.5.10). But Barbaro may also imply a distinction between higher-minded physicians and hands-on surgeons (cf. Palmer 1979, esp. 451), in advance of the contrast that he draws immediately below between theoretical and applied medicine.

ei praesertim qui se ab humana sotietate deduxit. Nam, quor artem illam adipisci velit quispiam, qua non sit unquam usurus, non videre se plane affirmant; quod si erat usurus, non erat utique illi ex oculis hominum abeundum. **34** Sed ignorare videntur hi duplicem esse usum medicinae: unum qui rationibus, alterum qui constet experimentis; empiricum hunc, logicum illum appellari, sive, ut alii melius fortasse expresserunt, unum esse qui in speculatione, alterum qui in actione consisteret; primum ad speculandum, alterum ad agendum repertum fuisse. Quare sic scissa in duo genera medicina non frustra sciri poterit etiamsi careat actione. **35** Scientiam itaque esse in coelibe, non usum, velim: quo circa[124] neque turpi ministerio addicetur, neque cuiquam serviet. Haec [**108r**] enim contra illos dicta sunt, qui se ad agendum contulerunt: an sit autem indecorum munus id et minime liberale, non est operis instituti explicare; tueantur suas partis ii quibus obiecta illa opponuntur. Rationalem itaque disciplinam non ignoret is quem totius naturae volumus esse contemplatorem: ad quod perfecte assequendum plurimi refert scire quae vis herbarum, quae animantium omnium et quae sensu carentium sit innata complexio; morborum quoque ex quibus causis fiant et qua ope curentur non erit agnitio contemnenda. **36** Ita enim naturae varietas omnis et machinae admirabilis pulchritudo ex causarum omnium, tam evidentium quam obstrusarum abditarumque, proprietate optime deprehendetur. Haec autem ita coniuncta est cum ea quae physice[125] dicitur disciplina, ut, nisi morborum aegrotationumve mentio aliqua fieret, seiunc[**108v**]tae minime[126] scientiae viderentur.

---

[124] *quo circa* MS; see p. 76 n. 235 on 3.6.19.
[125] *-ae* MS.
[126] *-ae* MS.

concluded with strong reason, they reckon, that one's energies shouldn't be devoted to medicine, especially on the part of the person who's withdrawn from associating with humankind. For they flatly assert that they don't see why anyone would want to acquire that skill when he's never going to use it; but if he *was* going to use it, it was certainly imperative for him not to disappear from the eyes of humankind. **34** But these people seem not to recognize the two-fold value of medicine – the one, which consists of theoretical reasoning, and the other, which puts things to the test; that the latter is termed empirical, the former logical; or, as others have perhaps more aptly stated, that there is the one branch consisting of intellectual enquiry, the other of action, and that the first was devised for theoretical investigation, the second for practical engagement.[127] Hence, when medicine is divided in this way into two classes, it will be possible to be well versed in it to no useless effect even if it lacks direct action. **35** And so I would want the celibate to have knowledge of it, but not hands-on experience; hence he will neither attach himself to an unseemly form of service nor be anyone's servant. To be sure, this much has been said in opposition to those who've devoted themselves to action. It's beyond the remit of the task I've taken on to state whether that is an unbecoming form of employment that's anything but ennobling; let those against whom such charges are leveled defend their own role. Accordingly, the student whom I want to be an observer of nature as a whole shouldn't be unfamiliar with the theoretical [aspect of the] discipline. To achieve this most fully, it's of the utmost importance to know the potency of medicinal herbs, and the inherent constitution of all animate beings and insentient forms;[128] knowledge of diseases, too, should not be rejected, in terms of the causes that give rise to them and the means by which they are treated. **36** Why? Because in this way all nature's diversity and the wondrous beauty of its system will be very well understood from the special character of all its forms of causation, both apparent and removed from view in their hidden place. But this branch of learning is connected with that called natural science in such a way that, if no reference were made to diseases and illnesses, the [two] departments of knowledge would hardly seem separate at all.

---

[127] Barbaro thus aligns his approach to medicine with the larger tension in *De coelibatu* between the contemplative life and its active alternative.
[128] Surely telling about Barbaro's own intellectual proclivities and his later scholarly trajectory, given his engagement already with Aristotle's biological writings (cf. 2.4.17 n. 100; 2.6.19-20 nn. 175–6; 3.3.4 nn. 39, 41; 3.5.42 n. 128), his own botanical interests (on which Reeds 1976: 527), and his fundamental work from the early 1480s onwards on the text of Pliny's *Natural history* and on Dioscorides (see Vol. 1 Intro. pp. 22–4).

37 Quoniam vero quaeri etiam solet utrum ea quae ad mores attinet disciplina pertineat etiam ad studium contemplandi, quum sit tota in actione collocata, necessarium, ut arbitror, est ne pars illa tractatus praetermittatur, in qua per singulas percurrendo virtutes liquebit quae sint coelibi nostro potissimum requirendae. **38** Non solum enim animi contemplatione beati esse <non> poterimus,[129] nisi etiam et probi simus et iusti et reliquis, quae ad honestatem pertinent[130] offitiorum, virtutibus informati. Quod autem virtutes hae[131] cadant in sapientem, idem est autem coelebs et sapiens, latissime patet ea ratio, quod hanc vitam sibi videtur is iccirco delegisse, ut esse posset Deo quam simillimus. Deum autem virtutum omnium fontem et caput qui negat esse, ex eo numero hominum est qui non solum impie sed etiam inconsyderate[132] loquuntur.

39 Primum itaque a Iustitia, quae, [**109r**] ut inquit Plato, regina et princeps est omnis honestatis, incipiamus probemusque inesse hanc ei hominum generi oportere, qui se a civilibus etiam rebus abduxerunt. Divisa est in partis

---

[129] *esse poterimus* MS, Br.; but *non* required to offset *nisi* below.
[130] *-et* MS.
[131] *haec* MS.
[132] *-ae* MS.

37 Since, however, it's also customarily asked whether the branch of learning that concerns moral behaviour[133] is also relevant to the pursuit of contemplation (seeing that the moral branch is entirely lodged in action), it's necessary, I think, not to leave out that section of the treatise in which, by running through the individual virtues, it will be evident which are most to be sought by our celibate. 38 For not only shall we <not> be able to find happiness through mental contemplation unless we are also of upright character, fair-minded, and shaped by the other virtues that are relevant to the respectability of our duties. But because these virtues accrue to the sage, and because the celibate and the sage are the same,[134] that line of reasoning is very wide-reaching,[135] in that the celibate sage seems to have chosen this life for himself precisely so that he could be as like to God as possible. And anyone who refuses to accept that God is the fountainhead of all the virtues belongs to the category of people who talk not just irreverently but also without thinking.

39 Accordingly, let's take our start from Justice, which, as Plato says, is the queen and initiator of all uprightness,[136] and let's demonstrate that it necessarily has to be present in that class of people who have distanced themselves even from matters of civic involvement.[137] The guiding principle

---

[133] Barbaro's turning to moral philosophy again accords with the humanistic curriculum (cf. Verg. *De ingen. mor.* 40: '... to the truly noble mind, and to those who are obligated to involve themselves in public affairs and human communities, knowledge of history and the study of moral philosophy are the more suitable subjects'; tr. Kallendorf 2002: 49). But his particular agenda here is importantly conditioned by his engagement with Cicero's *De officiis* in Book 1: after thrice contesting Cicero's position that 'all the praise that belongs to virtue lies in action' (*Off.* 1.19; tr. Griffin and Atkins 1991: 9), Barbaro now maps on to the celibate's existence the four parts of the Panaetian *honestum* ('the honourable') as distinguished in *Off.* 1; see Vol. 1 Intro. p. 19.

[134] For this association, 3.5.48 n. 135; 4.1.13 nn. 38, 43.

[135] I.e., it culminates in the likeness to God spelt out in the next clause. Given the larger imprint of *Off.* 1 on this part of Book 4, Barbaro's wording here suggestively echoes Cicero's *latissime patet ea ratio* at *Off.* 1.20 (so ordered, and with superl. *latissime*, the phrase is unparalleled elsewhere in the classical Latin canon).

[136] In *Republic* 4 the analogical relation drawn between individual and state – the soul's three parts ('the thinking,' 'the spirited,' and 'the appetitive') correspond to the Guardian class, the 'auxiliaries,' and the merchant class that satisfies appetitive needs (cf. 3.5.76 and n. 178 and 4.2.56 n. 179) – confers a special value on justice: in both the just state and the just individual the rational part rules, thereby allowing the other virtues of wisdom, courage, and temperance to prevail (cf. 427e-434d, esp. 433b-c). But Barbaro apparently also draws on Cic. *Off.* 3.28: 'For that single virtue [i.e., justice] is the mistress and queen (*regina*) of virtues' (tr. Griffin and Atkins 1991: 110).

[137] Barbaro quotes extensively from *Off.* 1 in opening his treatment of justice before going his own way in 4.2.40-7 to argue that the celibate indeed embodies that social virtue. In quoting and then modifying Cicero in this way, this section on justice establishes a template of sorts for Barbaro's similar technique in the cases of liberality (4.2.48-9), greatness of spirit (4.2.50-4), and decorum (4.2.55-6); see Vol. 1 Intro. p. 19.

duas a plerisque iustitiae ratio: quarum altera est quae prohibet ne cui iniuria, nisi lacescenti, inferatur, altera ut communioni hominum consulatur. Non solum enim ne cui fiat iniuria proprium esse aequitatis putant, verumetiam, ut Plato inquit et Cicero meminit, commutatione offitiorum, dando accipiendoque, cum artibus tum opera tum facultatibus, devincire hominum inter homines sotietatem ad iustitiam maxime pertinere arbitrantur. Quae qui non praestet, iniustum videri et malum sit necesse. **40** Quae divisio, quoniam nostrae disciplinae contraria est, nisi diligentius extimetur, efficitque ut vita coelebs esse abiectissima videatur, non erit a nobis praesertim admittenda: negat enim [**109v**] esse virum quenquam bonum posse, qui non sit in re publica et negotio versaturus, quod nos locis suis falsum esse monstravimus. **41** Quod si eam iustitiam posuissent in iis solum, qui vitam aliquam negotiosam elegerunt, non essent unquam contemnendi: sunt enim plerique qui aut studio rei familiaris tuendae, aut, ut inquit Cicero, odio quodam hominum suis tantum et privatis rebus utantur, qui dum nemini facere[138] iniuriam videantur, satis sese assequutos putant. Quo fit, ut eam vitae sotietatem, quam tueri deberent, deserant omnem et parvipendant. **42** Hos ego errare maxime et esse iniustissimos illis assentio. Inserviendum enim erat illis communi utilitati potius, eoque omnia referenda ut humanae sotietatis primum ratio haberetur. Quod si de ea quoque iustitia intellexissent, quae iubet ut communi utilitati unusquisque consulat, non quae ad rempublicam universos [**110r**] et actionem accerseret, meliorem sententiam effecissent. Fieri enim potest ut communibus rebus opem feramus etiam si ad rempublicam non accedamus. **43** Mihi crede: nullum esse debet in rebus

---

[138] *-are* MS.

of justice is separated by most thinkers into two aspects: of these, the one prevents harm from being inflicted on anyone unless the latter provokes it; the other is to serve the shared interest of the human community.[139] For they not only consider it to be the defining mark of fairness that harm be done to no one; but they also think, as Plato says and Cicero recalls,[140] that it's of the greatest relevance to justice to bind fast the fellowship of humankind with each other by the exchange of services and by giving and receiving, in terms not just of expertise but also of effort and resources. The person who doesn't do so must necessarily seem unjust and evil. **40** Since this division runs counter to my teaching (unless it's more carefully appraised) by causing the celibate life to appear to be thoroughly worthless, I shall first and foremost have to refuse to allow it; for it means that no man can be good who isn't going to engage in public life and business – a position that I've shown in its proper context to be misguided.[141] **41** But if they'd located that concept of justice only in those who chose some life of busyness, they wouldn't ever have to be disparaged;[142] for there are very many who engage only in their own private affairs, either through devotion to preserving their personal wealth or (as Cicero says)[143] through some kind of dislike of humankind; and, provided that they appear to do harm no one, they think they have achieved enough. Hence they abandon all that communal fellowship of life that they were obliged to uphold, and they think it of little importance. **42** I agree with them[144] that such people are very much mistaken and extremely unjust. For they[145] should rather have served the communal benefit, and everything should have been directed towards ensuring that consideration for human fellowship was primary. If they[146] had understood this about that concept of justice as well – its instruction is for every single person to take thought for the communal benefit, but it wouldn't summon all without exception to a public life of action – they would have come up with a better way of thinking; for it can happen that we help the common cause even if we don't enter upon public life.[147] **43** Believe

---

[139] Barbaro's wording combines echoes of Cic. *Off.* 1.20 and 31.
[140] Pl. *Ep.* 9 358a, to which Cicero refers at *Off.* 1.22; Barbaro draws directly on that Ciceronian passage in 'to bind fast ... resources' (*commutatione ... sotietatem*) below.
[141] 1.3-4.
[142] I.e., had the two-fold definition of justice in 4.2.39 been restricted *only* to those engaged in active/public life, that restriction would have closed a loophole: many who shun public life would claim to harm no one, and so to qualify as 'just' on the first criterion set out in 4.2.39.
[143] *Off.* 1.29, largely reproduced in 'for there are very many ... enough.'
[144] Thinkers like Cicero.
[145] I.e., 'such people' above, those said in 4.2.41 to 'engage only in their own private affairs.'
[146] Thinkers like Cicero.
[147] So, e.g., the Stoics Zeno, Cleanthes and Chrysippus helped humankind through their philosophical contributions even though they never held public office (Sen. *Dial.* 8.6.4-5).

humanis emolumentum maius quam id quod afferre potest is vir in quo nihil est nisi integrum, nisi sanctum, nisi divinum. Quanta sit enim apud Deum eius hominis auctoritas, qui Deum imitari semper est conatus, licet inde colligere quod vel in terris quoque solent maxime boni principes eos habere charissimos, quos suae voluntati fuisse semper obsequentissimos sciunt. His favent maxime, hos coli ab omnibus gaudent, ab his quicquid rogantur largissime exhibent. **44** Peccant qui gratitudinem istam auferunt Deo, quo nihil esse aut dici benignius potest; quare huiuscemodi homines et amabit unice et incredibili pietate prosequetur: exoratur [**110v**] nanque facillime ab iis, quos suae naturae divinitatique proximos novit. **45** Quo circa et coelibem audiet lubentissime et illius preces admittet et faciet semper satis honesta requirenti: nam si non amet huius studium et voluntatem haud sane intelligo quidnam sit quod amandum putet. **46** Sive enim religio quaeritur, quae ex rerum divinissimarum contemplatione constantiaque studiorum solet maxime proficisci, nulla esse absolutior aut gratior Deo potest, quam ea quam castissimus et innocentissimus homo prae se fert; sive ea utilitas ducitur, quae ad curam rerum humanarum est necessaria, aut plurimum prodesse potest is cui[148] impetrare omnia ab imperatore est facillimum, aut certe plus poterunt qui magis[149] meriti sunt. **47** Quamobrem proferamus audacter sententiam nostram asseramusque utilitatis publicae neminem esse tantum servatorem quam eum qui ita coelebs est et contem[**111r**]plator. Alteram vero iustitiae partem, quae vetat inferre vim cuiquam non provocatum, nemo tam rudis est qui ambigat inesse iis oportere qui Deum verentur et imitantur. Quare tota iustitiae ratio, quae duas partes complectebatur, inesse videbitur <eis> qui[150] a nobis instituuntur.

---

[148] *qui* MS.
[149] *minus* MS; but *magis* (Br. 145 n. 2) is surely required by the context.
[150] *videbitur qui* MS; *eis* posited (Br. 145 n. 3) as antecedent for *qui*.

me: there must be no greater gain in human affairs than that which can be contributed by the man who has in him nothing except what is upright, sacred, and godlike. How much respect before God that man has, who has always tried to imitate God, can be inferred from the fact that even on earth, too, good rulers very much make it their practice to keep closest to them men whom they know always to have been most obedient to their own will. They show these people the greatest favour, they rejoice in the fact that these people are cherished by all, and they very lavishly provide whatever they are asked for by them. **44** A mistake is made by those who take that gratitude away from God, than whom nothing can be, or be said to be, kinder; hence He will both love such mortals to a singular degree and honour them with an unbelievable loyalty of affection; for He is very easily won over by entreaty from those He knows to be closest to His own nature and godliness. **45** In consequence, He will both very gladly give ear to the celibate and be receptive to his prayers, and He will always meet the respectable wants he expresses; for were He not to love his devotion and willing disposition, I really fail to understand what on earth there would be that He would think warranted His love. **46** Why? Because if a sense of holiness is looked for, which usually emanates to the greatest degree from reflection on the most divine matters and from persistence in one's studies, no such sense can be more complete or welcome to God than that which a mortal of the purest and most blameless integrity exhibits; and if the benefit derived is essential for the safeguarding of human affairs, either the person who finds it very easy to obtain all that he asks for from his ruler can be of the greatest help,[151] or in any case those who are more deserving[152] will be able to be more helpful. **47** For that reason let me state my opinion in no uncertain terms, by asserting that no one is as great a protector of the communal benefit as one who is a celibate and contemplative in the manner described. But as for the second aspect of justice, which forbids inflicting violence on anyone without provocation, no one is so ignorant as to be in any doubt that it is necessarily possessed by those who go in awe of and imitate God.[153] Hence the entire principle of justice, which embraced two aspects, will be seen to be possessed by <those> who follow my instruction.

---

[151] I.e., to the common good; the stress on communal benefit anticipates the inevitable conclusion in 4.2.47 that the celibate meets the 'common advantage' criterion of justice.
[152] Of God's favour.
[153] The stress on God's kindness in 4.2.44 now has delayed effect: emulation of God and His kindness itself affirms the celibate's commitment to the 'cause no injury' criterion of justice.

48 Liberalitatem quoque beneficentiamque esse assequuti debent; nam et suarum rerum tantum elargientur quantum ferre poterunt facultates, et in collocando beneficio et gratia inferenda eam diligentiam adhibebunt, ut et pro dignitate cuique tribuatur et iis ipsis, quibus benigne videbitur fieri, prosit potius quam obsit benignitas. Quod si quod erogent nihil habuerint (diximus etiam id alias),[154] nihilotamen minus liberales erunt atque benefici, si tametsi desint facultates non tamen desit dandi voluntas. **49** Virtutum enim omnium sedes est animus: is si rectus est, virtutibus quoque praeditus erit [**111v**] omnibus. Quare et liberales etiam erimus si nihil agamus etiam quod liberale sit, verumtamen, ut alio loco diximus, maximam semper opem egenti ferre poterimus, si tales coelibes evademus, quales esse oportere praeceptum est. Nihil enim est quod negare Deus iis velit, quos sibi esse quam simillimos videt.

50 Fortes etiam atque magnanimos esse illos oportet. Id autem inde probabitur quod, quum duas res praestare vir fortis debeat, quarum altera est externarum despicientia, altera rerum gestarum amplitudo et laborum periculorumque, si opus ea re fuerit, tolerantia, utrunque plenissime sint

---

[154] *habuerint, (diximus* Br.

48 They must also have attained generosity and kindness;[155] for they will both [i] freely bestow as much of their own wealth as their means can bear, and in conferring a benefit and extending a favour they will pay close attention to ensuring [ii] that kindness is granted to each according to merit, and [iii] that it helps rather than hinders the very people to whom the kind act will seemingly be done.[156] But if they have nothing to disburse (I've also mentioned that elsewhere),[157] they will be no less generous and kind all the same, if there's no lack of the will to give even though they lack the means. **49** For the mind is the seat of all the virtues: if it is upright, it will also be endowed with all the virtues. Hence we shall also still be generous if we actually do nothing that counts as generous;[158] nevertheless, as I've said elsewhere, we shall always be able to give the greatest assistance to the needy if, as celibates, we shall turn out to be just as we are required to be by formal instruction.[159] For there is nothing that God would wish to deny to those whom He perceives to have the closest possible resemblance to Himself.

50 They also have to be brave and of noble spirit.[160] That will be demonstrated by the fact that – since a brave man must show two qualities, one of which is disdain for external circumstances, the other a distinguished record of exploits and, if need be, an ability to endure toils and dangers – each of these two properties has been acquired to the fullest degree by those who have had

---

[155] The second subdivision, after justice, in Cicero's treatment of social virtue in *Off.* 1. Cf. *Off.* 1.42: 'Next, I must do as I proposed [cf. 1.20] and speak about beneficence and liberality (*de beneficentia ac de liberalitate*)' (tr. Griffin and Atkins 1991: 19).

[156] Barbaro echoes the three caveats that Cicero registers about liberality at *Off.* 1.42: for [i], cf. Cicero's 'one must see ... that one's kindness does not exceed one's capabilities (*facultates*)' (tr. Griffin and Atkins 1991: 19); for [ii], cf. 'one must see ... that kindness is bestowed upon each person according to his standing (*ut pro dignitate cuique tribuatur*)' (tr. Griffin and Atkins ibid.); and for [iii], cf. 'one must see that kindness harms (*ne obsit benignitas*) neither the very people whom one seems to be treating kindly (*iis ipsis quibus benigne videbitur fieri*), nor others' (tr. Griffin and Atkins ibid.).

[157] 2.4.3-6.

[158] Intention is all (2.4.4), the celibate therefore no less beneficent than Cicero's man of action.

[159] Cf. 1.4.4-5: the contemplative celibate is hardly averse to helping others, given his respect for dutifulness and the claims of justice; but he will not bind himself to the active, public life.

[160] Barbaro moves to the third virtue in *Off.* 1, greatness of spirit, drawing directly on 1.66 in his division of the topic: 'A brave and great spirit (*fortis animus et magnus*) is in general seen in two things. One lies in disdain for things external (*in rerum externarum despicientia*) ... The second thing is that you should ... do deeds which are great, certainly, but above all beneficial, and you should vigorously undertake difficult and laborious tasks which endanger both life itself and much that concerns life' (tr. Griffin and Atkins 1991: 27). As in the cases of justice and liberality, after beginning with the Ciceronian starting-position on greatness of spirit in 4.2.50, Barbaro goes his own way (in 'each ... path') to vindicate the celibate's fortitude even at a far remove from the Ciceronian active life.

assequuti ii qui ita rei publicae gubernationem et rerum omnium agendarum molestiam contempsere, ut meliorem viam ingrederentur. **51** Quis enim, per deos, est qui tantum humana contemnat quam is qui ea, quae eximia plerisque et praeclara [112r] videntur, parva ducit et ut vilia aspernatur? Dolore etiam frangi quis minus potest, quam is qui ea, quae et acerba sunt et habentur, ita ferre potest, ut nihil mali putet in iis quae in hominum vita varia et molesta versantur, praeter id quod sit sapientia et constantia alienum? Quis rursum est, qui res gerat maiores aut utiliores aut vehementius arduas quam is qui potentissimus est et prudentissimus? Quis autem esse potentior potest quam is qui prope tantum valet ut Deus et tantum sapit ut Deus? **52** Risuros esse aliquos scio dum ista praelegent profusurosque ea verba quae impiissimi solent, negaturosque esse aliquam opem posse, nisi eam quam praesentes corporis vires et manus armatae ferant. O incredibilem et rudem inscitiam et non nullorum etiam pertinacem! Experimur inter homines plurimum posse auctoritatem, amicitiam, propinquitatem, chari[112v]tatem, et parvas plerunque hortationes minimosque respectus maximum habuisse momentum: hunc Stagiras praeceptoris merito condonasse, illum coniugis matrisque reverentia obsidionem ab urbe solvisse, alios alia in diversas

nothing to do with state governance, and with the nuisance of managing all manner of affairs, in such a way that they embarked on a better path. **51** For who is there, in heaven's name, who shows as much disregard for human affairs as he who considers trivial the things that seem to most people exceptionally valuable, and rejects them as worthless? Who, too, is less able to be broken by distress than he who can endure afflictions that are harsh – and are so regarded – in such a way that he thinks that there's nothing bad in the different vexations involved in human life except that which is incompatible with wisdom and firmness of character?[161] Again, who is there who deals with matters of greater importance, more usefulness, or graver difficulty[162] than he who has superlative capabilities and the greatest wisdom? And who can be more capable than he who is almost as strong as God and [almost] as wise as God? **52** I know that some will laugh while reading such things, and that they will pour out the words usually uttered by the unholiest types, denying that there can be any meaningful help at all except that given by a ready show of physical strength and hands wielding weapons. How incredibly boorish is the ignorance of some people, and how stubborn as well![163] Experience tells us that personal influence, friendship, closeness of association, and personal affection have very great force among people, and that on many occasions a few words of encouragement and the merest gestures of regard have carried the greatest weight; that one man granted pardon to Stagira in reward to his teacher,[164] and that another raised a siege from a city by showing regard for his wife and his mother;[165] and

---

[161] A close adaptation thus far in 4.2.51 of the complex final sentence in *Off.* 1.67.

[162] Barbaro reapplies to the fortitude of the celibate the Ciceronian sequence of adjectives at *Off.* 1.66 (*magnas* [*res*], *utiles, arduas*).

[163] Barbaro condenses Cicero's own spirited qualification at *Off.* 1.74-84 of the importance commonly attached to military as opposed to civic exploits, and his stress instead on the benefits of counsel and foresight rather than any rush to arms.

[164] Stagira, Aristotle's birthplace in the Chalcidic peninsula, was according to some sources destroyed by Philip II of Macedon in 348 BCE (see Flensted-Jensen 2004: 844 no. 613); it was restored at Aristotle's request by either Philip (Plut. *Alex.* 7.2-3, D. L. 5.4) or his son, Alexander the Great (Plin. *NH* 7.109 with Beagon 2005: 299–300). Beyond illustrating the communal benefit achieved by Aristotle's exertion of personal influence, Barbaro's allusion also underscores the special favour shown by rulers to those who serve them well (cf. 4.2.43).

[165] Barbaro alludes (albeit with distortion) to the Jewish historian Flavius Josephus' attempt to persuade the Judean rebels to cede to the Romans during the siege of Jerusalem in 70 CE (*B. Jud.* 5.418-19): '... at least have pity on your own families: all of you should hold before your eyes your children, your wives, your parents, all soon to be victims of either famine or war. *I know that I have at the same risk a mother, a wife, a family of some distinction, and an illustrious house going back generations: and you may think that this is influencing the advice I give you. So kill them! Take my flesh and blood as the price of your own salvation!* I too am ready to die, if that will bring you to your senses' (tr. Hammond 2017: 290; my emphasis). Josephus 'raised the siege' only in the sense that his speech encouraged some desertion among the populace (cf. 5.420-3) even as the rebels refused to budge.

sententias retorsisse. **53** Negabimus non[166] licere iis haec omnia impetrare, quibus non ut coeteris frigidum quicquam aut mancum inest, sed summa omnia, sed absolutissima, sed constantissima et propemodum sempiterna? Aut ingratum est Dei numen aut, ut poetae dixerunt, invidiae plenum erga mortales, aut putandum est nihil esse debere potentius quam is qui et charissimus est et simillimus Deo. **54** Quamobrem et fortis esse animi poterit et robusti et, quod magnae constantiae signum est, semper amabit humanum genus: merebiturque hanc etiam potestatem, ut non modo cum rogaverit, verum et quum aliud egerit, sponte[167] sequatur utilitas atque [**113r**] permaneat;[168] prodesseque hominum sotietati id solum poterit, quod eius generis homo quispiam sit, qui ita vivat, ut, quam maxime queat, Deum vereatur, imitetur, observet.

55 Sed quoniam esse non potest quispiam fortis, qui non idem sit et continentissimus, neque consentaneum est eum qui[169] nullo metu frangatur aut labore vincatur vel[170] capi voluptatibus vel cupiditate aliqua irretiri, non est credendum non esse temperantissimum eum quem excelsi et magni animi esse probavimus. Id autem facilius persuadere poterimus, quum nihil esse in coelibe praecipuum magis et proprium videatur, quam despicientia affectionum et contemptio voluptatum. **56** Hoc enim est, quod ut potissimum est in hoc homine ornamentum, ita requiri primum debet et maxime. Liquet ergo ex his eas omnis virtutes, quas Plato in partibus animae duabus [**113v**]

---

[166] As pleonastic negator, Pinkster 2015: 730 8.48 (cf. 3.6.24).
[167] *egerit sponte* Br.
[168] *-et* MS.
[169] *eum esse qui* MS, Br., but see p. 6 above.
[170] *vincatur, vel* Br.

that different people have reversed course on different issues to an opposite way of thinking. **53** Shall we deny that it's permitted for all such things to be obtained by entreaty by those in whom (unlike all the rest) there's nothing torpid or feeble, but all that is most excellent, most fully developed, most steadfast, and almost everlasting? The divine essence of God is either unappreciative[171] or, as the poets have alleged,[172] full of ill will towards mortals, or we have to suppose that nothing must be more powerful than he who is both most dear to God and very much like Him. **54** For that reason he will be able to be brave and firm of mind and – the mark of great steadfastness[173] – he will always love the human race; and he will also be rewarded with the capability that, not just when he's made a request for something, but even when he's been otherwise occupied, advantage ensues by itself, and endures.[174] And that alone will be able to benefit the fellowship of humankind – the fact that there is a particular mortal of that sort who lives in such a way that, to the greatest degree possible, he is in awe of God, imitates Him, and honours Him.

55 But since someone cannot be brave without also being most self-controlled, and since it's not consistent for one who is broken by no fear or beaten by no toil to be either captivated by pleasures or ensnared by any passionate desire, it's impossible to believe that the person I've shown to be of sublime greatness of mind is not of the greatest moderation.[175] But I shall be able to win acceptance of that rather easily, since nothing seems to be more outstanding in and characteristic of the celibate than his disdain for the emotions and his scorn for pleasures.[176] **56** For this is a quality that is the foremost mark of honour in this man, and it must accordingly be looked for first in him, and most of all. It is clear from all this, therefore, that all those virtuous qualities, which Plato located in the two parts of the soul that lacked

---

[171] Already discounted in 4.2.43-6.
[172] Esp. in the maverick divine conduct on display in the pagan tradition of the Homeric epics, Virgil's *Aeneid*, Ovid's *Metamorphoses*, etc.
[173] Barbaro returns (cf. 4.2.51 and n. 161) to explicit evocation of *Off*. 1.67, from which he draws *animi . . . robusti* and *magnae constantiae*.
[174] I.e., advantage for the common good, in line with justice as defined in 4.2.39.
[175] Barbaro turns to the fourth virtue in *Off*. 1, decorum, which itself embraces restraint and modesty (*temperantia et modestia*, 1.93; for Barbaro's *continentissimus* and *temperantissimum* cf. the combination of *moderatio*, *continentia* and *temperantia* at *Off*. 3.96, 116). As before, Barbaro effortlessly configures for his celibate the virtue that Cicero mandates for the man of action.
[176] Markedly Ciceronian phrasing: *despicientia* and *affectio* are first extant in Cicero, and for *contemptio voluptatum* cf. *Ac*. 1.23. For the special weight that Barbaro attaches to this 'scorn for pleasures,' see Vol. 1 Intro. pp. 31-2.

ratione carentibus collocavit, Aristoteles vero idem sane autumans, sed aliter conatus ostendere, in ea parte constare dixit, quae vacua ratione quum sit, rationi tamen ut imperatori atque patri parere possit et obedire; eas, inquam, virtutes omnis perspicuum fecimus[177] consummate[178] in coelibatu reperiri.

57 Sed et illis quoque, quas in parte animi praestantiore rationis et mentis plenissima constare Peripatetici atque illustres omnes philosophi asseruerunt, omnino non carere illorum vitam facillime ostendemus: omnem itaque animi agitationem rationi subiectam in sapientiam atque prudentiam dividi tam Peripatetici quam Achademici voluerunt. **58** Sapientiam dicunt esse indagationem inventionemque veritatis: prudentiam vero eam esse virtutem, qua quis quid in re quaque, quam tractat, optimum sit et verissimum, [114r] celerrime et acutissime perspicit, rationemque potest earum rerum videre et explicare; seu et alii diffinierunt prudentiam esse rerum expetendarum fugiendarumque scientiam. Utranque virtutem necesse est coelibem fuisse consequutum: nam et res maximas assiduo contemplatur et diligentissime in unam hanc cogitationem incumbit. **59** Quo fit, ut si est in rebus humanis aliqua, qua sciri res possint, ars aut ratio aut etiam disciplina, hic unus omnium sit, qui maxime eam assequi possit et debeat: unde evenit ut brevi sit

---

[177] *perspicuum est fec-* MS.
[178] *-ae* MS; *consum-* MS, Br., but cf. Br.'s *consumm-* for MS *consum-* at 3.2.6, 4.1.1.

reason,[179] whereas Aristotle – certainly thinking the same but trying to demonstrate it differently – said that they reside in that part which, though it is devoid of reason, can nevertheless submit to and obey reason as its ruler and father;[180] I have made it very clear, I say, that all those virtuous qualities are found in the most perfected form in the celibate.

57 But I shall also very easily show that their existence is not at all lacking in those qualities as well which, the Peripatetics and all distinguished philosophers have maintained, reside in the superior part of the soul that is fully endowed with reason and intellect. Accordingly, the Peripatetics as much as the Academics[181] have wanted all mental activity that is subject to reason to be divided into wisdom and prudence. **58** They state that wisdom is the search for and discovery of truth,[182] but that prudence is the virtue by which someone very quickly and sharply perceives what is best and truest in each matter that he handles, and by which he can see and explain the underlying logic of those matters;[183] or rather, others have also defined prudence as the knowledge of what is to be sought after and what avoided.[184] The celibate must necessarily have attained each of these two virtues; for he both continually ponders the most important matters and applies himself most attentively to this process of reflection alone. **59** Hence, if in human affairs there is any skill or method or even training by which things can be known, it is he alone of all people who can and must above all attain it; as a result, he is soon going to turn out to be extremely wise. As for prudence, too,

---

[179] I.e., the 'spirited' and the 'appetitive' parts (see 3.5.76 n. 178 and 4.2.39 n. 136); the 'spirited' element functions as the ally of reason in controlling the 'appetitive' part, thereby following the commands of the ruling *logistikon* (*Resp.* 4 441e-442b). Plato 'located' virtuous qualities in the 'spirited' and the 'appetitive' in the sense that such qualities are operative only when those two soul-parts are obedient to reason (cf. 442b-d).

[180] Cf. *EN* 1.13, esp. 1102b13-1103a3. The soul is in two parts, one non-rational (*alogos*), the other with a rational principle (*logos*: 1102a27-8). The non-rational side is itself twofold: one part is the 'nutritive' or 'vegetative' element (i.e., common to all species, and, because hardly distinctive to humans, with no share in human excellence: 1102b11-12); the other is the 'appetitive' element (*to epithūmētikon*, 1102b30). '[T]he vegetative element in no way shares in a rational principle, but the appetitive and in general the desiring element in a sense shares in it, in so far as it listens to and obeys it; this is the sense in which we speak of "taking account" of one's father or one's friends...' (1102b29-32; tr. Ross 1980: 27). After 1102b32, Aristotle again (1103a3) speaks of the 'appetitive' element heeding *logos* as one does a father; hence surely Barbaro's own 'father' analogy in *patri*.

[181] I.e., the Aristotelian as well as the Platonic tradition. In now turning to 'wisdom and prudence' Barbaro circles back to the first of the four parts of the *honestum* distinguished in *Off.* 1, once more modifying Cicero's stress on the primacy of the active life.

[182] A direct echo of *Off.* 1.15 (fundamental to the first virtue, encompassing wisdom and prudence, is *indagatio atque inventio veri*).

[183] A close adaptation of the first sentence in *Off.* 1.16.

[184] The definition is reproduced from *Off.* 1.153, where Cicero now distinguishes *prudentia* from *sapientia*.

sapientissimus evasurus. Prudentiam quoque nemo sibi facilius perfectiusque paraverit, quam is qui nihil agit in vita quod aut fieri melius possit aut tutius gubernari. Quamobrem duplicem prudentiam colligemus: una quae in rerum corpore agendarum ratione versatur, altera quae in rerum mente conceptarum [114v] dexteritate consistit. 60 Aeque et iustitiam duplicem et fortitudinem liberalitatemque faciemus, ut unum scilicet genus sit earum virtutum, quae ad contemplativum, alterum quae ad activum et administrativum attineant. Utraque autem eodem nomine vocabuntur, quoniam et utrarunque effectus eiusdem erunt nuncupationis: nam et iustum et liberale et forte et prudens praestabit offitium, et qui aget et qui speculabitur; plenius autem atque perfectius id omne erit quod a contemplante[185] quam quod a res gerente nascetur. 61 Ostensum est enim illius virtutem excellere et potestatem, qui secundus et proximus diis est: is autem erit qui ita ut praeceptum est vixerit in coelibatu.

62 Diximus iam quae oporteat caelibem contemplari quantumque in quaque re sit studium impendendum: non enim eodem ardore atque intentione scire omnia velle debebit aut ean[115r]dem operam singulis artibus indulgere, sed tantum in scientia qualibet laborare quantum ad cognoscendam Opificis magnitudinem infinitatemque videbitur opportunum. 63 In qua re quoniam non fuit propositum scientias laudare, ea causa fuit ut libatim et cursim[186] prope ea omnia, quae materiam iuvabant, attingerentur: quantum me hercle[187] putas in ea praeceptione ruboris et verecundiae toto corpore, praesertim vero ore, contraxisse, quum mihi ipsi viderer in alieno propemodum agro alienas fruges emetere? Pudebat autem

---

[185] *-platione* MS, corrected to *-plante*.
[186] *libatum et cursum* MS.
[187] *me hercle* MS; *quantum, mehercle,* Br., but see p. 6 above.

no one will have more easily or more completely obtained it for himself than one who does nothing in life that could either be better done or more safely steered. For that reason we shall infer prudence of two kinds: one engaged and concerned with physical actions, the other consisting in the apt handling of the ideas formed in the mind.[188] **60** Likewise, we shall make justice twofold, and bravery and generosity, so that there is evidently one class of those virtues that relate to the contemplative, another of those relating to the man of action and practical management. But each of the two will go by the same name, since the outcomes of both branches, too, will be called the same. For both the active man and the contemplative will render a service that is just and kind and brave and prudent; but the service arising from the contemplative will in each case be fuller and more complete than that from the man of action.[189] **61** For it has been demonstrated that the virtuousness and mental power of the contemplative, who is second only to the gods and very close to them, are pre-eminent; and he it will be who will have lived as instructed in celibacy.

62 I have now said what subjects the celibate ought to study, and how much application is to be devoted to each matter; for he won't be duty-bound to want to know everything with the same passion and concentration, or to grant the same effort to every single pursuit, but to exert himself in any area of knowledge as much as seems suitable for recognizing the greatness and limitless capacities of the Maker. **63** In this matter, since it wasn't my intention to extol the particular departments of knowledge, my motive was for just about everything helpful to my topic to be touched upon lightly in passing. Good heavens! How much blushing embarrassment do you think I've contracted over my entire body in that tutorial, but especially on my face, since I seemed to myself almost to be gathering in someone else's crops in a field that's not my own?[190] But I felt shame not just because the topic wasn't my own, but also because it was well worn by doing the rounds on everyone's

---

[188] The contrast between the physical and the mental categories anticipates the distinction drawn in 4.2.60 between the active and the contemplative lives: by creating 'active' and 'contemplative' dualities of prudence, justice, etc., Barbaro completes his process of making the four virtues of *Off.* 1 fully compatible with celibacy. Hence Barbaro neatly underscores the celibate's 'active' credentials by couching his existence in the language of civic engagement and productivity in 'one who does nothing ... steered' (*agit in vita*; *fieri* lit. 'to be done,' 'to take place'; *guberno -are* lit. 'to steer,' 'direct').

[189] The language of shared duty now nicely binds the 'active' celibate and the active citizen before the former's service is hailed as the greater. The crowning point of 4.2.37-61 as a whole is that Barbaro not only renders the 'four virtues' apparatus of *Off.* 1 compatible with celibacy; he also overturns the active life's superiority in Cicero by giving primacy instead to its contemplative opposite.

[190] Cf. 3.5.79 for Barbaro's unabashed justification of his infringement on medical matters (his tone is more conciliatory at 3.6.51).

non solum materiae alienae, verumetiam tritae et per omnium ora vulgatae, quum nemo iam sit qui nesciat et scindere disciplinas et in membra plura dispartiri. Verebar item ne, dum ea tractarem quae scire coelibem oportebat, viderer de doctrinis earumque inventione per ostentationem quandam percurrere voluisse. **64** Quod ne suspicari quisquam [**115v**] possit, fateor non esse rem arduam quam videri videor assequutus. Id enim nunc pueri etiam factitant; verum, ut ordo praecipiendi servaretur, necessariam duximus istam egressionem fore, si tamen egressio dicenda est ea, quae non sit egressa materiam, sed egressionem dici patiamur damnemusque hoc saltem nomine diligentiam nostram; qua confessione fortasse favorem aliquem extorquebo mereborque vel apud iniustos hanc veniam, ne pro egressore ostentatorem et pro diligente curiosum me fuisse arbitrentur. **65** Solet enim residere aliquantulum et refrigescere inimicorum impetus quum se hostis hosti sua sponte summittit; expertum etiam est mitiorem iudicem nancisci reum consuevisse, si se non carere omni culpa fateatur. Sed quor benefactum excuso? Erunt fortasse non iniuria non nulli qui excusationem [**116r**] potius quam excusatum accusent.

    66 Nunc quoniam ad finem properandum est reliqua explicemus.

    67 Quoniam itaque non modo habere curam sciendi omnia contemplator[191] debet, verumetiam quomodo id possit efficere, traditis iis, quae sunt potissimum cognoscenda, reliquum est ut modum etiam explicemus quo faciliter praestare offitium speculandi possit. Extrinsecus enim pleraque sunt adhibenda, quorum ope illa, quae supra praecepimus et intrinsecus sunt, optime exerceantur. Illa enim et interiora sunt et in animo cuiusque posita: haec vero, quae sumus tradituri, velut exteriora erunt. **68** Superioribus nanque libris diximus ex sese nullius rei esse indigum animum contemplantis, sed ex corporis, in quo clauditur, necessitate evenire, ut ope multa atque aliena indigeret. Quare neque hanc quidem praetermitti curam oportuit, [**116v**] ut

---

[191] *-atur* MS.

lips, since nowadays there's no one who doesn't know how to divide up the branches of study and to separate them into several divisions. I was likewise afraid that, while I was dealing with the things that the celibate ought to know, I would appear to have wanted to offer a survey of areas of learning, and of their discovery, through some wish to show off. **64** So that no one could suspect as much, I admit that what I supposedly seem to have accomplished isn't a difficult thing. For even boys nowadays do this sort of thing all the time; but, for my program of instruction to be properly observed, I thought that that digression would be essential – if, however, that which hasn't digressed from the topic is to be called a digression, but let's put up with it being termed a digression, and let's censure my own careful efforts at least by so terming them.[192] Through this admission I shall perhaps extort some measure of goodwill, and earn even from the harshly disposed this reprieve – not to think that I was a show off rather than just digressing, and meddlesome rather than painstaking. **65** For the violent impulse of enemies usually subsides somewhat and cools down when a foe voluntarily surrenders to a foe; experience also shows that a defendant normally finds a judge less severe if he admits that he's not devoid of all possible guilt. But why do I make excuse for my good deed? There will perhaps be some – not unjustly – of the sort to find fault more with the excuse than with the excused.

66 Now, since we must hurry on to the end, let's set out the matters that remain.

67 Well then, since the contemplative must pay serious attention not just to gaining a knowledge of everything, but also to how he can accomplish it, and now that I've registered the forms of knowledge that are especially to be mastered, it remains for me also to set out the way in which he can fulfill the task of contemplation without difficulty. For many factors have to be applied from without, so that by their help those qualities on which I've given instruction above,[193] and which are embedded within, are employed to the best effect. For the latter are internal and lodged in each person's mind; but the ones I'm about to tell of will be outside him, so to speak. **68** Now I've said in the preceding books that the mind of the contemplative wants for nothing from itself, but that the constraints of the body in which it's confined mean that it needs considerable assistance from outside itself.[194] Hence it was necessary for not even this concern to be overlooked – that though I'd

---

[192] Nicely ironic: Barbaro digresses in 4.2.64-5 to vindicate the (non-)digression of his curricular coverage down to 4.2.61 – a timely show of personality that anticipates the genial liveliness of mind that he calls for in 4.2.72-80.
[193] Justice, etc., in 4.2.39-61.
[194] See 2.4.1, 7-9; 2.5.10; 3.2.3; cf. 1.4.6-7.

quum ea omnia, quibus esse opus posset ad conservandam mentis intentionem, tradidissemus, desyderari profecto pauca liceret, quae si ad nostram rem pertinuissent, non essent mediocriter saltem his voluminibus pertractata.

69 Primum itaque sciri debet ea omnia quae valitudini faciunt contemplationem etiam iuvare: nequit enim corpore invalido animus exerceri. Tunc autem maxime viget opus animi, quum bene est corpori: bene autem est corpori, si pro sua quisque natura vivat. Diximus hac de re alias in ea parte, in qua ei puero, qui coelebs est futurus, necessariam esse corporis firmitatem ostendimus, sed hoc loco quoque non est ea cura ex toto abigenda. Verum breviter illa praecipiemus, quae prope peculiaria[195] iis videbuntur, qui sunt in coelibatu victuri.

70 Usus veneris non solum quia abhorret a vitae genere, quam elegit, verumetiam quia mentis [117r] intentionem tollit abesse debet ab eo qui contemplatur. Similiter cibus et potus et somnus timendus est: haec enim omnia, ut dictum est, saepius non solum nocent corporis incolumitati, sed etiam animi viribus. **71** Ita demum coniunctae sunt et caste vivendi ratio et contemplandi, ut non solum ea omnia, quae pudicitiam pariunt, iuvent etiam speculantis, verumetiam[196] ex abstinentia fugaque cupiditatum mirum in modum eveniat ut opus mentis strenue peragatur, et ex cogitatione rerum altissimarum fiat ut honeste et pudice vivatur. Haec autem omnia valitudinem faciunt et conservant. **72** Illud quoque non est in his praetermittendum[197] quae subinde admonemus: animi alacritate opus esse ei qui et bene vivere, hoc est bene valere, et bene contemplari volet. Sunt enim non nulli, et boni interim viri, qui nunquam supercilia de ruga moveant, sed tristi ore, tristioribus oculis et quasi [117v] plagis caesi, uno habitu semper videantur; graeci [μεμψιμοίρους[198]] vocant, moerentes maxime et subabsurdos. **73** His risisse nunquam aut facetius aliquid dixisse praeclarum est. Nescio an Socrates hac in re plurimum sit laudandus, quoius uxor Xantippe gloriata

---

[195] -ularia MS.
[196] *verum etiam* MS, Br., but cf. 1.3.7, 1.5.12, 3.5.80, etc.
[197] *pret-* MS.
[198] Proposed by Br. 150 n. 3 to fill the blank in the MS.

propounded everything that could be needed for maintaining the mind's concentration, it would certainly be possible for a few matters to be found missing which, had they been related to my topic, would have been treated at least to some reasonable extent in these volumes.

69 Accordingly, it must first be understood that everything that's conducive to good health also helps contemplation; for the mind cannot be busily employed if the body is weak. Mental activity most flourishes precisely when all is well with the body; but all is well with the body if each person lives in conformity with his own nature. I've spoken of this matter elsewhere,[199] in the section where I showed that bodily strength is essential for the boy who's going to be celibate; but in this context, too, that concern is not to be wholly spurned. Briefly, however, I shall set out the qualities that will seem almost exclusive to those who are going to live in celibacy.

70 Erotic experience has to be far removed from the contemplative, not just because it is incompatible with the kind of life he's chosen, but also because it puts an end to mental concentration.[200] Likewise, food and drink and sleep are to be viewed with apprehension; for all these things (as has been said)[201] too often do harm not only to our soundness of body but also to our strength of mind. **71** In sum, the guiding principles of living chastely and of contemplation are connected in such a way that not only do all the factors that give rise to sexual purity also help contemplatives; but also a remarkable result of refraining from and avoiding desires is that the work of the mind is briskly accomplished, and reflection on the loftiest matters leads to an upright life of decency; and all these things bring about and preserve good health.[202] **72** Not to be overlooked amid the points of advice I give next is also the following: one who will want both to live well (that is, to be vigorously well) and to contemplate well will need a lively frame of mind. For there are quite a few – and good men in some instances – who never shift their eyebrows from a state of wrinkled frowning, but are always seen with one and the same expression, with a bleak face and bleaker gaze, as if they've been pummeled with blows; these especially mournful and rather absurd types the Greeks term [*mempsimoirous*].[203] **73** Their outstanding achievement is never to have laughed or said anything rather witty. On this point I'm inclined to think that Socrates should be praised to the skies: his wife, Xanthippe, is said sometimes

---

[199] 2.5.
[200] Cf. 2.2.2; 2.3.10; 3.4.5; 3.5.32-9, 65, 67; 3.6.41.
[201] Cf. 3.5.17-31, 69-82; 3.6.49-53.
[202] The circle is complete: good health both promotes (4.2.69) and is promoted by contemplative celibacy.
[203] For the stock figure of 'the ungrateful grumbler' see Theophr. *Char*. 17, with Fraenkel 1957: 92-4 on his familiar presence in ancient diatribe and satire.

interdum dicitur, quod virum eum fuisset nacta, quem nunquam alio vultu domo egredientem alio domum redeuntem vidisset.

74 Mihi profecto non probatur tanta austeritas, in eo praesertim qui sit in maxima voluptate constitutus, qualem esse coelibem nostrum ex multis probavimus locis: huic enim esse alium contemplanti habitum, alium alloquenti, alium comedenti, alium ambulanti velim. Sed neque satis idonea ad negotium nostrum eius natura videbitur, qui ita sit tristis. Id enim ex atrae bilis excessu defectuque provenit, quoius ea est vilitas ut [**118r**] quatuor, quas habent animantes, concretionum sit proculdubio extima atque deterrima. **75** Et prius etiam dictum est sanguinem potius quam alium liquorem requiri in eo puero oportere, qui ad coelibatum est perducendus. Malencholiam[204] vero, sic enim graeci vocant nigram eluviem, quis nescit esse contrariam sanguini? nam ut aerem,[205] cui est sanguis comparatus, terrae, cui est quam simillima melencholia, adversari philosophi collegerunt, ita et sanguinem obstare melencholiae arbitrati sunt. At nimium in re aliena expatior.

76 Tristis ergo non erit is, qui se institui hoc modo patietur, sed neque nimium hilaris et effusus, extima siquidem omnia in vitio sunt: verum periocundus[206] et medii semper habitus sit, et qui servet pro temporis et rei, in qua est, dignitate temperamentum. Neque pugnant haec iis quae semel

---

[204] *Malen-* MS, Br.
[205] *aer est* MS.
[206] *-ius* MS, corrected to *-us*.

to have boasted that she'd acquired as her husband one whom she'd never seen leaving home with one expression and returning home with another.[207] **74** I certainly don't think well of so much sternness, especially in the sort of person who is settled in the most pleasurable condition, such as I've shown our celibate to be on multiple grounds; for I'd want him to have one demeanor when he contemplates,[208] another when he converses, another when he dines, another when he takes a walk. But as for the sort who is severe in this way, his temperament will not seem well enough suited to the business that concerns me. For that condition arises from a surfeit or a deficiency of black bile, which is of such baseness that it's undoubtedly the lowest and worst of the four clusters of matter that animate creatures possess.[209] **75** And it was also remarked before that blood rather than any other fluid ought to be looked for in the boy who is to be guided towards celibacy.[210] But who is unaware that melancholy (for so the Greeks call the black discharge) is opposite in kind to blood? For just as philosophers inferred that the air (to which blood has been compared) stands opposed to the earth (to which melancholy has the closest possible resemblance), so they also thought that blood stood in contrast to melancholy.[211] But I digress too much in a matter that is foreign to me.

76 Therefore, one who will allow himself to be trained in this fashion will not be severe, but neither will he be too unrestrainedly lighthearted, seeing that all extremes are at fault.[212] But he should be very agreeable and yet always of an intermediate disposition, and of the sort to observe moderation according to the needs of the moment and of the situation in which he finds

---

[207] If this anecdote is improvised by Barbaro (sources for it are elusive), it amounts to a timely flash of wit of his own after 'Their ... witty' above. For Xanthippe's reputation for shrewishness cf. 2.2.19-20 and nn. 42-3. Her boast here is humorously ambiguous in implication: she either fails to see – with a conspicuous lack of Socratic self-knowledge – why his equanimity is so remarkable (how can he *not* leave home looking happy, sad when he returns?); or she more knowingly boasts of his remarkable even-temperedness *despite* her famous ill-temper towards him.

[208] Cf. 4.2.78.

[209] For the four humours cf. 2.6.21 and n. 177; 3.6.28 and n. 250; 3.6.53 and n. 281.

[210] 2.6.19-21.

[211] The post-Galenic correlation drawn between the elements (air, fire, earth, water), the four bodily humours, and human temperament saw blood equated with air in the anonymous Greek *On the constitution of the universe and of man*, for which Ideler 1841: 303-4. Those in whom very pure blood predominates are friendly and full of laughter (Ideler 304.5-6), and 'rosy, reddish, and fine-coloured' in bodily complexion (304.7; cf. Barbaro at 2.6.19-21), but the temperament associated with black bile (which corresponds to earth: 303.10-11) is sluggish, fainthearted, and sickly (304.10-11); see further Jouanna 2012: 341-3 – part of a larger survey of other post-Galenic materials that similarly correlate the humours and temperament. Barbaro may claim to digress in 'But I ... to me' below; but in touching indirectly here on the joyous connotations of blood of high purity, he sets the stage for his ensuing description of the celibate's cheerfulness in 4.2.76-8.

[212] See 3.6.15 for the golden mean.

diximus, non esse in eo, qui se a rei publicae [**118v**] administratione eripuerit, varios et multiplices animi et corporis habitus retinendos. **77** Id enim etiam nunc asserimus et requirimus maxime: dicebamus autem in eo homine, qui esset ad res gerendas instructus, diversam operam exigi, ut mentiretur interdum, accusaret bonos, defenderet malos, faceret ea omnia quae utilitatem afferre rebus publicis possent. In eo vero quui curae esse illa non debent, frustra expectari talem operam dicebamus. **78** Nunc vero, quia non prohibetur ullus ut rideat, ut laetetur, hilaritatem exegimus, ut his, habita temporis ratione, modo gaudere palam videatur, modo alium vultum induere, non animum, et ad mediocritatem demum omnia referre meminerit. Ita enim fiet ut, quum in opere contemplandi versabitur, habitum oris intentissimum praestet,[213] et quum ab eo studio per intermissionem cessabit, una cum cogitationibus remittat etiam vultum aliquantisper [**119r**] subcissivique illius temporis aliam habeat rationem.

79 Quom itaque vacaverit, amicorum fruetur consuetudine: hos autem habere debebit, si licuerit, coniunctissimos, quibuscum, quoniam solus non facile vixerit, honestissime iocundissimeque confabuletur. Id enim tempus, in quo studium est intermissum, teri consumique aliquo modo est necesse: nequit autem id suavius fieri quam amici alicuius comitatu. Quare in hoc etiam activi hominis mutuabitur partis: id autem faciet, ut saepe dictum est, non ut contemplativus sed ut is homo quoius vita sine iis, quae ad victum sint necessaria, constare non potest. **80** Nam si fieri posset ut animum quis semper exerceret negligeretque corporis curam, utpote nulla ope indigentis, non essent haec tam multa extrinsecus requirenda. Palam autem est opus esse externo auxilio iis, quorum vita fragilis imbecillaque est et iugium indiga fomentorum. [**119v**] Ob id locupletes esse et sotietate amicorum munitos et

---

[213] *-ent* MS.

himself. Nor do these points conflict with what I said on one occasion[214] – that one who's escaped from managing the affairs of state should not keep up a great and varied assortment of dispositions of mind and body. **77** For I still very much affirm and demand the following: I was saying that in the sort of person equipped for engaging in public affairs, a versatility of performance was required, to the effect that he'd sometimes lie, bring charges against good men, defend the bad, and do everything that could be of benefit to the common interest.[215] As for one who isn't obliged to concern himself with such matters, however, I was saying[216] that it was vain to anticipate that sort of performance in such a person. **78** Now, however, because no one is prevented from laughing or feeling joy, I've called for cheerfulness so that, taking account of the given moment, he's seen by these people[217] now to be openly rejoicing, and now to be assuming a different expression but not a different mindset, and, finally, he remembers to judge everything by reference to the middle course. The result will be that, when he's engaged in the task of contemplation, he shows on his face an expression of the utmost concentration, and when he pauses for a break from that devoted study, he also relaxes his expression for a bit, together with his thoughts, and regards that spare time differently.

79 Accordingly, when he has free time, he will enjoy the company of friends; and he should regard them, if possible, as very close intimates with whom to converse in the most respectable and congenial fashion, since he won't easily exist on his own. For the time in which he takes a break from his studies has to be used up and spent in some way, and that can't happen more agreeably than through the companionship of some friend. Hence in this respect, too, he'll borrow the role of the active man;[218] but he'll do so, as has often been said, not as a contemplative but as a being whose existence can't continue without the essentials for living.[219] **80** For if it could happen that someone would always put his mind to use and show no concern for his body (as might be expected if it needed no help), these manifold essentials wouldn't have to be sought from outside the self. But there is plainly a need for outside help in the case of those whose existence is frail and weak and constantly requiring forms of alleviation. For that reason I want them to be well-to-do

---

[214] 2.6.8.
[215] 2.6.2-7.
[216] 2.6.8 again.
[217] The sort 'equipped for engaging in public affairs' in 4.2.77, and hence with an eye for 'a versatility of performance.'
[218] I.e., the contemplative's enjoyable interaction with friends reflects – like the active man's public service – the fact that humankind is social by nature; see Cic. *Off.* 1.157-9, and cf. 1.4.6 and n. 61.
[219] Cf. 1.4.6-9 for the life-requirements (basic sustenance, etc.) that necessitate a certain sociability in the contemplative.

bonam habere valitudinem volumus: hilares etiam laetosque fecimus, ut animus vacatione curarum vegetior redderetur. Haec autem ita commisimus[220] coniunximusque ut et valitudinem facere et fieri ex valitudine videantur.

81 Ut enim ex alacritate incolumitas nascitur, ita ex incolumitate alacritas proficiscitur: alacritatem vero pleraque faciunt, et non modo omnia quae valitudinem, sed et propria quaedam et maxime opportuna, quemadmodum sunt ea quae a medicis desyderantur, aëris puritas, domus lata atque illustris, spatiosi prospectus, viridaria, montes, rivuli, veris clementia,[221] exercitii gestationisque genera. **82** Non enim idem efficitur eademque utilitas procreatur, quocunque id modo[222] fiat, sed alius equitando, alius venando, alius ambulando, alius saltando, alius circa unam rem [**120r**] operamque insudando. Nam quae maiori cum voluptate fiunt, ea maiorem pariunt alacritatem. Tempori tamen inserviendum est et rei quam geris, ut si parvum sit omnino tempus in quo sit vacandum, brevioribus exercitiis sit agendum, si contra multum, longioribus sit utendum: neque deerunt virorum clarorum mores, quos in hac re imitentur. **83** Sive enim in littore calculos colligant, sive pila sive lucta oblectentur, habebunt quos sequi voluisse dicantur, Lelium, Scevolam, Platonem. Nam ...[223] nunquam nisi XL emensis stadiis, quo

---

[220] -issimus MS.
[221] rivuli veris Br., thereby construing *clementia* as abl., not nom.; *clae-* MS.
[222] modus MS.
[223] A two- or three-word blank is left in the MS.

and supported by a community of friends, and to have good health; I've also made them cheerful and joyous, so that the mind would be rendered livelier by taking a respite from its responsibilities. And I've brought these points together and combined them in such a way that they seem both to give rise to good health and to arise from it.[224]

81 For just as physical soundness is generated from a condition of liveliness, so liveliness proceeds from physical soundness. Very many factors bring about that liveliness, however, and not just all those that make for good health, but also certain personal factors that are especially advantageous, in the manner of the conditions wished for by doctors – clean air, an expansive home with good light, views over a wide area, green spaces, mountains, little streams, the mildness of spring, and various types of physical exercise and riding.[225] **82** For the outcome isn't the same [for everyone] or the same benefit derived regardless of how that outcome arises, but one person achieves it by riding, another by hunting, another by walking, another by dancing,[226] another by building up a sweat over one particular activity and effort. For the greater the pleasure with which activities are performed, the greater the liveliness they produce. However, close attention should be paid to the time and to the activity you engage in, so that if the time-span in which you're to take a respite is altogether short, it's to be spent on briefer exercises, but if it's considerable, longer ones are to be employed; and there'll be plenty of examples of distinguished men's behaviour for them to imitate in this matter. **83** For whether they gather pebbles on the shore or take pleasure in ball playing or wrestling, they'll have models they may be said to have wanted to follow – Laelius, Scaevola, Plato.[227] Moreover, ... never came home to eat

---

[224] Cf. n. 202 above.

[225] Given Barbaro's advocacy in Book 3 of living at a remove from the temptations of the city (3.6.18-20, 25-39), the healthful charms that he describes here offset his stress on the celibate's need for occasional company in 4.2.79-80; he evokes instead the claims of solitude in the vein of, notably, Petrarch's *De vita solitaria* (*On the solitary life*, written between 1346-56), on which Enenkel 2018.

[226] In light of the striking overlap between Barbaro's allusion to Laelius and Scaevola in 4.2.83 and Verg. *De ingen. mor.* 69 (see n. 227 below), this listing of recreational pursuits is suggestively modeled on Vergerio's parallel overview in his 69-70 (tr. Kallendorf 2002: 85-7), incl. riding, hunting, walking and dancing.

[227] Verg. *De ingen. mor.* 69 (tr. Kallendorf 2002: 85) similarly mentions two of the three examples (Plato the exception) that Barbaro cites here – suggestively Barbaro's direct source (cf. n. 226 above), unless both he and Vergerio share a common reference-point (V. Max. 8.8.1-2?). For Laelius, 3.3.1 and n. 28; for his penchant for collecting pebbles on the seashore, Cic. *De or.* 2.22, V. Max. 8.8.1. The distinguished jurist and politician Q. Mucius Scaevola Augur (*c.* 169-88 BCE, cos. 117) was Laelius' son-in-law; for his skill as a ball player, V. Max. 8.8.2 (albeit Quintus is there confused with P. Mucius Scaevola, cos. 133: see Cic. *De or.* 1.217 with Briscoe 2019: 160). For Plato's alleged prowess as a wrestler, Apul. *De dog. Plat.* 1.2.3, D. L. 3.4, and cf. 2.5.11 and n. 123.

ingesta cibi moles consumpto alimenti vapore consisteret, esum revertebatur. **84** Avus meus, quum se multum et tamen celeriter volebat exercere, saxum ingens, quod ad usum hunc appenso rudenti alligaverat, ter aut quater ab imo ad summum, hoc est in altissimam contignationem, labente per ro[**120v**]tam funiculo attollebat: quum vero manare sudor videretur, tum ad studia se recipiebat.[228] **85** Ex horum genere id sibi seligere debebit coelebs quod naturae suae propius[229] et conducibilius et ad id, quod agit, accommodatius esse existimabit. Mutare etiam quandoque proderit, si ita tempus aut ocasio postulabit, et illa ipsa varietas afferet etiam voluptatis plurimum. **86** Quae omnia ita sunt pertractanda, ut valitudinis ratio inprimis habeatur: scire enim nos oportet omnia facilius tolerari quam morbum posse. Quare ab hoc metu incipiendum est et ad reliqua tunc demum accingi, quum fuerint plane perspecta non esse valitudini nocitura: huc enim omnia sunt referenda, quae solent extrinsecus adhiberi.

87 Quamobrem modus erit in unaquaque re huius temperamenti, ut neque nimium neque parum sit quod aggredientur: ita fiet ut a cupiditatibus ferri minime sinant, neque [**121r**] iis credendum putent quae non modo corpus sed etiam animum solvunt atque corrumpunt. Quae omnia si praestare potuerit coelebs, poterit autem si volet, volet autem si debere velle se noverit, finem erit suum plenissime assequutus. Erit enim adeptus et pudicitiae gloriam et contemplandi recte omnia facultatem; quorum utrunque divinum opus est et munus deorum ante omnia admirandum.

---

[228] *ricipi-* MS.
[229] *proprius* MS, corrected to *-pius*.

unless he'd covered forty stades, so that his heaped-up mass of a meal would be left to stand and the burning heat of the food all spent.[230] **84** My grandfather,[231] when he wanted to give himself a strenuous but quick workout, used to raise up with a cord moving through a wheel-hoist a great rock that he'd fastened to a hanging rope-system for this purpose; [he would raise it up] three or four times from the bottom to the top, that is, to the highest point of the upper story; but when his sweat was visibly flowing, he'd at that point return to his studies.[232] **85** In keeping with activities of this sort, the celibate will have to choose for himself the kind that he believes to be closer to and more expedient for his own nature, and better suited to the task he's engaged in. It will sometimes also be beneficial to change it, if the time or ripe circumstance so demands it, and that shift of approach will itself also bring a great deal of pleasure. **86** All of these matters are to be carefully handled in such a way that consideration is given first and foremost to good health; for we must know that everything can be more easily endured than illness. Hence we should take our start from this fear [of illness], and only gird ourselves for all other pursuits at the point when they are clearly recognized as posing no threat of future harm to our health; for all the factors that are usually applied from without are to be assigned to this end.[233]

87 Just as restraint will figure in every single aspect of this compromise, so that no undertaking of theirs will be either too much or too little, so they won't in the least allow themselves to be carried away by any desires; nor will they imagine that any faith is to be placed in those desires that enervate and damage not just the body but also the mind. If the celibate can bring all these qualities to bear (and he *will* be able to if he'll want to, and he *will* want to if he knows that he *must* want to), he will have achieved his end-goal to the fullest degree. Why? Because he'll have acquired both the distinction of sexual purity and the capacity to contemplate all things properly; each of the two is a divine achievement, and a gift of the gods that is to be marveled at before all else.

---

[230] Difficult: perhaps, alternatively, 'so that when the bulk of his meal was consumed (cf. OLD *ingero* 1c), it would settle down [in the stomach] because the burning heat of the food was all spent'? The identity of the pre-prandial rider[?] covering forty stades before eating is lost in the two- or three-word blank in the MS. If a stade is taken to be just over 600 feet (see Engels 1985), the distance covered is approximately 4.5 miles/7.3 kilometres.

[231] Presumably his paternal grandfather, Francesco.

[232] A possible play on *su_do_r*/*stu_di_a*, with variation on the idea that one's studies should *themselves* induce sweat (cf. Hor. *Ars P*. 412-13, Sen. *Dial*. 1.2.5).

[233] I.e., of supporting good health. For these external factors cf. 4.2.67-9, the starting-point for the sequence of argument concluded here.

88 Quare erit is exemplar quoddam in terris et testimonium felicitatis Dei. Hunc colent et venerabuntur nationes, huic templa condent civitates, huic fundet populus preces et vota componet et sacra faciet. Proximus est enim et maxime secundus Deo, cuius numen non alius placare potest, quam is qui aut est coelebs aut ut coelebs. **89** Durat adhuc apud singulas gentes durabitque semper mos ille religionis, quo nemini ante licet precari numina aut sacrificare, quam sint [**121v**] vitia omnia, praesertim libidinis atque impuritatis, expiata. Quod munus coelibi maxime proprium fecimus, neque alia re differunt nisi quia perpetuo hic, illi ad tempus se abstinent foeditate. Quamobrem charissimum illum esse diis est necesse: quod, si cui delubra dicanda sunt, huic vivo et mortuo honestissime dicabuntur. **90** Consecratus est vivus Apollinis et Iovis oraculo Eutimius poeta, quoniam in olympicis certaminibus semel tantum victus, victor alias semper perdurasset, et Ephestionem Alexander templis ornavit, quia fidissimo eo uno et amicissimo usus fuisset. Quantum autem iis praestare debeat coelibis[234] virtus non explicamus: manifestum enim est id, et nos alio loco monstravimus. Quare si

---

[234] -*ibiis* MS.

88 Hence he will be a kind of likeness on earth, and an attestation, of the blessedness of God. Peoples will worship and revere him, states will establish temples for him, to him the general public will pour forth their entreaties, lay out their prayers, and perform their holy rites.[235] Why? Because he is very close to God and very much the next greatest to Him, whose divine power no one can conciliate other than he who is either celibate or like the celibate. **89** There still persists in individual nations – and it will always persist – that custom of religious observance whereby no one is permitted to pray to the gods or perform a sacrifice before all his moral defects are atoned for, especially of lust and defilement. I have made this task very much the celibate's own, and they[236] differ in nothing else save the fact that the latter permanently refrains from foul behaviour, the former only for a time. Hence the celibate is necessarily most dear to the gods; but if temples are to be dedicated to anyone, they will most becomingly be dedicated to him both in life and when he's dead. **90** While yet living, the poet Eutimius was recognized as divine by the oracle of Apollo and Jupiter, since he'd only been defeated once in Olympic competitions, and he'd elsewhere held out as a permanent winner;[237] and Alexander honoured Hephaestion with temples, because he'd found him, and him alone, a most faithful and committed friend.[238] I refrain from setting out the extent to which the celibate's virtue must surpass these cases; for that much is perfectly clear, as I've shown elsewhere.[239] Hence, if honours were

---

[235] Despite the hyperbolical pitch, the public acclaim and reverence for the celibate underscore the importance of his service to the community even though he remains detached from conventional active life.

[236] The celibate on the one side, and, on the other, those '[not] permitted to pray to the gods' until they have atoned for their sinfulness.

[237] Barbaro's source is Plin. *NH* 7.152, and his wording in *Eutimius poeta* reflects a reading disseminated in early printed editions of Pliny; but in his *Castigationes Plinianae et in Pomponium Melam* of 1492-3 (for which, Vol. 1 Intro. pp. 24, 29, 32) Barbaro himself emended the reading to *Euthymus pycta* (see Pozzi 1973-9: 2.557-8). The brilliantly recovered Plinian allusion is then to 'the boxer Euthymus [of Locri] who always won at Olympia [in 484, 476, and 472 BCE], suffering only one defeat, [and] was to his own knowledge deified while still a living man' (tr. Beagon 2005: 92, with pp. 353-4 on the evolution of Euthymus' cult).

[238] By one tradition Alexander the Great ordered that his most intimate friend, the Macedonian Hephaestion, be worshipped as a god after his death in 324 BC (cf. Diod. Sic. 17.115.6, Just. *Epit.* 12.12.12). According to Diod. ibid., Alexander's order was corroborated when he received report that the oracle of Ammon commanded that sacrifice be made to Hephaestion as a god (the historical reality appears to be rather that Alexander established hero-cult for Hephaestion, not deification: see McKechnie 1995: 426-7 and n. 47). The oracular dimension is implicit but important in Barbaro's allusion because (i) it complements the role of the oracle of Apollo and Jupiter in Eutimius' case above, and (ii) that oracular support matches the special divine favour that Barbaro claims for the celibate.

[239] Cf. esp. 4.2.44-6, 51-4 (on the celibate's matchless favour before, and likeness to, God).

iuste honores habiti illis sunt, iustius longe coelibi habebuntur: est enim is, ut diximus et concludamus, proxi[**122r**]mus et secundus Deo, eiusque exemplar quoddam in terris et testimonium foelicitatis.

91 Verum in extrema operis nostri parte non est omittenda ratio respondendi iis, qui quaesituri plerunque sunt an fieri possit ut foeminae quoque et sine marito vivant pudice et contemplentur recte ea omnia, quae huic offitio subiecta esse voluimus. Quum itaque foemina homo sit et rationis particeps animal et intelligentiae capax, sui etiam arbitrii et mali et boni non ignarum, quorum alterum ad sciendum satis est, alterum ad pudice vivendum idoneum, haud sane intelligo quor eripere illi sexui hanc gloriam debeamus.

92 Si mihi ea virgo detur quales Sibillae traduntur, qualis Lala Sizicaena, quae perpetuam pudicitiam adamavit, nonne sperandum erit posse eas ad finem, quem praescripsimus, pervenire? Negari nequit esse id saltem [**122v**] opinabile atque possibile; quod si detur, iam tunc non licebit foeminas pellere.

93 Quod si iccirco illas abigendas esse putaremus, quia difficile videretur hanc virtutem cadere posse in foeminam, viros etiam non liceret admittere, quia esset et id viris perquam difficile; quamvisque minus laboriosum sit, ut inquit Aristoteles, omne negotium masculis, non tamen prorsus est id foeminis intolerabile. Nam et foeminae esse possunt quas plerunque non secus atque viros ad hoc vitae genus videtur natura procreasse: has ego magno animo, ut ad castitatem et contemplationem incumberent, hortatas esse voluerim. Ut enim non est naturae repugnandum, ita ea maxime retinenda sunt ad quae quisque natus esse videatur. **94** Non modo autem hoc in foeminis requiri debet, verumetiam in viris est maxime providendum, ne

rightfully paid to *them*, they will be far more rightfully paid to the celibate; for he is, as I've said,[240] and to conclude, very close and second only to God, and a kind of likeness of Him on earth, and an attestation of His blessedness.

91 But in the very last section of my work, I'd be remiss if I offered no way of answering those who are often going to ask whether it can happen that women, too, both live respectably without a husband and contemplate in the desired manner all the things I've wanted to be subject to this calling. Accordingly, since a woman is a human and a living being who both [i] shares in reason and is capable of intelligent thought, and [ii] is also of independent judgment and not unaware of good and bad (of these two qualities, the one is sufficient for knowledge, the other appropriate for a life of sexual purity), I certainly fail to understand why we should rob that gender of this mark of distinction.[241] **92** If I consider the kind of virginal woman such as the Sibyls are said to have been,[242] or Lala Sizicaena,[243] who deeply loved her permanent state of chastity, isn't it to be anticipated that they are capable of reaching the end-goal I've set out? It can't be denied that that is at least imaginable and possible; if this is granted, already then it will be impossible to exclude women.

93 But if we'd imagine that they are to be spurned precisely because it would seem hard for this quality of virtue to be able to befall a woman, it wouldn't be possible to admit men either, because that would also be extremely hard for men; and though, as Aristotle says, every task is less burdensome for males,[244] that one is nevertheless certainly not beyond bearing for women. Why? Because there can also be women whom nature often seems to have produced for this kind of life no differently from men; those I would wholeheartedly want to be encouraged to devote their energies to a chaste existence of contemplation. For just as nature isn't to be resisted, so we should very much hold fast to the things for which each appears born. **94** But not only should this be looked for in women, but also in the case of men the greatest care should be taken to ensure that no one wishes to pursue what, as

---

[240] 4.2.88.
[241] For Barbaro's boldness of initiative in configuring the female celibate here, see Intro. pp. 2, 3.
[242] The term *Sibylla*, first attested in Heraclitus (D42 LM = B92 DK = T151 Graham 2010: 176–7), is found as a proper name by the fifth century BCE, denoting a prophetic woman; the Sibyl became intimately connected with Rome through the hallowed tradition of the Sibylline books (see Takács 2008: 62–70).
[243] An elusive figure – if the text is sound.
[244] Cf. [Arist.] *Oec*. 1.3 1343b30-1, but Branca 1969: 154 tentatively also cites *Gen. an.* 4.6 775a9-16 via Francesco Barbaro's *De re uxoria* IV.2 (Griggio 2021: 196 [Gnesotto 1915–16: 38.1-4]; tr. King 2015: 76).

ea sequi quisquam velit quae, ut inquit Cicero, assequi minime possit. Quare expendere opor[**123r**]tebit et quantum valeat et ad quod natura feratur, qua adversante scire licet nihil confici, nihil fieri posse absolutum: quo fit ut non minus ea cura marium sit quam foeminarum, quin et longe magis sit propria iis ad quos ea gloria videtur maxime pertinere. **95** Turpe est enim iis desistere ab incepto, qui adipisci finem facilius poterant: facilius autem eum viri quam faeminae nanciscuntur. Quare maiore admiratione prosequimur si quam praestare in iis rebus mulierem videamus, quae virorum sunt propria: qualem fuisse Corneliam Gracchorum matrem historia omnis asseruit. Non solum enim quia rara sunt haec laudare et admirari solemus, verumetiam quia neque petita neque sperata. Quis enim aut eloquentiam in foemina requisivit unquam, aut robur et fortitudinem expectavit? Utrunque tamen praestitisse plurimas memoriae traditum est. **96** Eas itaque foeminas, quae natura ad id deducente vitam [**123v**] coelibem comprobabunt, ea sequi praecepta[245] velim omnia, quae sunt superius explicata, uno tantum excepto potissimum, ne cum viris, si fieri possit, uspiam[246] diversentur, sed cum foeminis ubique vivant, et cautiones omnis adhibeant ne aut sotios habeant qui moribus et vitae quam delegerunt minime congruant, aut omnino consuetudine careant. Caetera cum viris debent habere communia, ut quemadmodum illi ex hac vita quam simillimi Deo fient, ita et foeminis evenire posse concessum sit ut Deo proximae efficiantur.

97 Succensebunt mihi fortasse viri pauperes atque infortunati, quod se, ut ex iis quae dicta sunt patere potest, ita omisimus atque contempsimus, ut eos tantum instituere videremur qui et locupletes essent et opulenti. Quibus

---

[245] *praec-* MS, *prac-* Br.
[246] Br.'s conjecture (155 n. 1) for MS *quispiam* (impossible because of its gender and number).

Cicero says,²⁴⁷ he can't in the least attain. Hence it will be necessary to weigh carefully both the extent of our capacities and the direction in which nature is carrying them; if nature stands in the way, you can be sure that nothing can be accomplished and nothing made complete. The result is that this preoccupation [of celibacy] applies as much to males as to females – yes, and that it belongs far more particularly to those to whom that mark of distinction appears especially relevant. **95** For it's shameful for those who were more easily able to achieve their end-goal to cease from their undertaking; and men reach that end more easily than do women. I therefore honour with greater veneration any woman I see to be excelling in those pursuits that are the preserve of men – the sort of woman that the entire historical record declares that Cornelia, the mother of the Gracchi, had been.²⁴⁸ We generally praise and respect such qualities [in women] not just because they are rare, but also because they are neither sought nor hoped for; for who either expected ever to find eloquence in a woman or anticipated seeing physical strength and bravery? Tradition has it, however, that very many women have shown both of these qualities. **96** Accordingly, those women who will wholly approve of the celibate life, with nature drawing them in that direction – I'd want them to follow all the injunctions that have been set out above, with just one very important exception: that, if possible, they don't lodge anywhere with men,²⁴⁹ but in all circumstances live with women, and that they take all precautions against having the sort of companions who aren't in the least suited to the ways and existence they have chosen, or entirely lack familiarity with them. They should regard all the other precepts as shared in common with men so that, just as those men will become as like as possible to God as a result of this existence, so too it's granted as a possible outcome for women that they are rendered very close to God.

97 Men who are poor and unfortunate will perhaps be angry at me because (as can be evident from what's been said) I left them out and showed them scant regard in such a way that I seemed to train only those who were both rich and well supplied.²⁵⁰ To all of these I'd want this to be said in reply:

---

²⁴⁷ *Off.* 1.110, explicitly drawn on from 4.2.93 'For just as nature ...' onwards; for the importance of heeding one's individual nature cf. 3.6.34-6 and n. 261.

²⁴⁸ For the cultured Cornelia as an exemplary wife and mother who steadfastly endured the violent deaths of the famous revolutionary tribunes Tiberius and Gaius Gracchus in (respectively) 133 and 121 BCE, see, e.g., Sen. *Dial.* 6.16.3, 12.16.6, Tac. *Dial.* 28.5, Juv. 6.166-9.

²⁴⁹ Cf. the similar injunction to males at 3.5.56 (the same verb *diversor -ari* in both cases).

²⁵⁰ This flash of anger from the impoverished suggestively modifies (Branca 1969: 155) the comparable interlocutory outburst in Francesco Barbaro's *De re uxoria* VIII.1 (Griggio 2021: 220 [Gnesotto 1915-16: 53.21-54.2]; tr. King 2015: 88), a passage itself modeled on [Plut.] *De lib. educ.* 11 (*Mor.* 8e).

velim ita[251] responsum sit omnibus: non consulto me illos despexisse sed ea tantum [124r] voluisse ut tractarentur, quae meliori via et breviori ad eam metam, quam figebamus, perducebant. Nunc vero,[252] ut etiam vobis faciamus satis, viri inopes atque egeni, ne vestram probitatem, quae[253] plerunque maxima sub vestris palliis latere solet, omnino aspernemur, brevissime ea complecti poterimus, quae requirere haud iniuria a nobis videmini.

98 Primum igitur id vobis ante oculos sit, ut vestrum ingenium cognoscatis. Si prompti eritis ad contemplandum, si fortes ad resistendum voluptati, aut non longe a fine eritis aut ad finem proculdubio pervenietis: sed maiore difficultate, grandiore periculo, laboribus etiam vehementius arduis. Quod si stadium iam percurreritis, tum vos latissime vobis ipsis opem feretis, tum vobis omnia abunde suppeditabunt. 'Quo pacto?' inquies. Quia mediusfidius Deus est nunquam defuturus vobis, quom sui causa [124v] viderit tot esse labores a vobis perlatos, tot difficultates toleratas: quin etiam, ut vobis ampliorem spem faciamus, merito vestro perinde ac maiore et laudabiliore movebitur, ut vos esse in tuto possitis.

99 Habes iam a filio munus, Pater optime, quatuor de coelibatu libros, quos siquis reprehenderit merito ita me sibi devinciet, ut sit a me hanc gratiam relaturus: me nunquam ea pertinaciter defensurum, quae male a nobis scripta iudicabuntur. Vale. Kalendis Februarii MCCCCLXXII.

---

[251] *ita velim ita* MS; for one *ita* omitted, Br. 156 n. 1.
[252] *Nunc, vero* Br., but he prints no comma at 2.5.19, 3.6.2, 24, etc.
[253] *qua* MS.

that I didn't deliberately disdain them, but wanted only those topics to be treated that led by a better and shorter route to the goal I was setting. Now, however, to meet your desires as well, needy men of poverty, and so that I don't altogether scorn your good character (which is generally of the highest degree but in the habit of lying hidden beneath your outer garments), I'll be able very briefly to sum up the points that you appear to be asking of me, and not unreasonably.

98 The first priority for you to have in view, then, is that you recognize your natural aptitude.[254] If you will be readily disposed to contemplation, and if strongly committed to resisting pleasure, you will either not be far from your end-goal or doubtless reach that goal – but with more difficulty [than if you were rich], a greater degree of risk, and also toils that will be more strenuously challenging. But if you'll have now completed your circuit of the running track, to a very broad extent you'll come to your own aid at that point; at that point all your needs will be supplied in abundance. 'How?' you'll say. Because (on my word of honour!) God is never going to fail you, since He will see that so many hardships have been shouldered by you for His own sake, so many troubles endured; and furthermore – so that I provide you with greater hope – He will be touched by your claim to merit just as if it were greater and more praiseworthy [than that of the affluent], so that you can be on a safe footing.

99 You now have as a gift from your son, my dear father, four books on celibacy. Anyone who finds fault with them with just cause will make me obliged to him in such a way that he's going to get back from me this expression of thanks: that I'll never stubbornly defend what will be judged to be poorly written by me. Farewell. February 1 1472.[255]

---

[254] Cf. 3.6.34-6 and n. 261; 4.2.93-4.
[255] On the date see Vol. 1 Intro. p. 6 and n. 30.

Introduction to *On the Duty of the Ambassador*

I: To Milan

In January 1488 Ermolao was appointed as Venice's ambassador to the Sforza court in Milan. Although he had accompanied his father on various of the latter's ambassadorial assignments,[1] he had little diplomatic experience of his own before going to Milan. He had served in only one delegation, to the Holy Roman Emperor Frederick III and his son Maximilian I in Bruges in 1486; but that assignment was largely ceremonial in purpose, offering congratulations on Maximilian's installation as King of the Romans.[2] His assignment to Milan posed a very different challenge, but one he enthusiastically embraced, at least to judge by a letter that he addressed on 21 January 1488 to his humanist friend Giorgio Merula (*c.* 1430–94), who was himself then resident in Milan. His appointment was precious to him for many reasons, wrote Ermolao, not least family pride:

> Is there any other family at all, any house, in the whole of Italy apart from ours, from which three members, in a continuous sequence, grandfather, father, and son, set out with this title from the same [Venetian] senate to the same [Milanese] rulers?[3]

Ermolao had recently accompanied Zaccaria when his father served as ambassador in Milan in 1485,[4] and in his letter to Merula he fondly recalls the warmth with which he himself had been received by their hosts. He was glad to be going back, and gladder still at what he found there shortly after his arrival on 23 March 1488.[5] Other Venetian envoys felt the strain of trying to make time for their humanist studies amidst their diplomatic duties,[6] but apparently not Ermolao: in a letter penned on 13 April he wrote of his delight at having so much free time that he was completely absorbed in his studies;[7] in a separate letter on that same day, he wittily surmised that the shades of Dioscorides and Aristotle had secured his position for him so that he could finish editing their works.[8] 'It was in this same positive mood,' writes Patricia

Labalme, 'that Ermolao Barbaro wrote, sometime between 1489 and 1490, his *De officio legati*, whose strictures against disobedience to one's government he himself would so shortly violate.'[9] Hence the challenge before us: how to understand Ermolao's own actions – his acceptance of the Patriarchate of Aquileia in 1491 without Venetian permission[10] – in light of, or despite, the charter of ambassadorial discipline and obedience that he set out only months before in his *De officio legati*?

II: The text: its history, completeness and content

The text of *De officio legati* as presented in this volume reproduces with slight adjustment[11] that published by Vittore Branca alongside *De coelibatu* in his 1969 edition of both works. An Italian translation has appeared in the last decade,[12] and extracts also exist in English in at least two important studies;[13] but to my knowledge the translation offered here is the first complete Anglophone version. Branca based his text on the ten manuscripts that were known to him, none of them autograph or in the hand of Barbaro's long-term secretary, Tommaso Didimo Zanetelli (*c*. 1450–1514).[14] Branca identifies three groups of manuscripts and conjectures that 'the archetypes of the three groups derive directly or indirectly from a version approved by the author'[15] – a version that may nevertheless have been left incomplete, as the extant ending appears suspiciously abrupt.[16] But the available manuscripts are sixteenth-century or later: given the lateness of the transmission, another possibility is that Ermolao never sanctioned or circulated an 'official' original, and that the work was transmitted posthumously from a draft left among his papers.[17] The text was first printed in 1761 and then in 1906, on both occasions on the basis of the same manuscript but with numerous transcriptional errors;[18] hence the importance of Branca's edition in establishing a new foundation for the text.

It has been claimed that the treatise enjoyed a wide diffusion in the Italian courts, and that it shows an affinity to the prescriptive mode of 'how-to' manuals for rulers in the *institutio principis* tradition; the abrupt ending of the text as we have it is then symptomatic of what Maria Doglio presents as a brief and pointed compendium of easily grasped lessons.[19] But six of the ten manuscripts known to Branca are located in Venice or existed there before being moved elsewhere, and none of them shows the careful and decorous 'finish' that might be expected of a version destined for the courtly library. Given these considerations, and also the relative lateness of the extant transmission, the manuscript evidence hardly tells in favour of the work's wide circulation in courtly circles soon after it was written,[20] and few scholars would now straightforwardly accept that it is complete in its ending. The connection with the *institutio principis* tradition may still be valid, at least by loose association; but Doglio's reading leaves much room for further speculation about Ermolao's motivation for penning the treatise, as we shall see.

The work is conveniently divisible into three movements.[21] In the introductory section (§§1–6), Ermolao's broad definition of the duty of the ambassador gives way to his closer focus on the so-called resident ambassador, i.e., a permanent representative of one state to another, as opposed to the 'special' envoy sent on pressing matters of ad hoc business.[22] For all the protocols governing the ambassador's role, much stress is placed from the outset on his capacity for shrewd initiative in the moment: this *prudentia* (§2) will figure prominently in the rest of the work, not least in practical illustrations drawn from Ermolao's own ambassadorial experience in Milan. Even though the treatise purports to address the theme of diplomacy in general,[23] the Venetian imprint on it is deep and far-reaching, as is that of Ermolao's father, Zaccaria: the inextricable linkage between family and state in Quattrocento Venice is amply reaffirmed in *De officio legati*.[24]

In the main body of the treatise (§§7–46), Ermolao sets out the main principles that should guide the ambassador's conduct, chief among them his absolute obedience to his mandate, his duty to uphold in every aspect of his own behaviour the dignity of the state he represents, and the need for a cautious guardedness at all times. The ambassador drawn in this section is in many ways permanently an actor whose adherence to the official script is importantly supplemented by his own powers of quick-thinking dissimulation. In the third section (§§47–57) Ermolao turns from positive instruction to the consequences of any scandalous or criminal behaviour on the ambassador's part. After his main focus on the envoy's public role, he finally addresses the domestic arrangements within the ambassadorial residence: in his family life and the management of his household retinue, the ambassador must naturally uphold the standards of dignity and decorum that characterize his official life.

In his perfected form, the ambassador configured by Ermolao is less a Platonic ideal[25] than a model of Aristotelian completeness, his measured disposition and poise an applied version of Aristotle's 'middle way' (*mesotēs*; cf. §18 *mediocri ingenio*).[26] This Aristotelian emphasis is in keeping with the strong Venetian accent of the work, given Aristotle's centrality to the Republic's civic ideology.[27] The Venetian ambassador was not so much a representative of the state as its incarnation, as if the symbolic embodiment of its values. In this respect Ermolao's vivid verbal portrait of him is directly comparable with visual portraiture of the Venetian nobility in the same period: just as the brush captures not merely the outer appearance of the man but also his inner essence and the patrician values encased within him,[28] so

Ermolao looks beyond the envoy's public image and the surface protocols of his office to the qualities of the man within – a textual fashioning of the person that suggestively anticipates the formational techniques emblematized by Baldassare Castiglione's *Il libro del Cortegiano* (*The Book of the Courtier*) some four decades later.[29] The further implication is that through his autobiographical touches Ermolao engages in a form of self-portraiture, at least partially inserting himself into his vision of the ideal envoy. But if he sought to burnish his own credentials as a loyal and committed servant of the state in *De officio legati*, that self-fashioning dramatically disrupts the long-term life-narrative of his strained relationship to the Venetian *cursus*. Hence the split approach to the work in what follows: we turn first to the public face and function of the treatise, but then to the more personal story that it reflects, or implies, about Ermolao himself.

III: The originality of *De officio legati*

A helpful departure-point for gauging Ermolao's originality of approach is provided by the French jurist and prelate, Bernard de Rosier (1400–75), author of the *Ambaxiatorum brevilogus* (1435–6), apparently 'the first textbook of diplomatic practice written in Western Europe.'[30] This work was meant as a practical guide for diplomats that was informed by de Rosier's expertise in the law and his own experience of diplomatic missions. In its thirty chapters it offers global coverage of (in partial sketch) the personal and moral qualities that are to be sought in the ambassador (§2), the reasons why he would be deployed (§4), the need for absolute clarity in the instructions he is given (§9), how the ambassador is to be received at his destination (§11), the assured and methodical way in which he should engage in negotiation (§§12–15), how the proceedings are to be brought to appropriate closure (§§17–20), the rights, protections and honours attaching to the office (§§23–7), and how he is to be received upon returning from his mission (§29). The work follows the ambassador in real time, as it were, from his selection for the given assignment to his return home after its completion. In reviewing the scenarios in which the ambassador could feasibly be deployed, de Rosier portrays the function of the diplomat in highly idealized terms: the long list includes always striving for good, never for discord or evil, advancing the honour of the Holy See and the unity of the Church, upholding the Christian faith, and promoting the causes of peace, justice, friendship, and goodwill (§4). Hence, at the work's conclusion in §30, de Rosier reaffirms that the ambassador's duty is to serve the interests not just of the given state but of the whole world (*rei public[a]e et toti orbi*). This universalist perspective generates a tension between his duty to the state or the ruler he serves and his 'public' duty in the wider sense (cf. *ambaxiatorum officium publicum est*, §6): to serve the interests of the larger Christian commonwealth and even, in theory, the commonwealth of humankind.[31]

Bernard de Rosier was no humanist, and so the contrast is immediately striking when we encounter the relatively unaffected style and lucid flow of Barbaro's Ciceronian Latinity in *De officio legati*.[32] So too in terms of his content and thematic approach, Barbaro inhabits a conceptual world far from that of de Rosier some half-century before. Ermolao wastes no time in stressing the ambassador's duty solely to the utilitarian advantage of the state or ruler he serves (§1): the medieval view of diplomacy as working for the good of a single and like-minded Christian community persisted in de Rosier, but now it gives way to a thoroughly modern charter for competitive self-interest on the chessboard of inter-state rivalry.[33] The language of Ermolao's title and opening words (*legati munus/officium*) echoes that of medieval canon law and of secular as well as pontifical diplomacy.[34] But in contrast to the scholastic, medieval approach to the topic, Barbaro's trajectory from the outset is strikingly novel because he is the first humanist writer on diplomacy to mention, and focus explicitly on (§§4–5), the permanent 'resident' ambassador as opposed to the 'special' envoy.[35] Residents proliferated after the Treaty of Lodi of 1454 gave rise to a regional balance of power that lasted among the northern Italian states down to 1494. Precursors of the 'official' concept of the resident ambassador arguably extended back at least to the fourteenth century,[36] but a residential arrangement between Venice and Milan in particular (cf. §10) was apparently not formalized before 1485,[37] when Zaccaria Barbaro served there. More generally, in 'pass[ing] over in silence all the customary medieval phrases about an ambassador's office,' Ermolao's is for Garrett Mattingly 'the voice of the new age'[38] – one that breaks with the medieval tradition in preferring, as Douglas Biow puts it, 'brevity to discursivity, ethical to legal concerns, the personal example to the impersonal precept, the immediate present to the remote past, unified and focused discourse to the technical information provided in often extended *quaestiones*.'[39]

Whereas de Rosier focuses on procedures and protocols in following the envoy in a linear fashion from the beginning of his mission to its conclusion, Barbaro's approach is less mechanical in its structure, more finely attuned to the inner person of the envoy, and more 'real' in the concrete anecdotes he adduces to exemplify his strictures.[40] But despite this human touch, and despite the feel it conveys of a certain ease of exposition, there is nothing casual about the conceptual design of Barbaro's de facto tribute to the myth of Venice in his treatise. In an explicit patriotic turning roughly at the midpoint of the work (§§25–8), he surveys the characteristics – their distinctive laws, way of life, imperial power, etc. – that have apparently caused the Venetians to be 'called arrogant by their enemies and the envious, stern by the more respectful' (§25). Venice is literally central to the treatise as we have it[41] through its prominent positioning here; but its figurative centrality is already evident from the outset. The marked Venetian stress on allegiance above all to the state and its collective *unanimitas*, not on the individual interest or viewpoint, gives a special topical force to Barbaro's opening words on the ambassador's obligation to his mandate. Thereafter, the close correlation in Venetian ideology between the patriarchal structure of the aristocratic family and the Republic's order of government is reflected in the tight-knit patrilineal economy of the work. Ermolao refers three times to the senatorial fathers (*patres*, §§11, 14, 31), and three times also to his own father, Zaccaria (*pater*, §§6, 16, 21), all within a structure of overall devotion to the fatherland (*patria*, §46).[42] Ermolao follows in Zaccaria's footsteps as Venetian ambassador to Milan, but loyalty to his father's example is inseparable from his obedience to the civic fathers. At the same time, his own work *De officio legati* is pointedly informed by the thorough discussions that he shared with Zaccaria 'about the ambassador's duty' (*de officio legati*, §16): if Ermolao shapes himself in his father's ambassadorial image, his treatise is itself cast as a textual replica or extension of the conversations he shared with Zaccaria, as if it is the product of inherited cross-generational wisdom.[43]

In one pattern of movement, then, the treatise 'spirals out from the *patres*, to the *pater*, to the son,'[44] a process that inevitably subordinates the individual to the paternalistic machinery of state. But another pattern features a movement inwards from the public sphere to the private, from the ambassador's external persona to his inner character and moral disposition (§§47–53), and from his official responsibilities to his domestic arrangements (§§54–7).[45] Fundamental to this second pattern is the correlation it posits between the inner condition and the outer aspect; so, e.g., the tone of orderly calm that the ambassador sets in the household reflects his stability of bearing in the public eye and arena. By extension, this correlation has reflexive implications for the treatise itself: to what extent does the work embody or perform the qualities and techniques that distinguish the skilled ambassador? Take, for example, Barbaro's vignette in §§34–7 about what happened in Pavia when the rumour spread that he was in good standing with Ludovico Sforza, the Regent of Milan, and he consequently received many requests from the local community of the lettered and learned for him personally to recommend them before the Regent. Barbaro turned those requests down on the grounds that such advocacy in a private capacity was impermissible for an ambassador; but he pledged to offer a general recommendation of them, 'and this I did' (§36). He has it both ways, impressing Ludovico with his apparently sincere praises of those he commends, but also with his restraint in requesting a special favour for no on. The learned who flocked to him did so not so much as a mark of respect for him, Barbaro suspects, but to discover 'what sort of person I was' (§34). The anecdote serves a double function, first as a good example of the kind of tact that the ambassador is expected to show, but secondly as *itself* an artfully contrived projection of Barbaro's own nature: his measured dissimulation in §§36–7 reflexively offers its own telling demonstration of 'what sort of person he is.'

This reflexive dimension extends to many other features of the treatise, notable among them Ermolao's stress on how much the busy prince appreciates brevity of speech in an ambassador (§29): the point is neatly underscored by Barbaro's own concise simplicity of expression in the work.[46] The ambassador will sometimes have to apply his practical judgment (*prudentia*) in the moment to address situations not accounted for in textbook guides to diplomacy (§2): Ermolao himself models such resourcefulness in deftly amending his instructions from the Republic at a tense moment in its relations with Milan in §§10–12, or in dealing with indiscreet lines of questioning that were put to him when he first arrived in Milan (§43) – another test of his character that he passed with flying colours (§44).[47] On a different front, a skilled envoy such as Zaccaria knows how to use a strategy of deliberate diversion so as to win an interlocutor's trust even when that interlocutor is already telling him what he wants to know (§21). So at a textual level Ermolao uses 'a similar strategy of calculated indirection'[48] by going off on tangents that nevertheless prove to have real point. In §25, for example, he turns his focus to the adroitness that is desirable in the envoy, and 'a seriousness of demeanor (*gravitas*) combined with that adroitness; and along with that seriousness, a gentle kindness of instinct, *especially in a Venetian*.' The leading phrase in these last words allows him to embark on his paean to Venice in §§25–8, but there too indirection is all. Instead of directly praising the Republic, he views it through the eyes of others in §25, and with a negative valence (Venice's reputation for arrogance or sternness) that nevertheless bespeaks formidable power. Ermolao takes an overtly non-committal stance in 'neither commend[ing] nor completely condemn[ing] what was said by a certain senator of ours' (§27). That senator goes on to speak in his own reported voice – an emphatic assertion of Venetian greatness that is nevertheless presented with a carefully contrived indirectness on Ermolao's part: ever the diplomat, he delivers high praise of the Republic without explicitly endorsing that praise himself.[49]

Masking and dissimulation are staple techniques in *De officio legati* at the level of both the individual and the state, again with patrilineal significance: Zaccaria proves to be an adept dissimulator in his seemingly disinterested intelligence gathering (§21); Ermolao emulates his father in skillfully deploying a form of sincere pretense that impresses Ludovico when the envoy is forced by sudden circumstance to change the message that he bears from the Republic (§§10–12); and the paternalistic Republic will itself occasionally take advantage of 'pretend[ing] not to know' (§9).[50] But such dissimulation is also embedded performatively within the text, as Biow well observes: Ermolao 'even translates many of the requisite virtues discussed in his treatise into a prose that prudently stages what it preaches – by being deceptively simple, by dissimulating, by concealing its own shrewdness, by not being showy.'[51] A further layer of dissimulative masking has yet to be considered, however – for present purposes, the most important one of all: the possibility that the treatise as a whole functions as a mask, or a means by which Ermolao projects to the world (and perhaps even to himself) a version of himself that disguises a hidden reality.

IV: Behind the mask

Beyond the saga of Barbaro's nomination to the Patriarchate of Aquileia in 1491, a separate storyline complicates any attempt to gauge his possible motivation(s) in writing *De officio legati* after his term of service in Milan. This storyline centers on the incident precipitated by events at Forlì in §§10–12: the sudden news of Milan's success there in a quick military action meant that the message that Barbaro had been authorized by the Venetian Senate to relay to Ludovico Sforza – that Milan should lay down its arms – was instantly irrelevant. Instead, Barbaro offered congratulations on Milan's success in the field and then improvised further: 'I pretended that I had come to them to ask that they take steps to provide for a calm state of affairs in Italy, and to allow the war to be decided not by arms but by legal procedure' (§11). He thereby explains why and how he reluctantly but necessarily departed from his official script over the Forlì business – a maneuver for which he was duly 'praised by the Fathers' (§11).

Such at least is Barbaro's version of events; but the fuller story casts matters in a rather different light.[52] Some three weeks after Ermolao arrived as ambassador in Milan on 23 March 1488, Girolamo Riario, Lord of Imola and (from 1480) Forlì, was assassinated on 14 April. Forlì was taken over in the name of the Pope, Innocent VIII, but Riario's widow, Caterina Sforza, appealed to her uncle, Ludovico Sforza, for Milanese support; through Milanese intervention, Caterina was quickly restored as regent of Forlì for her eldest son, Ottaviano. Barbaro's version in §§10–12 of his dealings both with the Venetian Senate and with Ludovico captures only part of the picture offered by other sources: he was received at the Sforza court on 3 May, and the message he bore from Venice stated the hope that a peaceful outcome could be attained; for the Venetian understanding was that Innocent VIII was aggrieved at the Milanese intervention in Forlì, and that he was supported in this stance by another (unnamed) power.[53] Summoned by the agitated Ludovico on 4 May and asked about the identity of this other power, Ermolao replied, apparently with a touch of ingenuousness, that it could only be the Florentines – an indiscretion that prompted a rapid denial from Florence, while the Venetian Senate quickly distanced itself from its ambassador by insisting that he had distorted his instructions. Barbaro's faux pas duly received an official reprimand in Venice, but his good relations with Ludovico were soon restored; and given his appointment to significant offices even before he was sent as ambassador to Rome in 1490, this unfortunate incident hardly derailed his career.[54]

Against this background, his own account of the quick thinking that earned him the Venetian Senate's praise and Ludovico's admiration appears one-sided at the very least. It robustly asserts the ambassador's need for a certain freedom of maneuvre within (or despite) the rigid codification of his role, but Ermolao quickly checks himself by rounding out the episode with tactful praise of Venice itself (§12);[55] his account also stresses his obedience to his original instructions, and his departure from them only because of sudden necessity. But if the tract was written for public circulation in the spring or summer of 1489, soon after his return from Milan, can Ermolao's favourable account of events have failed to raise official eyebrows in the Venetian Senate?[56] How to reconcile his faux pas with his assertion that he was 'praised by the Fathers'? One solution is to conjecture that Ermolao's misstep – and the impression of naïveté that went with it – lingered in the Venetian memory and on people's lips after he returned to Venice in April 1489. A general tract on ambassadorship gave him the opportunity to defend his actions over Forlì and indirectly to advertise his skills as a deft and polished envoy; but that motive of self-justification became less pressing when he was appointed to fresh posts as early as June 1489.[57] The work was therefore laid aside (hence the impression of incompleteness at its transmitted end), and his one-sided version of events never came to light in his own lifetime.

For all the plausibility of this scenario, much uncertainty remains about the date of *De officio legati*, Barbaro's full motivation in writing it, and whether or not the work as it survives is complete. In the discussion that follows, these different strands are woven into the composite storyline of Barbaro's last years down to his death in Rome in 1493. But to declare my own tentative position at the outset: the work was written soon after his return to Venice from Milan in spring 1489, and it was never completed in the sense that Barbaro did not live to give it the 'finish' that would render its extant ending less abrupt. His appointment to other offices even before he was announced as Venetian ambassador to Rome meant that the self-exculpatory motive that he had for the work (in light of the Forlì business) became less pressing in the second half of 1489; but that private agenda was hardly incompatible with a genuinely committed reflection on the duties, the necessary attributes, and the behaviour to be expected of the late-Quattrocento ambassador. Nor was his private yearning for a life devoted to his beloved literary studies incompatible with his writing on the nature of ambassadorship, however ambivalent he may have felt in his own case about actively serving as a Venetian envoy. On this approach, the work is multi-sided in its possible motivations and goals, and much room for speculation remains. Hence the experimental lines of enquiry that are pursued in the rest of this section, the first of them revisiting the chronology of *De officio legati* from a different angle: what of its likely *terminus ante quem*?

It is hard to believe that *De officio legati* could have been written after 6 March 1491, when Ermolao was nominated as Patriarch of Aquileia.[58] Despite Ermolao's protestations that he accepted the Patriarchate in forced obedience to Pope Innocent VIII,[59] Riccardo Fubini balances the picture by pointing out[60] that the Barbaro family had close ties to the Papal Curia that extended back at least to Zaccaria's term as ambassador to Rome in 1480–1; that in Milan in 1488–9 Ermolao was notably close to the Papal Nuncio there, Jacopo Volterrano (1434–1516), and encouraged by him to take holy orders on what Volterrano foresaw as a sure path of progress to the Cardinalate; and that when Ermolao left to become Venice's ambassador to Rome in 1490, word spread in Venice that he was already intent on an ecclesiastical future in Rome. In his letter to Jacopo Antiquario of 7 January 1492, Ermolao stands by his record of honourable service to the Republic before his nomination to Aquileia, but he also unambiguously affirms his true allegiance:

> I have held the greatest offices in the Republic, with what dutifulness, integrity, and attentiveness (all others may or may not know) God is my witness. He alone meets my needs – He whose standards I follow, and under whose leadership and command I serve as soldier and subject.[61]

Fubini cites the first part of this passage to illustrate what he characterizes as Ermolao's desire to justify himself and to affirm his continuing awareness of the responsibilities incumbent upon the Venetian patriciate. Hence Fubini's further suggestion that *De officio legati* was written in this same spirit of self-justification *after* Ermolao's nomination to Aquileia.[62] An intriguing proposal that Fubini offers with due caution; but how then to reconcile any such justificatory strategy with Barbaro's insistence in that same treatise that the ambassador will under no circumstances act contrary to his instructions (cf. §§1, 13–15, 31), and never seek or accept any personal benefit from the host state (cf. §§38–9)?[63] That stress on blind obedience surely signals that the work cannot have been written after he became Patriarch of Aquileia in March 1491.

We revert, then, to a date of composition between April 1489 (when Ermolao returned to Venice from Milan) and May 1490 (when he departed for Rome), even though the *terminus ante quem* could conceivably be as late as February 1491, just before the Aquileia crisis arose in early March.[64] For Vittore Branca, the treatise marks a major shift in Barbaro's attitude to the Venetian patriciate's civic calling. If some two decades earlier Ermolao had been irresistibly drawn to the contemplative life of study at a remove from the Venetian *cursus*, his experience in Milan was in Branca's view transformative: through his social and political interactions there, Ermolao felt afresh the rich tradition of Venetian humanism that stressed continuity and fusion between contemplative study and civic life, not their antithetical separation.[65] Pausing for reflection in the restful months after his return from Milan, a period that Branca characterizes as one of the happiest and most serene of Ermolao's short life,[66] he gave voice in *De officio legati* to the belief that the fullest self-realization of the individual lay in the mindset and actions of 'civic wisdom':

> [T]he human space in which a man could realize himself was that of the state, not the family, a state whose sound and aristocratic oligarchical constitution and high ideal of liberty could truly offer conditions suited to the harmonious development of human dignity.[67]

By appeal to this 'sapienza civile',[68] this mediation between the *vita contemplativa* and the *vita activa*, the treatise leaves far behind it the rebellious instincts of *De coelibatu*: the young man who turned his back on public life in that early tract has at last found peace with the civic role to which he was born.

But Branca's position is open to challenge on at least two fronts. First, he prioritizes the treatise's role in the macro-scheme of Ermolao's shifting attitudes over time, but at a cost: a less clear-cut picture of Ermolao's development emerges from the textual evidence. In his letters from Milan, his devotion to his philological studies appears constant and all-important, and his contemplative energies seem overwhelmingly committed in that direction, as opposed to being channeled towards 'civic wisdom'; he also voices considerable irritation and frustration at the worries and encumbrances of his official life, and at how they distract him from his studies.[69] Secondly, it is striking that Ermolao chooses to mention so early in the work, in §§10–12, his quick thinking in amending the official Venetian message to Ludovico

Sforza over the Forlì incident. The impression conveyed is that he set about writing what was on his mind, and that he sought to put the record straight on the Forlì matter, at least as he saw it, before getting into his stride on the duties of the ambassador.[70] But the further implication then is that a certain anxiety impelled his writing – a scenario that sits uneasily with Branca's vision of him penning the work in a period of relaxed serenity. If Ermolao did indeed configure the treatise as a way of articulating his shifting attitude towards the civic *cursus*, the high-mindedness of that trajectory is in tension with what looks like the more immediate tactical utility of his undertaking; Branca's interpretation may capture an important dimension of the work, but not the totality of its meaning.

A still more radical response to Branca's position is to argue that the treatise offers no decisive shift in Ermolao's attitude to civic duty in the patriciate tradition, but amounts instead to yet another manifestation of the divided loyalties that had pulled him in different directions from his youth onwards – his devotion to his studies on the one hand, the call of the civic *cursus* on the other. On this approach, the dissimulation that he illustrates and performs within the work is powerfully suggestive: to what extent does Ermolao fashion himself as a committed servant of state even though his truer sense of mission lay elsewhere? The tumultuous events of his nomination as Patriarch of Aquileia in March 1491 now become all-important. In his letter to Antonio Calvo of 22 July 1491, Ermolao hails his downfall:

> O blessed disaster, which has restored literary studies to me, me to literary studies, or rather my very self to myself! O happy calamity, which has given me back my peace! O lucky storm, which has brought me freedom from care! O sweet bitterness, which has drawn me back into the most agreeable haven from my long rough-ride at sea, not to say from shipwreck![71]

In his extant letters dating from April 1491 onwards, Ermolao directs these and other expressions of joy to three correspondents, Ugolino Verino (the recipient of one letter), Antonio Calvo (five letters), and Jacopo Antiquario (four letters).[72] If we accept that such expressions are sufficiently consistent and widespread across the letters to reflect a true inner condition, how to read *De officio legati* in hindsight?

Short of positing his straightforward insincerity in casting himself as a devoted public official who offers a blueprint for fellow travellers, Ermolao arguably writes without genuine conviction, perhaps as a disinterested theorist in the art of diplomacy, or as if trying to persuade himself of an ideal that he struggles truly to internalize for himself.[73] Alternatively, or in addition, how easy is it to believe that Barbaro, that 'freeman of the timeless and cosmopolitan commonwealth of letters,'[74] could have truly and viscerally felt the blind, uncompromising patriotism that is the bedrock of his treatise? Perhaps the pragmatist in him found it prudent in that work to apply on the home front the dissimulation that fortifies the ambassador abroad; to gesture, that is, at a patriotic zeal that would satisfy the watchful eye of the Republic. After all, as Mattingly well puts it, '[t]he new omnicompetent, egotistic states were beginning to demand the external signs, at least, of this kind of total allegiance, and in making the expected gestures men were coming to feel the appropriate emotions.'[75] But if in *De officio legati* Ermolao donned a mask, projecting a self that was devoted first and foremost to the Republic, that very exercise of presenting a front to the world perhaps precipitated his final reckoning: the disguise could not be sustained, his own happiness was ultimately more important than meeting the societal and familial expectations that weighed on him in Venice, and something had to give.[76] He was pressured by Pope Innocent VIII, he insists,[77] to accept the Patriarchate of Aquileia early in 1491, a claim that (at least in his own mind) absolves Ermolao of disloyalty to Venice. But if his Venetian mask had already begun to slip, his nomination to Aquileia, fortuitous or not, was exquisite in its timing: release at last.

Whatever the (now irrecoverable) psychological truth of the matter, the ambiguity that had long characterized Ermolao's relationship to the patrician *cursus* at Venice is captured all too painfully in the chronological proximity of *De officio legati* on the one hand, his renunciation of his own duty as an ambassador at Rome on the other. And if in February/March 1491 his treatise was still a work in progress, its ending incomplete, that lack of finish is now readily explained: there was nothing more to say after he succumbed to the happy tragedy and the sad euphoria of release that accompanied his appointment to Aquileia.[78]

Notes

1 See Branca 1969: 24–5 n. 1.
2 On this mission, Figliuolo 1999: 17–19; for the oration that Barbaro delivered on August 5 1486, Branca 1943: 2.110–20 (*Orat*. IV) with 1.xcix-cvi and 2.7–8 *Ep*. LXXXII (August 4 1486, to Jan I Carondelet, Chancellor of Burgundy 1480–96 and secretary to Maximilian), and now Rothkamm 2016: 87–172.
3 Branca 1943: 2.11 *Ep*. LXXXVII; 1488 by the Julian calendar, but Ermolao assigns the letter to 1487 by Venetian fashion (cf. Vol. 1 Intro. p. 6 and n. 30). Francesco Barbaro had served in Milan in 1444, Zaccaria in 1476 and then 1485 (King 1986: 324, 326).

4   Branca 1969: 25 n. 1; 1973: 239 n. 6.
5   See Figliuolo 1999: 20–1.
6   See Robuschi 2013-14: 270 for Girolamo Donato and Bernardo Bembo.
7   Branca 1943: 2.14–15 *Ep.* XCI, to Marco Dandolo.
8   Branca 1943: 2.14 *Ep.* XC, to Girolamo Donato; on this letter and that to Dandolo (n. 7), Figliuolo 1999: 22 with Fubini 1996: 655–6. For Barbaro's work on Aristotle and Dioscorides see Vol. 1 Intro. pp. 22–4.
9   Labalme 1996: 334 n. 5.
10 See Intro. pp. 1–2; Vol. 1 Intro. pp. 1–4.
11 See p. 196 n. 32 on §30 *ultro* †*sese*†.
12 Rinaldi 2013-14.
13 See King 1986: 202–3 and esp. Biow 2002: 108–20.
14 See Branca 1969: 25–31; for Zanetelli, Branca 31 and n. 1 with M. Zorzi 1996: 382–3 and N. Zorzi 2008.
15 Branca 1969: 31–48, here at 47.
16 See Branca 1969: 21–3, observing (23 n. 1) that the copyists of several MSS themselves register doubt about the work's completeness.
17 See on this line Fubini 1996: 659.
18 See Branca 1969: 48–50; the MS in question is Vat. lat. 5392.
19 Doglio 1983, esp. 300–1, 309.
20 On these points, Figliuolo 1999: 87–8.
21 After the model of Biow 2002: 109–10.
22 Despite the broad claim made by Mattingly 1964: 87 ('... all four of the great secular states [Naples, Milan, Venice, and Florence] had [by the 1450s] established permanent embassies with each other'), 'permanence' and 'residentiality' remain problematic in terms of their exact definition and variable applicability to different states: see Fletcher 2015: 23–4 with Anderson 1993, esp. 5–15. For general overviews of the nature and duties of resident diplomacy see Fletcher 36–58 with Mattingly 94–102. But Beverley 1999: 189–226 argues that permanent resident embassies were hardly the Venetian norm in the fifteenth century, that special embassies were still frequently deployed, and that the complexity of Venetian diplomatic practice in this era in any case resists easy generalization. Venice was relatively slow to innovate through the adoption of resident missions in the second half of the fifteenth century, partly because the Republic 'was allied with relatively few states in these decades' (p. 218), but still more because, unlike the trend towards 'career diplomats' in other states, Venetian patrician ambassadors tended not to be specialists in diplomatic affairs; those ambassadors also served relatively short terms, partly because Venice was wary of the risks of disloyalty if its diplomats were too close to a host government, and partly also because long absence from domestic politics and from the *cursus* at home was often unappealing to the ambassadors themselves. Hence (p. 226) '[t]he republicanism of Venice led to a system of diplomacy which preferred short term *ad hoc* missions to longer term resident or permanent embassies.'

23 As emphatically signaled by the allusion to both 'republican' and 'princely' states in the opening sentence (Fletcher 2015: 39).
24 For the linkage of family and state see Vol. 1 Intro. pp. 12–13; for the imprint of Venice in general, of Zaccaria in particular, pp. 171–2.
25 Cf. Doglio 1983: 298: on the sixteenth-century Italian poet Torquato Tasso's reading in a Platonic key, Barbaro's ambassador is an idealization akin to the perfect Ciceronian orator.
26 See Biow 2002: 111 with Robuschi 2013–14: 282.
27 See Vol. 1 Intro. p. 22.
28 Further, Robuschi 2013–14: 285–6.
29 Cf. Doglio 1983: 309; Fedele 2017: 46.
30 Mattingly 1964: 25. Further on de Rosier, Mattingly 25–6, 30–40; Behrens 1936, esp. 618–19; Arabeyre 1990; Fubini 1996: 645–55; Gilli 2015; Fedele 2017, esp. 41–4, 104–6, 168–71, and 2018. For his *Ambaxiatorum brevilogus*, Hrabar 1906: 3–28 (with Barbaro's *De officio legati* on pp. 65–70 – the 1906 edition referred to above, p. 168 and n. 18).
31 For this universalist emphasis, Mattingly 1964: 42–3 with Fubini 1996: 650–2 and Fedele 2017: 104–6. It is hard not to detect 'a certain stubborn optimism' in such idealism (Mattingly 43, continuing with: 'Bernard [de] Rosier and his colleagues were surely not unaware that diplomacy... sought less than the noblest ends... Probably they knew that they were putting the ideal higher than the possible, in the hope that men might thus be pricked into climbing a little higher').
32 On this Ciceronian accent, McLaughlin 1995: 245 with Vol. 1 Intro. pp. 29, 32, 35.
33 Further, Fedele 2017: 45, 110 with Biow 2002: 103, 107.
34 See Fedele 2017: 83–118, with stress (pp. 109–10) on Barbaro's use of the traditional terminology to a new effect (the ambassador serving not the *respublica universa* but the interests of his own state).
35 On this point, Mattingly 1964: 94; Beverley 1999: 209; Fubini 1996: 654; Fletcher 2015: 38; Lazzarini 2015: 65; Fedele 2017: 45.
36 In overview, Mattingly 1964: 61–70 with Queller 1967: 76–84.
37 Cf. Fubini 1996: 655; the point directly undercuts Mattingly's broad claim (above, p. 180 n. 22) that Venice and Milan had a permanent arrangement in place already by the 1450s.
38 Mattingly 1964: 95.
39 Biow 2002: 107.
40 See §§10–12, 34–7, 43–4.
41 Perhaps an argument in itself for the completeness of the extant work (cf. on the question pp. 168, 175 with 207 n. 63).
42 Points well made by Biow 2002: 113–14.
43 Biow 2002: 114.
44 Biow 2002: 114.
45 On this 'movement... from the outside in,' Biow 2002: 110.
46 Biow 2002: 116.
47 On this latter episode, Biow 2002: 118.

48 Biow 2002: 116–17.
49 Further, Biow 2002: 119.
50 On this nexus of dissimulation, Biow 2002: 116.
51 Biow 2002: 119.
52 Further on what follows, Figliuolo 1999: 22–33 with Robuschi 2013–14: 265–7; Pellegrini 1999: 37–65; Hairston 2000, esp. 687–94.
53 See on Barbaro's delivery of the message Figliuolo 1999: 27, with p. 28 on the difficulty of gauging the extent to which, in his interview with Ludovico, he elaborated on or departed from the precise wording of the dispatches he had received from Venice.
54 On this outcome, Figliuolo 1999: 33 with Robuschi 2013–14: 267.
55 Cf. Robuschi 2013–14: 283: Barbaro drops the point because it amounts to 'un'esplicita critica al profilo tradizionalmente richiesto dal Senato,' and he duly reaffirms the ambassador's general lack of autonomy (§§13–14).
56 See Figliuolo 1999: 81.
57 See Figliuolo 1999: 77 (Barbaro's post-Milan appointments), 81.
58 See on this possibility Fubini 1996: 659–61 with Paschini 1957: 38, but cf. for critique Figliuolo 1999: 78 and n. 3.
59 See Vol. 1 Intro. pp. 1–2.
60 1996: 660–1.
61 Branca 1943: 2.76 *Ep.* CLIV.
62 Fubini 1996: 661.
63 Cf. already Branca 1969: 18–19.
64 Cf. Mattingly 1964: 94: 'While resident ambassador at Rome, Ermolao spent his leisure in polishing, in the best Ciceronian tradition, a little essay intended as advice to a friend entering the Venetian diplomatic service.'
65 Branca 1969: 24–5; cf. on the same line Bigi 1964: 97–8 and Doglio 1983: 299.
66 Branca 1969: 23.
67 Branca 1973: 232; cf. in Italian 1998: 80.
68 Branca 1998: 80.
69 On these points, Figliuolo 1999: 89 with King 1976: 41–2 and n. 89 = 2005 V 41–2 and n. 89 and 1986: 202–3 and n. 320.
70 See on this line Figliuolo 1999: 88–9.
71 Branca 1943: 2.70 *Ep.* CLII; see already on this letter Vol. 1 Intro. p. 3.
72 Verino: Branca 1943: 2.65–6 *Ep.* CXLVII; Calvo: Branca 2.64, 66–7, 69–72, 81–2 *Epp.* CXLV, CXLVIII, CLII, CLIII, CLVIII; Antiquario: Branca 2.64–5, 68, 72–7 *Epp.* CXLVI, CL, CLI, CLIV. See also Branca 1998: 178 for Barbaro's similarly positive tone in a letter to Giorgio Merula of May 24 1492 (not included in Branca 1943).
73 Cf. King 1986: 204: 'He adopts [in *De officio legati*] ... the perspectives of *unanimitas* ... characteristic of Venetian humanism, and has suspended his dissent from those values. But he has not wholly accepted them, in spite of his words: they are, perhaps, signs of his intention to conform to a patrician norm still inimical to him, or they may be, perhaps, insincere.'
74 Mattingly 1964: 102.

75 1964: 102.
76 See on this line Robuschi 2013–14: 275–6, also relating (p. 277) Ermolao's naiveté ('un' eccessiva ingenuità') in failing to appreciate the possible consequences of accepting the Aquileia nomination to the ingenuousness he showed in the Forlì affair.
77 See Vol. 1 Intro. pp. 1–2.
78 On the tragic aspect, King 1986: 205 and n. 330 with Labalme 1996: 341: 'This was Ermolao's tragedy: that he believed too fervently in the integration, in the ultimate harmony of his dedications to literature, to natural philosophy, to Christ, to the authority of the Church as represented by the Pope, to the Venetian Republic and to his own family's long tradition of service to the state. *He did not tolerate the tensions of contrary commitments . . . He did not acknowledge that heroes must make choices between competing goods*' (my emphasis).

De Officio Legati

1 Legati munus est mandata Reipublicae suae vel Principis obire diligenter et ex usu eius, a quo legati nomen habuit. **2** Huius officii praecepta quamquam tradi possunt, plus tamen nescio quid in hominis prudentia situm est, quam quod mandari scripto queat. Multa dabit occasio consilia, multa etiam temeritas, quae omnia comprehendi nullo modo possunt utique, sicuti neque praevideri quae futura sunt.

3 Legati autem aut ad internuntiandum, aut ad pacem cum hoste componendam, aut ad foedus societatemve iungendam aut conservandam mittuntur. Causae sunt et aliae, sed illustriores et magis insignes hae sunt. **4** Porro, quia et belli denunciandi ratio ac condendae pacis opus et ineundae societatis raro non intra paucos dies absolvitur, de uno tantum genere legatorum dicemus, qui tuendae societatis aut benevolentiae gratia ultro citroque mittuntur, brevissima unius manus syngrapha, uti curent eum, ad quem legati sunt, quam studiosissimum et amicissimum civibus suis aut principibus efficere continereque. **5** Non habet praefinitum aliquod tempus

On the Duty of the Ambassador

1 The duty of the ambassador is to carry out the instructions of his own State or Sovereign[1] scrupulously and to the advantage of the party from whom he received the title of ambassador.[2] **2** Although the principles of this office can be set down, something more nevertheless depends on a person's practical judgment than the directives that can be given by written prescription. Opportunity will offer many suggestions, as will boldness – all of which can in no way be covered for certain, just as it is also impossible to foresee what lies ahead.

3 Now ambassadors are sent either to relay messages between different sides or to arrange a peace with an enemy or to join or preserve a treaty or alliance. There are other reasons as well, but these are the more distinguished ones, and the more noteworthy. **4** Moreover, because the process of declaring war and the task of establishing a peace and of entering an alliance are rarely not completed within a few days, I shall speak only of the single class of ambassadors who, for the sake of protecting an alliance or terms of goodwill, are sent on both sides. Their general charge is very straightforward in its brevity,[3] namely to see to it that they render – and keep – the party to whom they are ambassadors as warmly attached and as well disposed as possible to the ambassadors' own citizens or leaders.[4] **5** An embassy of this sort does not

---

[1] With pointed allusion to diplomacy in general, spanning both 'republican' and 'princely' states: see Intro. p. 169 and n. 23.
[2] The language in the work's title and opening words (*legati munus/officium*) echoes that of medieval canon law and of secular as well as pontifical diplomacy. But Barbaro's trajectory remains strikingly 'modern' from the outset, esp. in his focus on the permanent resident ambassador and the envoy's duty to serve not the general interest of the *ius commune* but the self-interest of his home state: see Intro. pp. 169 and n. 22, 170–1.
[3] Lat. *unius manus* lit. 'of a single hand,' hence 'straightforward,' 'simple.' On these instructions, Queller 1966: 13–14: 'When it was deemed appropriate to appoint an ambassador the objectives of the mission and the means by which the ambassador should seek to achieve them were set forth in his commission. Elsewhere this document might have been called "instructions." It was intended primarily for the guidance of the envoy, not for presentation at the court to which he was dispatched.'
[4] On the rise of resident ambassadors see Intro. pp. 169 and n. 22, 171. For their role and responsibilities in general, Fletcher 2015, esp. 42–58; on the specifically Venetian ambassador (special as well as resident), Beverley 1999: 203–16.

huiusmodi legatio, sed apud nos anno fere concluditur, poscentibus legatis et interim valetudinem et interim familiarem rem suam, quaerentibus quibusdam pudorem ne amare videantur quod alii fastidiunt. **6** Pater Romae plus anno egit, Neapoli biennio, non quia nollet redire, sed quia successorem haud impetrare posset, quod apud eos principes auctoritate et gratia valere dicebatur.

7 Sed ad praecepta veniamus. Finis legato idem est qui et caeteris ad Rempublicam accedentibus; ut ea faciant, dicant, consulant et cogitent, quae ad optimum suae civitatis statum et retinendum et amplificandum pertinere posse iudicent. Hoc si spectaverit legatus et si huc totum se converterit, haud temere unquam labetur.

have any prescribed duration, but in our case it is usually completed in a year,[5] with ambassadors sometimes invoking their health and sometimes their own personal finances,[6] while some strive for self-respect, so as to avoid giving the impression that they adore what others disdain. **6** My father acted as ambassador in Rome for more than a year,[7] and in Naples for more than two years,[8] not because he was reluctant to return home, but because he was unable to secure a successor, as he had the reputation of commanding considerable prestige and influence among those rulers.[9]

7 But let's come to the points of instruction. The ambassador has the same object as all the rest who serve the Republic:[10] to do, say, advise, and reflect upon what, in their judgment, can be relevant to maintaining and augmenting the optimal condition of their own state. If the ambassador looks to this objective, and turns his complete attention in this direction, he will never go heedlessly wrong.

---

[5] Venetian embassies far from the Republic could be extended for longer, but they generally lasted no more than two years for reasons including (i) the Venetian need to recall able ambassadors for political service at home; (ii) the reluctance of ambassadors themselves to prolong their absence from the Venetian *cursus*; and (iii) through relatively short terms of service, less risk that an ambassador's loyalty to Venice might be compromised over time (further, Beverley 1999: 62–3, 223–5, and cf. Intro. p. 180 n. 22).

[6] For the considerable financial burden incumbent on ambassadors, Queller 1966: 14–28 with Beverley 1999: 145–52; hence the frequent phenomenon of seeking to avoid election in the first place, and/or to evade taking up an assignment (see Queller 1969: 229–32).

[7] 1480–1.

[8] 1471–3. In light of §5 'with ambassadors ... finances,' it is striking that in his dispatches back to Venice Zaccaria began in June 1472 to seek recall; when his efforts fell on deaf ears, he invoked the physical as well as financial strains of his prolonged stay that lasted down to September 1473 (see Robuschi 2013–14: 281–2 n. 69, with documentation) – hardships frequently voiced by other ambassadors (Fedele 2017: 134–5), albeit see on Zaccaria's purported wealth Beverley 1999: 150–1. Zaccaria's missions to Rome and Naples were but two (albeit major) of at least twelve ambassadorships that he held from 1459 onwards, for which King 1986: 325–6.

[9] Zaccaria's Neapolitan ambassadorship coincided with a period of relative accord between Naples and Venice (Bertelli 2001: 812–14). Zaccaria's introduction so early in the work has important implications for the self-serving aspects of Ermolao's agenda (see Intro. pp. 172, 173–4): his father's high standing at Naples, here underscored by the notably Ciceronian combination of *auctoritas* and *gratia* (e.g., *Brut.* 97, *Flac.* 14, *Leg.* 3.39, *Mur.* 59, etc.), sets an early benchmark for ambassadorial conduct as explicated in what follows – a programmatic stimulus for imitation (cf. Doglio 1983: 306), and even, we infer, a model *already* emulated by Ermolao.

[10] Barbaro here reflects (Fubini 2000, esp. 31, 46, with Fedele 2017: 83–4) the 'normalizing' effect that the rise of the resident ambassador in late fifteenth-century Italy had in reconfiguring the diplomat's function as an external equivalent to the state's internal political offices – albeit Barbaro's 'vague expression' here is 'indicative of the difficulty of the concept when transferred from actual reality to doctrine' (Fubini 31).

8 Hoc amplius praestare debent legati, ut mandata ediscant et exsequantur, nunquam committant, ut se prudentiores iudicent. **9** Incidunt quidem causae nonnunquam, ut mollienda quaedam et quasi repolienda sint mandatorum genera, quoties videlicet aliquid fortuito supervenit, quod Senatus, decreti sui tempore, nescierit. In quo tamen multiplex adhibenda prudentia est: quid enim, si tale sit, ut nescire Respublica voluerit, aut scire dissimulaverit, aut nihilominus, etiam si scisset, constitura idem fuisset?

10 Mediolani agebam legatus: iubet Senatus denunciem principibus ut arma ponant, quae in foroliviensem agrum movissent. In ipso temporis articulo nuncius victoriae, et quod peracta essent omnia, supervenit. **11** Consilium e re cepi, gratulatus sum: venisse me ad eos finxi rogaturum ut providerent ac prospicerent tranquillitati Italiae, utque non armis bellum sed iure decerni paterentur. Tantum mutare sensum nolui, verba coactus sum novae rei superventu: laudatus sum a Patribus. **12** Mediolanensem quoque principem, qui, quamquam haud sciret quid afferrem, coniectura tamen ceperat cur venissem, admiratum scio, quod, rebus iam compositis, omnino tale aliquid retulissem; tum conversum ad suos dixisse aliud esse Reipublicae, aliud tyranni legatum agere; quod et verum est.

8 In addition, ambassadors must ensure that they learn their instructions by heart and carry them out, and never allow it to be said that they consider themselves shrewder [than those instructions].¹¹ **9** Admittedly, reasons sometimes arise for having to soften and, so to speak, polish some kinds of instructions, evidently whenever some chance development comes along that the Senate knew nothing about when it made its own decision. In this circumstance, however, a layered form of discretion is to be applied;¹² for what if the matter is such that the Republic wanted not to know it, or pretended not to know it, or, even if it had known, would nevertheless have been set on making the same decision?

10 I was acting as ambassador in Milan:¹³ the Senate ordered me to call on their rulers to lay down the arms that they had deployed against the territory of Forlì. At the most critical moment a report of victory suddenly arrived, to the effect that it was all a *fait accompli*. **11** I formed a plan in keeping with the situation, and offered congratulations. I pretended that I had come to them to ask that they take steps to provide for a calm state of affairs in Italy, and to allow the war to be decided not by arms but by legal procedure. I was reluctant to change the sense of so important a message, but I was forced by the sudden new development to change my words; I was praised by the Fathers.¹⁴ **12** As for the Regent of Milan as well,¹⁵ although he had no knowledge of what message I was bearing, he had nevertheless inferred why I had come. I know that he admired the fact that, after matters had already been settled, I had delivered any such message at all; and that he then turned to his own advisers and said that it was one thing to be an ambassador of a Republic, another to act as the ambassador of a tyrant; and that is true.¹⁶

---

[11] A likely echo of the Venetian act of 13 July 1478 reprimanding ambassadors for going beyond or against their mandate (Queller 1966: 116 no. 87, with tr. on p. 45).

[12] Reversion to the theme of practical *prudentia* (cf. §2, and see Intro. pp. 169, 173).

[13] Beyond illustrating the capacity for initiative highlighted in §§2 and 9, Barbaro's version in §§10–12 of what transpired in Milan in April–May 1488 affirms his credentials as a worthy successor to Zaccaria (cf. n. 9), himself ambassador to Milan in 1476 and 1485. But given his molding of the facts to his own advantage, this passage also reveals much about Ermolao's wider personal agenda in this work: see Intro. pp. 174–6.

[14] For the Fathers of the Senate (cf. §§14, 31) in the patrilineal economy of the work, see Intro. p. 172.

[15] Ludovico Sforza (1452–1508) ruled as Regent for his young nephew, Gian Galeazzo Sforza, from 1480–94; after Gian Galeazzo died in mysterious circumstances in 1494, Ludovico became Duke of Milan.

[16] The first of many touches that render the work 'in large measure an encomium to Venetian ambassadorial work' (Biow 2002: 112); see Intro. pp. 171-2, 173.

13 Legatus, nisi affectus omnes et opiniones de Republica statim digressus urbe posuerit, exuerit, induxerit, nec sibi, nec Reipublicae suae consulet. Extrema dementia, et propius sceleri quam dementiae peccatum, non dico praeterire aut in contrarium ire, sed aut malignius aut negligentius obire mandata curiae, quia ipsi aliter aut urbe proficiscentes sentiremus aut modo sentiamus. **14** Nunquam satis dictum est quod in aliqua praeceptione caput est. Legatus, nisi se multo inferiorem et iudicio et usu rerum quam Patres existimet, protinus legati fine decidit. **15** Solet hoc plerumque rationibus publicis officere, sed privatis antevertere, praesertim in nostra civitate, ubi nihil severius expenditur, quam aut factum aut dictum legati: nulla parte delinquitur minus, nulla parte delinquitur odiosius. Commisereri solet in magistratibus et urbanis et peregrinis quandoque, in legato nunquam.

16 Curare debent legati ut gratia et auctoritate valeant apud eos ad quos mittuntur: id autem omnis quidem virtutis, sed praecipue bonitatis et integritatis opinione consequentur, et, ut pater mecum de officio legati disserens diligenter expressit, liberae cuiusdam et ingeniosae simplicitatis; nam servilis et rustica non auctoritatem, sed contemptum efficit. **17** Ingenium quoque negotiosum et callidum sollicitudinis et ostentationis plus habet quam utilitatis; et vitatur ab omnibus fraus publica, quo nihil adversius his, qui ad gratiam et benevolentiam conciliandam profecti sunt. **18** Nonnulli,

13 The ambassador, unless he lays aside, throws off, and erases all his feelings and opinions about the Republic immediately upon departure from the city, will act in the interests neither of himself nor of his own Republic. It is the utmost folly – and a mistake that is closer to a crime than to folly – I do not say to ignore or go directly against the government's instructions,[17] but to attend to them either rather grudgingly or carelessly, because we ourselves either held a different view when we left the city or began to do so only recently.[18] **14** What is of prime importance in any issuance of instruction is never stated enough: the ambassador, unless he believes himself to be far inferior to the Senate in both judgment and experience of affairs, automatically lapses from an ambassador's purpose. **15** This generally tends to impede public business, but instead to give priority to private interests, especially in our city, where nothing is more seriously weighed than what an ambassador either does or says:[19] on no front is misbehaviour less concerning, on no front more heinous. Compassion is customarily sometimes shown in the case of officers of state both at home and abroad, but never in the ambassador's case.[20]

16 Ambassadors must take steps to acquire a weight of influence and prestige[21] in the eyes of those to whom they are sent. This they will achieve through a reputation for all possible moral excellence, certainly, but especially for honest conduct and soundness of character, and, as my father put it in his thorough discussions with me about the ambassador's duty,[22] for a certain guilelessness of independent-minded intelligence; for guilelessness that is slavish and unsophisticated gives rise not to a weighty prestige but to scorn. **17** Likewise, a temperament that is busy with clever scheming has a greater degree of watchful anxiety and showiness than of practical usefulness; and deceit in public is shunned by all, as there is nothing more counterproductive to those who have set out to gain influence and goodwill. **18** A number of

---

[17] See §8 and n. 11 above.
[18] This charter of blind obedience has important implications for the ethical status of the ambassador, whose obligation to loyalty offers one way of resolving the dilemma of how to serve a utilitarian political end that potentially compromises him morally; for discussion in direct relation to Barbaro's tract, Hampton 2009: 46–7.
[19] '[W]eighed' not least through the final report (*relazione*) which, from the thirteenth century onwards, the returning ambassador was obliged to present before the Venetian Senate – a synthesis of such range and depth that the Venetian *relazione* evolved into a unique cultural form (see Queller 1967: 142–8 and 1973 with de Vivo 2011), albeit one vulnerable to cultural bias and Veneto-centric myopia (see Dursteler 2011, esp. 234–6).
[20] Perhaps with wry reflection on the fallout of the Forlì incident: see n. 13 above and Intro. pp. 174–6.
[21] Cf. §6 *auctoritate et gratia* and n. 9 above.
[22] In terms of patrilineal succession within the work (cf. n. 14 above), Zaccaria's discourse *de officio legati* is as if continued in Ermolao's *De officio legati*: see Intro. p. 172.

propter nimiam calliditatis et astutiae famam, legationes suas nunquam non infeliciter concluserunt; contra alii, mediocri ingenio viri, nunquam non feliciter.

19 Legatum esse te non exploratorem memineris; alioquin rescire quid agatur facilius est his, qui negligere videntur, quam qui dissimulare curam talem haud possunt. **20** Lustrare debent omnia non furtim, non latrunculorum more, sed interim simpliciter et aperte, interim per gradus et quodam quasi sensu, nec strepitu sed silentio. Multa sunt quae non continenter, sed membratim et vellicatim interrogare oporteat; quaedam ita ut aut negligenter aut invitus audire videaris. **21** Interpellabat et interrumpebat aliquando Zacharias pater etiam narrantem quae scire cupiebat, ne sollicitudinem suam detegeret et ut maior fides sibi haberetur si ultro sciscitari vellet.

22 Quidam, ut industrios et satagentes se civibus suis ostentent, non modo scrupulatim quid geratur, perminima quaeque perscribunt, sed quo nihil est scelestius, confingunt aliqua atque comminiscuntur, aut quae non fecerint fecisse aut quae non responderint respondisse praedicando, multo saepius quod fecerint aut responderint tacendo. **23** Haec semper vanitas est, plerumque perfidia, utique si ex huiusmodi mendacio aliquid incommodi

envoys, because of an excessive reputation for clever cunning, have invariably brought their ambassadorships to an end without success; by contrast, others of a measured disposition[23] have always ended theirs successfully.

19 Remember that you are an ambassador, not a spy;[24] besides, to find out what is happening is easier for those who seem not to be paying attention than for those who cannot disguise such a concern. **20** They must survey everything not with stealth, and not like bandits, but sometimes straightforwardly and openly, sometimes in stages and with a certain feeling of the way, as it were, and not noisily but in silence. There are many questions that should be asked not in one unbroken sequence, but severally and piecemeal; and some asked in such a way that you seem to listen either carelessly or with reluctance. **21** My father Zaccaria would occasionally break in on and interrupt someone even when he was saying what Zaccaria wanted to know; he did this to avoid laying bare his own anxiety to know, and so that he might be held in greater trust if he wanted to ask questions on his own initiative.[25]

22 Some, to show themselves to their own citizens to be diligent and with their hands full, not only compile a record of every tiniest detail in scrupulous coverage of their activities, but – there is nothing more villainous than this – they fabricate and invent some items, by declaring either that they did what they have not done or that they gave replies that they have not given, but far more often by keeping silent about what they *have* done or about the replies they *have* given.[26] **23** This is always folly, and on many occasions treachery, especially if the Republic suffers any amount of harm from a falsehood of this

---

[23] I.e., neither too calculating nor excessively naïve, in keeping with the Aristotelian mean (Robuschi 2013–14: 282 with Biow 2002: 111; for the mean, *De coelibatu* 3.6.15–16).

[24] But cf. Queller 1966: 53: 'By the fifteenth century ... the ambassador was regarded, at least in one of his functions, as a lawful spy, though this was not so true in an age of only intermittent and *ad hoc* diplomacy like the thirteenth and fourteenth centuries.'

[25] Zaccaria is again (cf. §6 and n. 9) pictured to totemic effect, his skillful dissimulation (cf. §19 *dissimulare*) matching that of Venice itself in §9 *dissimulaverit*, the only other occurrence of the verb in the work (further, Intro. pp. 173–4); for Ermolao's conspicuous silence on other methods of information gathering (esp. buying or trading for it), Mattingly 1964: 99–100.

[26] The different sets of prefixes neatly demarcate the faults of an over-scrupulous thoroughness on the one hand (*per-* ... *per-*), unscrupulous contrivance on the other (*con-* ... *com-*); the latter's artificiality is then nicely conveyed through the highly contrived verbal/syntactical balance, contrast, and repetition in *aut quae non fecerint ... tacendo*. The extremes Barbaro faults here are presumably egregious even by the normative Venetian standard of copious dispatches (Mattingly 1964: 96); even though his father, Zaccaria, was criticized for the excessive length and detail of his dispatches when ambassador in Naples in 1471–3 (Robuschi 2013–14: 283 n. 76), he never – the thought goes – approached the excesses that Ermolao deplores.

Respublica patiatur. Adde quod damnosa Reipublicae mendacia raro unquam occludi diu possint. **24** Cum primum laesam se senserit, reclamat offensa civitas, auctor deposcitur, inquiruntur circumspiciuntur miscentur omnia, donec veritas elucescat; tum poenitentia mendacii cooritur, tum tanta mentis aestuatio, ut nihil habeat praeter se quod accuset, unicum videatur perfugium ut mendacia mendaciis operire tentet, atque ita funditus etiam maiori iactura pereat.

25 Multum placet principibus et populis in legato dexteritas, et cum dexteritate coniuncta gravitas, et cum gravitate lenitas et humanitas, praesertim in veneto; qui, sive quod separatis legibus utuntur, victu quoque atque vestitu, sive quod severius in sontes animadvertunt, sive quod gentis antiquitate libertatis et imperii diuturnitate gloriantur, ab inimicis et invidis superbi, a reverentioribus tetrici cognominantur. **26** Proinde summo studio adniti decet, ut veterem nominis invidiam, non disputatione aut sermone tantum, sed opere atque facto coarguamus, ita tamen, ut publicae dignitatis nunquam obliti esse videamur. **27** Nec probo nec admodum damno senatoris

sort. Besides, falsehoods that are damaging to the Republic can rarely ever be long prevented from getting out. **24** As soon as it recognizes that its interests have been damaged, the displeased Republic cries out in protest, the perpetrator is demanded for punishment, and everything is looked into, closely examined, and put together until the truth becomes clear; then regret for the falsehood arises, and then a turmoil of mind so great that it has nothing to blame apart from itself, the only means of escape seems to be for it to try to cover lies with lies, and in this way complete ruin follows with even greater loss.[27]

25 Adroitness is much approved in an ambassador by rulers and peoples, and a seriousness of demeanor combined with that adroitness; and along with that seriousness, a gentle kindness of instinct,[28] especially in a Venetian.[29] Whether because they observe a distinct set of laws, and also a distinct way of life and dress, or because they punish the guilty more severely, or because they pride themselves on the antiquity of their people's independence and the longevity of their imperial power,[30] the Venetians are called arrogant by their enemies and the envious, stern by the more respectful. **26** Accordingly, it is fitting that we strive with the utmost effort to show that this longstanding resentment at our name is wrong, not only by debate or dialogue,[31] but also by action and deed – in such a way, however, that we never seem to have forgotten the dignity of our official standing. **27** I neither commend nor

---

[27] Barbaro's control of active and passive verb forms is itself telling in §24: after the hurtful discovery and outcry (*senserit, reclamat*), the Republic's investigative machinery goes through its impersonal motions in a sequence of passive verbs (*deposcitur ... miscentur*) until the truth becomes clear in intransitive *elucescat*. But the wayward ambassador only worsens his situation by actively taking matters into his own hands (*mendacia ... tentet*) until disaster inevitably follows (*pereat*); in terms of the ambassadorial theatricality and performative masking portrayed in the wider work (see Intro. pp. 172-4), the maverick legate is in every sense a bad actor.

[28] Given that eloquence was the hallmark of the fifteenth-century ambassador, and the term *orator* synonymous with him (see Mallett 1994, esp. 235-6, with Beverley 1999: 9), the qualities here sought in him predictably match the affective qualities inculcated by Roman rhetorical training (see esp. Cic. *De or.* 2.212 with Hampton 2009: 19).

[29] On Barbaro's indirect praise of Venice in §§25-8, as if he writes with the deceptive simplicity of the dissimulating ambassador, see Intro. pp. 171-2, 173.

[30] A suitably patriotic summation of the myth of Venice, which was by legend founded on 25 March 421 CE, as if heir to the greatness of classical Rome (see Vol. 1 Intro. p. 10). Dress: for the traditional patrician toga see Newton 1988: 9-12 with Robuschi 2013-14: 273-4. Sumptuary laws regulated the finery of dress to project a uniformity of appearance and status (see Allerston 2000: 373 with de Vivo 2016: 131); for such robes were 'a statement of republicanism, patriotism, puritanism, and communality' while also emphasizing 'the exclusivity of the patriciate as a closed, hereditary body' (Finlay 1980: 24).

[31] For such deployment of the written/spoken word in second-generation Venetian humanism to defend the Republic's values and reputation, see Vol. 1 Intro. pp. 10-11.

cuiusdam nostri dictum: 'Notent,' inquit, 'in veneto superbiam, modo, ut ait Flaccus, meritis partam esse fateantur; superbum non esse venetum, sed si foret, multa tamen esse, quamobrem fieri posset; immensas opes, innumerabilia et belli et pacis decora, imperium terra et mari praepotens ut uni tantum romano cedat, diuturnum ut nulli. **28** Expende aliarum civitatum mores, finge haec in illis esse, quae in nobis sunt: quid, obsecro, aut illi facerent aut quid nos facimus, quod illi non facerent?' Sed haec alterius loci sunt.

29 Brevissima esse debet cum Principibus oratio; occupati enim sunt, et sibi parci gaudent, et hanc in legatis magni faciunt. Rarus quoque aditus ad eos laudari solet fere quod et privatam existimationem et publicam dignitatem conservat. **30** Faciles se omnibus praebere legati debent, populares esse et vulgares ultro †sese†[32] cum omnibus atque semper non debent. Hic mos veneto peculiaris est et maxime apud omnes commendatur: nunquam, nisi aut rogatus aut missus, in regiam proficiscitur, caeteris propemodum assiduis; quod quidem eos et principi molestos reddit.

31 Ante omnia cavere debet legatus ne pro se neu pro aliquo aut de aliqua re cum Principe unquam loquatur, nisi Patres mandaverint. **32** Magnam personam legati sustinent, adeo ut, cum controversia inciderit, Respublica de finibus per advocatos non per legatos sua iura defendi velit; tantum abest ut

---

[32] *ultro sese* Br., but *sese* is hard to construe in relation to *esse* ... *debent*.

completely condemn what was said by a certain senator of ours: 'Let them censure arrogance in the Venetian,' he said, 'provided that they acknowledge, as Horace said,[33] that it was acquired deservedly; that the Venetian is not arrogant, but that if he were, there are nevertheless many reasons why he could become so: vast wealth, countless glories in both war and peace, and an empire superior enough in power on land and sea that it yields to the Roman empire alone, in terms of longevity to none.[34] **28** Weigh the character of other states, and imagine that the qualities that are in us are in them: what, I beg you, would they be doing, or what do we do that they would *not* be doing?' But this is for another context.

29 Speech with Sovereigns ought to be very brief:[35] they are busy and are pleased to be spared, and they value this brevity of speech highly in ambassadors. Likewise, infrequent approaches to them tend to win approval, mainly because they leave unhurt both the ambassador's personal reputation and his public standing. **30** Ambassadors should present themselves as accommodating to all, but they must not show popular sympathies and a spontaneous ordinariness of manner with everyone and in all situations. The following practice is a special characteristic of the Venetian ambassador, and wins very great approval from all: he never goes into the palace unless either asked for or sent, whereas the other ambassadors do so almost constantly – which in fact makes them annoying to the sovereign ruler as well.

31 Above all, the ambassador must take care never to speak with a Sovereign on his own behalf, nor for anyone or about any matter, unless the Fathers[36] have commanded it. **32** Ambassadors take on an important role, so much so that when a dispute arises, the Republic wants its rights about territorial boundaries to be defended through the agency of lawyers, not ambassadors; so far from the truth is it that an ambassador is permitted to

---

[33] *Carm.* 3.30.14–15, with *superbia* there surely of justifiable pride, not arrogance (Nisbet and Rudd 2004: 376–7 ad loc.) – a distinction now reapplied to Venetian *superbia*.
[34] The Venice lauded here as yielding only to Rome may moderate the strongly pro-Venetian stance taken in Marcantonio Sabellico's recently published (May 1487, Livy his guiding model) *Historiae rerum venetarum ab urbe condita libri XXXIII*: see Fubini 1996: 657–8 with (on Sabellico) Fabbri 1992, esp. 389–95.
[35] The proximity to Roman rhetorical training is again striking (cf. n. 28 above): for brevity as one of the three virtues of narration (with plausibility and clarity), Lausberg 1998: 140–2 §§294–7. The brevity Barbaro enjoins characterizes this very work: see Intro. p. 173.
[36] See n. 14 above.

apud Principem intercedere legato liceat. **33** Philippus, Mediolanensium Dux tertius, cum legatorum preces nec respuere auderet nec admittere saepenumero fas esset, edicto sanxit ut, quaecumque legatorum interventu quilibet impetravisset, anno tantum valerent, abolita et irrita post tempus illud essent. **34** Ticini agebam legatus: confluebat ad me fere omnis litteratorum ordo, ut ad novos assolet, non tam honorandi, credo, quam explorandi gratia qualis essem. Frequentabat aedes meas et Ludovicus princeps: percrebuit fama bono me apud eum loco esse. **35** Tum qui ad praelectiones subscripti erant et qui iam praelegebant commendari per me Principi volebant. **36** Negavi privatim commendaturum esse quemquam: excusavi leges mandati, quibus, indicta gravi multa, omne patrocinii genus legatis interdicitur. Pollicitus sum tamen in communi laudaturum me litteratos omnes Principi, quod et feci. **37** Ita Princeps, laudari a me suos audiens, probavit candorem, sed cum nemini beneficium rogassem, modestiam.

intervene before a Sovereign.[37] **33** Philip, the third Duke of Milan,[38] since he was not prepared to reject out of hand the entreaties of ambassadors and it was improper to grant them access again and again, ordained by proclamation that whatever anyone had succeeded in obtaining through the intervention of ambassadors should hold good only for a year, and be null and void after that period.[39] **34** I was acting as ambassador at Pavia:[40] almost the entire order of the learned flocked to me, as it usually does to new arrivals, not so much for the purpose of showing respect, I believe, as of discovering what sort of person I was. The Regent Ludovico, too, often used to visit my residence; the rumor became widespread that I was in good standing with him.[41] **35** At that, those who were candidates for lecturing posts and those who were already lecturers[42] wanted to be recommended to the Regent through me. **36** I said that I was not going to recommend anyone in a private capacity; I cited in excuse the terms of my commission, according to which every kind of advocacy is prohibited for ambassadors, and a harsh penalty imposed upon it. I nevertheless promised that I would offer the Regent general praise of all those men of learning, and this I did. **37** In this way the Regent, when he heard me praising his own subjects, commended my sincerity, but also my restraint, since I had requested a favour for no one.[43]

---

[37] With a likely autobiographical resonance: in October 1488 Barbaro was instructed by the Venetian Senate to raise before Ludovico Sforza the matter of a contested frontier between the Venetian and Milanese territories in the Lombardy region. Ludovico deferred the matter, but Barbaro was ordered by Venice to press it further. Irked at this persistence, Ludovico saw no reason to reconsider a frontier that had been determined just years earlier, in the time of the War of Ferrara (1482-4; on the whole matter, Figliuolo 1999: 51-2, 59-60). In light of these developments, Barbaro's assertion that such disputes warrant lawyerly, not ambassadorial, intervention implies a veiled critique of the Venetian government (see Rinaldi 2013-14: 294 n. 97 with Figliuolo 83).

[38] Filippo Maria Visconti (1392-1447), Duke from 1412 until his death.

[39] I.e., if an ambassador's appointment was conventionally for one year (so Venice; cf. §5), concessions won in that year expired with his departure from office or soon thereafter.

[40] The Sforza court transferred to Pavia (ancient Ticinum, situated on the river Ticinus, a tributary of the Po) on 24 May 1488, returning to Milan on 11 July (Figliuolo 1999: 36, 44); the resident ambassadors followed.

[41] This rumour is well illustrated by the correspondence of Jacopo Trotti, the Duke of Ferrara's ambassador in Milan (Figliuolo 1999: 39-40); but for Ludovico's own tactical machinations in being seen to be on close terms with the Venetian ambassador, and for the mixed effects of that strategy, see Rinaldi 2013-14: 295 n. 100.

[42] The precise sense here is hard to determine: for connective *et*, Biow 2002: 113 n. 29: '... lettered men, who had attended my lectures at my house and were now lecturing themselves'; but for disjunctive *et*, and for *praelectio/praelegere* of university posts, Rinaldi 2013-14: 296: '... coloro che si erano candidati alle cattedre universitarie e quelli che già tenevano cattedra ...'

[43] See further on this episode Intro. pp. 172-3.

38 Laus haec veneto propria tribuitur, obaeratum esse nolle Principi, nihil ab eo petere, cum eo nunquam nisi de Republica disserere. **39** Nullius apud te vel auctoritas vel preces vel amicitia tantum possit propter quem ab instituti huius tenore decedendum putes. Testimonium castitatis et innocentiae nostrae Principes ipsi reddant; quis hanc ausit convellere?

40 Plerumque Principes de successoribus et decessoribus interrogant, et multae possunt esse causae quamobrem interrogent: nunquam committendum est, non dico ut cupide, sed oratione suspiciosa locuti esse videantur; nunquam decet, nunquam tempus est ut quis de cive inter alienos male respondeat. **41** Finge illum, de quo nunc quis te interrogat, interrogatum de te prius fuisse; nonne ille ingratus et malus vir, si tu honorifice loquaris de quo prius ipse male praedicasset? aut tu, si ille? **42** Et, hercule, successores decessoribus, et contra his illi, detrahunt invicemque carpunt mores et acta damnant; magnus et erectus ille fuerit, qui communem et promiscuam labem vitare poterit. **43** Deum testor, de nulla re prius percuntari me coeperunt, qui obviam mihi Mediolanum eunti prodiere, quam de vita et moribus et existimatione decessoris; nec male sentiebant illi de homine, sed qualis et quam prudens essem ipse periculum faciebant. **44** Verum illis ex sententia

38 To the Venetian ambassador is ascribed this praiseworthy quality as his own special characteristic – that he does not want to be indebted to a Sovereign, he seeks nothing from him, and he never discusses anything with him unless it is about the Republic.[44] **39** No one's prestige or entreaties or friendship should be so influential in your eyes that, on his account, you think that you should deviate from this consistent practice. Let the Sovereigns themselves bear witness to our blameless purity of conduct: who would have a mind to undermine such conduct?

40 Sovereigns often pose questions about successors and predecessors, and there can be many reasons why they do so. Ambassadors must never make the mistake of appearing to have spoken, I do not say with partiality, but in terms liable to arouse mistrust. It is never fitting, and never timely, for anyone to reply negatively about a fellow-citizen among foreigners.[45] **41** Imagine that the person whom someone is now asking you about had previously been asked about you: would that man not be unappreciative and unkind if you speak respectfully of him when he had previously spoken negatively of you? Or the other way around? **42** And heaven knows![46] Successors disparage their predecessors, and, conversely, the latter the former; they mutually criticize their characters and harshly judge their exploits. Noble and upright will be the man who can avoid this universal and indiscriminate stain. **43** God be my witness, those who came out to meet me when I went to Milan began questioning me, before any other matter, about the life, character, and reputation of my predecessor;[47] nor did they think ill of the person, but they were testing to see what sort of character I was myself, and how discreet.[48] **44** But it did not turn out to their liking; for I answered in

---

[44] The underlying principle is perhaps derived from ancient legal precedent (Rinaldi 2013-14: 296 n. 101, citing Cic. *Leg.* 3.9.5 *rei suae ergo ne quis legatus esto* 'Let no one be an ambassador for the sake of his own affairs'; tr. Zetzel 2017: 162). For Venetian legislation to curb ambassadorial conflicts of interest in the pursuit of private business, and for the temptations resulting from the financial burdens of being an ambassador, Queller 1966: 39–43, esp. 42 ('The stinginess of the Venetian government is really appalling').

[45] Seamless continuity from one ambassador to the next is all, as the office itself transcends any individual office-holder (cf. §46 'Grant … person': always the state before the individual).

[46] On the tonal shift introduced late in the work by this and other interjections (cf. §§48, 53), Biow 2002: 110 n. 24: this shift coincides with Barbaro's movement 'from the topic of duty to play, from the state to the family, from business (*negotium*) to leisure (*otium*).'

[47] Sebastiano Badoer, for whom King 1986: 317–18 with Cracco 1963. Other resident ambassadors were apparently among those who received Barbaro when he arrived at Milan on March 23 1488 (see Figliuolo 1999: 20 and n. 7, 82–3 and n. 15).

[48] For *qualis … ipse* cf. §34 *explorandi gratia qualis essem*. Through these anecdotes the text *itself* embodies the tact and dissimulation it describes; further in this direction, Biow 2002: 118–19 with Intro. pp. 172–4.

non cessit: ita enim respondi, ut eos suae sciscitationis et curiositatis poeniteret. Eos vero, qui me ad cavillandum et retaxandum invitabant, non solum refrigeravi hoc meo pudore sed etiam retudi penitus atque fregi. **45** Nunquam tantum aut bonae conscientiae aut simultatis in quoquam sit, ut successorem aut decessorem parum amice nominet: ubique et inter non suos nolo; si parcus, si flagitiosus, si inimicus infensusque Reipublicae, volo parcas. **46** Da hoc patriae, non homini; plus hoc veneto venetus debet, quam caeteri, cum haec dignitas imperii non alia tam ratione coaluerit, creverit, duraverit, quam civium inter se concordia: hanc qui odit, non eos odit, quos odit, sed ipsam plane Rempublicam odit.

47 Legatorum quoque crimina vel lege vel extraordinaria[49] vindicentur; non dico si quaestum aliquem exerceant (nam et hoc lege prohibetur, non quasi crimen sed quasi et dignitati et utilitati publicae contrarium); illud dico, si adulterium, si vim, si stuprum attulerint. **48** Et, hercule, par est ut, qui Reipublicae causa absunt, quemadmodum si honores petunt, ita si flagitiose vivant, abesse non dicantur. **49** Confundit iudicia sua vulgus et ex unius aut bene aut male facto metitur omnes; nullo discrimine aut respectu, non unius, qui peccat, sed totius gentis vitium esse praedicant. Et contra praesumptionem

---

[49] Sc. *poena*.

such a way that they regretted their own meddlesome line of questioning. In fact, through this reserve on my part I not only chilled the enthusiasm of those who were inciting me to offer petty criticisms and rebukes, but I also completely quelled them and crushed their spirit. **45** Never should anyone have so good a conscience[50] or such a degree of animosity that he speaks of his successor or predecessor in an unfriendly way. I am against it in all circumstances, including among non-citizens; and if he was ungenerous,[51] if scandalous in his conduct, if ill disposed and bitterly hostile to the Republic, I want you to show forbearance. **46** Grant as much to the fatherland, not the person; a Venetian more than all others owes this to a Venetian, since this greatness of our imperial power has taken root, grown, and endured for no other reason than the harmonious unity of its citizens:[52] one who hates this unity hates not just those he hates, but he evidently hates the Republic itself.

47 The crimes committed by ambassadors should also be punished either by the law or by special penalty. I do not mean if they pursue some way of making money (for this too is forbidden by law, not as a crime but as detrimental to the State's standing and interests);[53] I mean this – if they have engaged in adultery, violence, or sexual violation.[54] **48** And heaven knows![55] In the case of those who are abroad for the sake of the Republic, it is reasonable that, just as if they stand as candidates for public office, so if they live scandalous lives they are not regarded as being abroad.[56] **49** The general public blurs its own judgments, appraising all ambassadors by the actions, good or bad, of a single individual; without making distinctions or paying close regard, they proclaim it to be the fault not of the individual transgressor, but of an entire class of person. And indeed, to counter this presupposition

---

[50] I.e., to be so sure of one's own virtue as to venture criticism of another.
[51] I.e., one's predecessor, presumably ungenerous in his remarks about his successor.
[52] For this Venetian ideal of *unanimitas* see Vol. 1 Intro. pp. 10, 11, 22.
[53] In 1396 the Venetian Senate barred ambassadors and other officials abroad from engaging in business, whether directly themselves or through others, in their place of posting (Queller 1966: 42; cf. n. 44 above).
[54] Rinaldi 2013–14: 298 n. 103 refers to the scandalous case (sufficiently sensational and recent enough to be in Barbaro's mind here?) of the Venetian resident ambassador to Rome, Antonio Loredan (1446–1514), for whom Dal Borgo 2005: in late 1486 Loredan was investigated on charges of sodomy, as was his secretary, Bernardo Teatini; beyond sodomy, the case concerned the leaking of confidential information. Loredan was consigned early in 1487 to ten years of exile from Venice, only to be allowed to return in 1492; he went on to serve as ambassador on at least three further occasions. See further on the saga Canosa 1991: 126–8 with Beverley 1999: 51, 56–7; on the larger danger in the diplomatic community of state secrets being compromised through such incidents, Labalme 1984: 235.
[55] See n. 46 above.
[56] I.e., they will be liable to prosecution in Venice even when absent from there.

hanc severitate nova Reipublicae opus est, non ut saeviat, sed ut existimationem suam asserat, nec ut illum vel illum puniat, sed ut se redimat infamia. **50** Iam qui tantum et voluptati et cupiditatibus suis indulsit, ut civitati maculam inureret, postulare haud debet ut sibi parcat Respublica, qui Reipublicae nequaquam pepercit. **51** Ergo legatorum et magistratuum abstinentes esse debent et manus et oculi, perinde atque sacerdotum quoties ad aram stant et in divinis operantur; meminerint nulla re tantum de Republica benemereri posse benemerita de se prius, quam sanctitate morum et innocentia. **52** Quanquam usque adeo perversi quidam sunt et praepostere sibi consulunt, ut quum procul absunt ab auribus et oculis popularibus semoti sunt, praedam morum faciant. **53** Obscaena cogitatio ambire legationes et provinciam, ut occasionem impune delinquendi, hoc est sine testibus et arbitris, inveniant, luxuriosius et licentius vivant, cibo potuque mergantur, exoletos ac concubinas (proh scelus, proh monstrum, inusitato poenarum genere luendum) circumferant.

54 Unde tritum illud, nec uni notum Italiae, proverbium: 'Nunquam sine vase continentiae legatorum et comites et familia respondeant.' **55** Magnus

the Republic needs an unusual strictness of standard, not so as to act harshly but to protect its own reputation, and not to punish so-and-so or such-and-such but to save itself from disrepute. **50** Further,[57] a miscreant who has devoted himself to his own pleasure and desires to the extent of branding the state with disgrace must not demand that the Republic show him consideration, given that *he* by no means showed the Republic consideration. **51** Therefore, both the hands and the eyes of ambassadors and high officers of state must show restraint,[58] just as those of priests do whenever they stand at the altar and perform their religious rites. They should remember that through no quality can they deserve well of the Republic (which has first deserved well of them) as much as through their blameless purity of character. **52** However, certain individuals are so misguided and take thought for themselves in so wrongheaded a fashion that when they are abroad [and] far removed from the eyes and earshot of the public, they make plunder of virtuous habits. **53** Repulsive is their design of seeking to gain appointment to embassies and a provincial command in order to find an opportunity for transgressing with impunity (that is, without witnesses and onlookers);[59] to live with an excessively indulgent wantonness; to drown in food and drink; and (What villainy! What horror, to be atoned for by an extraordinary class of punishments!)[60] to parade catamites and concubines.

    54 Hence that well-worn saying, and known not just to Italy alone: 'Never without a store of containment may the ambassadors' retinue and household present themselves for duty.'[61] **55** Great is the number of those who, on the

---

[57] Cf. *OLD iam* 8a.
[58] A likely echo (Rinaldi 2013–14: 298 n. 104) of Cic. *Off.* 1.144: 'Pericles and the poet Sophocles were colleagues as praetor and had met about some shared duty. By chance, a beautiful boy went past and Sophocles said, "Pericles, what a lovely boy!" His answer was a good one: "It is seemly for a praetor, Sophocles, to abstain not only from touching, but even from looking (*decet non solum* manus *sed etiam* oculos abstinentes *habere*). But if Sophocles had said the same thing at an athletes' trial, it would not have been just to criticize him; so great is the significance of place and time' (tr. Griffin and Atkins 1991: 56).
[59] After the hallowed heights of §51 (the ambassador as priest-like), the deviant ambassador descends to depths of depravity; the envoy is meant *to be seen* to act with integrity (cf. §§16, 39), not to avoid accountability before 'witnesses and onlookers'.
[60] See n. 46 above.
[61] Fig. *vas vasis* n. (lit. 'vessel,' 'utensil') after *OLD vas*² 1a; and for *respondeo* so construed, *OLD* 6a. But it is also possible to interpret *continentiae* as dat. w. *respondeant*, to the effect of: 'Never without a store of containment may their retinue and household accord with the ambassadors' [own] containment' (cf. *OLD respondeo* 12a). Parallels for the saying remain elusive, but cf. the Jesuit Pierre Favre (1506–46) in his *Memoriale*: *Placeat Domino nostro dare mihi gratiam ut ego possim quotidie crescere ut fiam capacius vas continentius et mundius* (Faber 1914: 537 §88: 'May it please our Lord to grant me favour so that I can grow everyday to become a more capacious vessel, more measured and pure'). But in a MS of the *Memoriale* discovered in 2018 in the Historical Archives of the Pontifical Gregorian

eorum numerus est, qui ad legatum eo ipso die, quo renunciatus est, quasi nomina daturi confluant. Legendi sunt qui mansuetudine, modestia, probitate caeteris anteire videantur, honesta quidem specie, sed virili et ab omni suspicione remotissima, omnino ut formam virorum quam mores accusare posse malis. **56** Delicta familiae, quanquam ferri nulla debeant, duo tamen eiusmodi sunt ad quae si legati conniveant, plus ipsi peccant, quam qui deliquerunt: contumelia et impudicitia, sive domi sive foris. Alterum discordiae, alterum infamiae seminarium est.

57 In legati domo pax sit: aliter legatus ab omnibus contemnitur et ludibrio habetur, praecipue vero suis. Quia porro nihil est tam inimicum bonis moribus quam otium et desidia, optandum est atque adeo summopere quaerendum, ut alicuius omnes artis studio voluptateque ducantur, vel pingendi vel scribendi vel canendi, calculis etiam ludendi.

very day when the ambassador is announced, flock to him as if to enlist. Those to be chosen are the sort who appear to surpass all the rest in their gentleness, their unassuming manner, and their uprightness, with a handsome complexion, to be sure, but one that is manly and very far removed from all hint of suspicion – to the effect, in general, that you prefer to be able to find fault with the men's appearance, not their character. **56** As for misdeeds within the household, although none at all should be tolerated, two are nevertheless of the sort that, if ambassadors turn a blind eye to them, they themselves act more incorrectly than those who have committed the wrong: insulting behaviour and sexual impurity, whether at home or away from it. The one is a seedbed for dissension, the other for notoriety.[62]

57 The ambassador's residence should be peaceful: otherwise, the ambassador is looked down on and viewed as a laughing-stock by all, but especially by his own people. Because, moreover, nothing is as harmful to good character as leisurely slackness, there has to be the desire – and in fact the quest has to be made with the utmost effort – for them all to be drawn by the pursuit and pleasure of some skilled activity, whether painting or writing or singing, or even playing board games.[63]

University in Rome (shelf-number FC 1042), the reading is *ut fiam capacius vas continentiae et mundius* ('to become a more capacious vessel of restraint, and more pure': https://gate.unigre.it/mediawiki/index.php/Page:FC_1042.djvu/136). Given this parallel, emendation to *vade* (*OLD vas*[1] *vadis* m.: 'a surety') is unnecessary, but cf. Fletcher 2010: 531 and n. 67, apparently reading *vase* but understanding 'surety': 'Let no-one make accords without surety of the continence of the ambassadors, their retinue and household.'

[62] A recent case is supplied by Bernardo Teatini, Antonio Loredan's secretary, convicted of sodomy in 1487 (see n. 54 above).

[63] In moving from the ambassador's public role to his inner sanctum, from duty to leisure, and from his official persona to his 'real' self as reflected in his wholesome household, the work appears complete in its thematic arc. But if the work is yet considered unfinished (so, e.g., Fedele 2017: 44 ['sans doute inachevé']; Branca 1969: 21–3 is more circumspect), that incompleteness has important ramifications for the date of composition: see Intro. pp. 174–9.

Bibliography

Allerston, Patricia. 'Clothing and Early Modern Venetian Society,' *Continuity and Change* 15, no. 3 (2000): 367-90.

Anderson, Matthew S. *The Rise of Modern Diplomacy, 1450-1919*. Abingdon and New York: Routledge, 1993.

Arabeyre, Patrick. 'Un prélat languedocien au milieu du XVe siècle: Bernard de Rosier, archevêque de Toulouse (1400-1475),' *Journal des Savants* 3-4 (1990): 291-326.

Azzolini, Monica. *The Duke and the Stars: Astrology and Politics in Renaissance Milan*. Cambridge, MA, and London: Harvard University Press, 2013.

Azzolini, Monica, and Adam Mosley. 'Astronomy and Astrology,' in *Brill's Encyclopedia of the Neo-Latin World: Macropaedia*, edited by Philip Ford, Jan Bloemendal, and Charles Fantazzi, 667-77. Leiden and Boston: Brill, 2014.

Bakker, Egbert J. *The Meaning of Meat and the Structure of the* Odyssey. Cambridge: Cambridge University Press, 2013.

Bakola, Emmanuela. 'A Missed Joke in Aristophanes' *Wasps* 1265-1274,' *Classical Quarterly* 55, no. 2 (2005): 609-13.

Balme, David M., ed. and tr. *Aristotle*, History of Animals, *Books VII-X*. Loeb Classical Library 439. Cambridge, MA, and London: Harvard University Press, 1991.

Beagon, Mary. *The Elder Pliny on the Human Animal:* Natural History, *Book 7*. Oxford: Oxford University Press, 2005.

Behrens, Betty. 'Treatises on the Ambassador Written in the Fifteenth and Early Sixteenth Centuries,' *English Historical Review* 51, no. 204 (1936): 616-27.

Belfiore, Elizabeth. 'Wine and Catharsis of the Emotions in Plato's *Laws*,' *Classical Quarterly* 36, no. 2 (1986): 421-37.

Bertelli, Sergio. 'Diplomazia italiana quattrocentesca,' *Archivio Storico Italiano* 159, no. 4 (2001): 797-827.

Beverley, Tessa. 'Venetian Ambassadors 1454-94: An Italian Elite.' PhD diss., University of Warwick, 1999.

Bigi, Emilio. 'Barbaro, Ermolao,' *Dizionario biografico degli Italiani* 6 (1964): 95-9.

Biow, Douglas. *Doctors, Ambassadors, Secretaries: Humanism and Professions in Renaissance Italy*. Chicago and London: The University of Chicago Press, 2002.

Branca, Vittore, ed. *Ermolao Barbaro: Epistolae, orationes et carmina*. 2 vols. Florence: Bibliopolis, 1943.

Branca, Vittore. 'Un trattato inedito di Ermolao Barbaro: il *De coelibatu libri*,' in *Bibliothèque d'Humanisme et Renaissance* 14, no. 1 (1952): 83-98.

Branca, Vittore, ed. *Ermolao Barbaro*, De coelibatu, De officio legati. Florence: Leo S. Olschki, 1969.

Branca, Vittore. 'Ermolao Barbaro and late Quattrocento Venetian Humanism,' in *Renaissance Venice*, edited by John R. Hale, 218–43. London: Faber and Faber, 1973.

Branca, Vittore. *La sapienza civile. Studi sull'Umanesimo a Venezia*. Florence: Leo S. Olschki, 1998.

Briscoe, John, ed. *Valerius Maximus*, Facta et dicta memorabilia, *Book 8*. Untersuchungen zur antiken Literatur und Geschichte 141. Berlin and Boston: Walter de Gruyter, 2019.

Bury, Robert G., ed. and tr. *Plato:* Timaeus, Critias, Cleitophon, Menexenus, Epistles. Loeb Classical Library 234. Cambridge, MA, and London: Harvard University Press, 1929.

Canosa, Romano. *Storia di una grande paura: la sodomia a Firenze e a Venezia nel Quattrocento*. Milan: Feltrinelli, 1991.

Carey, Hilary M. 'Astrology in the Middle Ages,' *History Compass* 8, no. 8 (2010): 888–902.

Conte, Gian Biagio. 'Proems in the Middle,' in *Beginnings in Classical Literature*, edited by Francis M. Dunn and Thomas Cole, 147–60. Yale Classical Studies 29. Cambridge: Cambridge University Press, 1992.

Cracco, Giorgio. 'Badoer, Sebastiano,' *Dizionario biografico degli Italiani* 5 (1963): 124–6.

Dąbrowa, Edward. 'The Origin of the *Templum Gentis Flaviae*: A Hypothesis,' *Memoirs of the American Academy in Rome* 41 (1996): 153–61.

Dal Borgo, Michela. 'Loredan, Antonio,' *Dizionario biografico degli Italiani* 65 (2005): 747–9.

de Melo, Wolfgang, ed. and tr. *Plautus:* Amphitryon, The Comedy of Asses, The Pot of Gold, The Two Bacchises, The Captives. Loeb Classical Library 60. Cambridge, MA, and London: Harvard University Press, 2011.

de Vivo, Filippo. 'How to Read Venetian *Relazioni*,' *Renaissance and Reformation* 34, nos 1–2 (2011): 25–59.

de Vivo, Filippo. 'Walking in Sixteenth-Century Venice: Mobilizing the Early Modern City,' *I Tatti Studies in the Italian Renaissance* 19, no. 1 (2016): 115–41.

Dillon, John. *The Heirs of Plato: A Study of the Old Academy (347–274 B.C.)*. Oxford: Oxford University Press, 2003.

Dixon, Suzanne. 'The Marriage Alliance in the Roman Elite,' *Journal of Family History* 10, no. 4 (1985): 353–78.

Doglio, Maria L. 'Ambasciatore e principe: L'*institutio legati* di Ermolao Barbaro,' in *Miscellanea di studi in onore di Vittore Branca III: Umanesimo e Rinascimento a Firenze e Venezia*, 297–310. Florence: Leo S. Olschki, 1983.

Dunkle, Roger. *Gladiators: Violence and Spectacle in Ancient Rome*. Abingdon and New York: Routledge, 2013.

Dursteler, Eric R. 'Describing or Distorting the "Turk"? The *Relazioni* of the Venetian Ambassadors in Constantinople as Historical Source,' *Acta Histriae* 19, nos 1–2 (2011): 231–48.
Emilsson, Eyjólfur K. 'On Happiness and Time,' in *The Quest for the Good Life: Ancient Philosophers on Happiness*, edited by Øyvind Rabbås et al., 222–40. Oxford: Oxford University Press, 2015.
Enenkel, Karl A. E. 'Petrarch's Constructions of the Sacred Solitary Place in *De vita solitaria* and Other Writings,' in *Solitudo: Spaces, Places, and Times of Solitude in Late Medieval and Early Modern Cultures*, edited by Karl A. E. Enenkel and Christine Göttler, 31–80. Leiden and Boston: Brill, 2018.
Engels, Donald. 'The Length of Eratosthenes' Stade,' *American Journal of Philology* 106, no. 3 (1985): 298–311.
Everson, Stephen. 'The *De somno* and Aristotle's Explanation of Sleep,' *Classical Quarterly* 57, no. 2 (2007): 502–20.
Fabbri, Renata. 'La storiografia veneziana del Quattrocento,' in *La storiografia umanistica*, edited by Anita Di Stefano et al., 2 vols: 1.347–98. Messina: Sicania, 1992.
Faber, Petrus. *Epistolae, memoriale et processus, ex autographis aut archetypis potissimum deprompta*. Madrid: G. Lopez del Horno, 1914.
Farwell, Paul. 'Aristotle and the Complete Life,' *History of Philosophy Quarterly* 12, no. 3 (1995): 247–63.
Fedele, Dante. *Naissance de la diplomatie moderne (XIIIe-XVIIe siècles): l'ambassadeur au croisement du droit, de l'éthique et de la politique*. Studien zur Geschichte des Völkerrechts 36. Baden-Baden: Nomos Verlag, 2017.
Fedele, Dante. 2018. 'Rosier, Bernard de (1400–75),' in *The Encyclopedia of Diplomacy*, edited by Gordon Martel, 1654–8. Hoboken, NJ: Wiley Blackwell, 2018.
Figliuolo, Bruno. *Il diplomatico e il trattatista: Ermolao Barbaro ambasciatore della Serenissima e il* De officio legati. Naples: Guida, 1999.
Finlay, Robert. *Politics in Renaissance Venice*. London: Ernest Benn, 1980.
Flensted-Jensen, Pernille. 'Thrace from Axios to Strymon,' in *An Inventory of Archaic and Classical Poleis*, edited by Mogens H. Hansen and Thomas H. Nielsen, 810–53. Oxford: Oxford University Press, 2004.
Fletcher, Catherine. '"Furnished with Gentlemen": The Ambassador's House in Sixteenth-Century Italy,' *Renaissance Studies* 24, no. 4 (2010): 518–35.
Fletcher, Catherine. *Diplomacy in Renaissance Rome: The Rise of the Resident Ambassador*. Cambridge: Cambridge University Press, 2015.
Fraenkel, Eduard. *Horace*. Oxford: Oxford University Press, 1957.
Fubini, Riccardo. 'L'ambasciatore nel XV secolo: due trattati e una biografia (Bernard de Rosier, Ermolao Barbaro, Vespasiano da Bisticci),' *Mélanges de l'École française de Rome: Moyen-Age* 108, no. 2 (1996): 645–65.
Fubini, Riccardo. 'Diplomacy and Government in the Italian City-States of the Fifteenth Century (Florence and Venice),' in *Politics and Diplomacy in Early Modern Italy: The Structure of Diplomatic Practice, 1450–1800*, edited by Daniela Frigo, 25–48. Cambridge: Cambridge University Press, 2000.

Gill, Christopher. *The Structured Self in Hellenistic and Roman Thought.* Cambridge: Cambridge University Press, 2006.
Gilli, Patrick. 'Bernard de Rosier et les débuts de la réflexion théorique sur les missions d'ambassade,' in *De l'ambassadeur: les écrits relatifs à l'ambassadeur et à l'art de négocier du Moyen Âge au début du XIXe siècle,* edited by Stefano Andretta et al., 187–97. Rome: École Française de Rome, 2015.
Gnesotto, Attilio, ed. *Francesci Barbari* De re uxoria liber in partes duas, *Atti e Memorie della R. Accademia di Scienze, Lettere ed Arti in Padova* n.s. 32 (1915–16): 6–105.
Graham, Daniel W., ed. and tr. *The Texts of Early Greek Philosophy.* 2 vols. Cambridge: Cambridge University Press, 2010.
Granger, Herbert. 'The Theologian Pherecydes of Syros and the Early Days of Natural Philosophy,' *Harvard Studies in Classical Philology* 103 (2007): 135–63.
Graver, Margaret. *Cicero on the Emotions:* Tusculan Disputations *3 and 4.* Chicago and London: The University of Chicago Press, 2002.
Grendler, Paul F. *Schooling in Renaissance Italy: Literacy and Learning, 1300–1600.* Baltimore and London: The Johns Hopkins University Press, 1989.
Grendler, Paul F. 'Education in the Republic of Venice,' in *A Companion to Venetian History, 1400–1797,* edited by Eric R. Dursteler, 675–99. Leiden and Boston: Brill, 2013.
Griffin, Miriam T., and E. Margaret Atkins, eds. *Cicero,* On Duties. Cambridge Texts in the History of Political Thought. Cambridge: Cambridge University Press, 1991.
Griggio, Claudio. 'Francesco Barbaro, *De re uxoria.* II: Nota sul testo, testo critico, traduzione, commento,' in *Francesco Barbaro,* De re uxoria, edited by Claudio Griggio and Chiara Kravina, 151–343. Florence: Leo S. Olschki, 2021.
Gummere, Richard M., ed. and tr. *Seneca,* Epistles *1–65.* Loeb Classical Library 75. Cambridge, MA, and London: Harvard University Press, 1917.
Guthrie, William K. C. *A History of Greek Philosophy, I: The Earlier Presocratics and the Pythagoreans.* Cambridge: Cambridge University Press, 1962.
Guthrie, William K. C. *A History of Greek Philosophy, II: The Presocratic Tradition from Parmenides to Democritus.* Cambridge: Cambridge University Press, 1965.
Hairston, Julia L. 'Skirting the Issue: Machiavelli's Caterina Sforza,' *Renaissance Quarterly* 53, no. 3 (2000): 687–712.
Hammond, Martin, tr. *Josephus:* The Jewish War. Oxford World's Classics. Oxford: Oxford University Press, 2017. With an Introduction and Notes by Martin Goodman.
Hammond, Martin, tr. *Artemidorus:* The Interpretation of Dreams. Oxford World's Classics. Oxford: Oxford University Press, 2020. With an Introduction and Notes by Peter Thonemann.
Hampton, Timothy. *Fictions of Embassy: Literature and Diplomacy in Early Modern Europe.* Ithaca and London: Cornell University Press, 2009.

Hankins, James. 'Socrates in the Italian Renaissance,' in *A Companion to Socrates*, edited by Sara Ahbel-Rappe and Rachana Kamtekar, 337–52. Malden, MA, and Oxford: Blackwell Publishing, 2006.

Harris-McCoy, Daniel E. *Artemidorus' Oneirocritica: Text, Translation, and Commentary*. Oxford: Oxford University Press, 2012.

Hett, Walter S., ed. and tr. *Aristotle, On the Soul, Parva naturalia, On Breath*. 2nd edn. Loeb Classical Library 288. Cambridge, MA, and London: Harvard University Press, 1957.

Hicks, Andrew. 'Martianus Capella and the Liberal Arts,' in *The Oxford Handbook of Medieval Latin Literature*, edited by Ralph J. Hexter and David Townsend, 307–34. Oxford: Oxford University Press, 2012.

Hieatt, A. Kent, and Maristella Lorch, tr. *Lorenzo Valla, On Pleasure: De voluptate*. New York: Abaris Books, 1977.

Hrabar, Vladimir E., ed. *De legatis et legationibus tractatus varii. Bernardi de Rosergio* Ambaxiatorum brevilogus; *Hermolai Barbari* De officio legati; *Martini Garrati Laudensis* De legatis maxime principum; *ex aliis excerpta qui eadem de re usque ad annum MDCXXV scripserunt*. Tartu (Dorpat): C. Mattiesen, 1906.

Hulskamp, Maithe A. A. 'Sleep and Dreams in Ancient Medical Diagnosis and Prognosis.' PhD diss., University of Newcastle, 2008.

Hussey, Edward. 'Aristotle and Mathematics,' in *Science and Mathematics in Ancient Greek Culture*, edited by Christopher J. Tuplin and Tracey E. Rihll, 217–29. Oxford: Oxford University Press, 2002.

Ideler, Julius L., ed. *Physici et medici Graeci minores, I*. Berlin: Georg Reimer, 1841.

Inwood, Brad. 'Stoic Ethics,' in *The Cambridge History of Hellenistic Philosophy*, edited by Keimpe Algra et al., 675–705. Cambridge: Cambridge University Press, 1999.

Inwood, Brad. *Seneca: Selected Philosophical Letters*. Oxford: Oxford University Press, 2007.

Jocelyn, H. D., ed. *The Tragedies of Ennius*. Cambridge Classical Texts and Commentaries 10. Cambridge: Cambridge University Press, 1969.

Johnson, David M. 'Aristippus at the Crossroads: The Politics of Pleasure in Xenophon's *Memorabilia*,' *Polis: The Journal for Ancient Greek and Roman Political Thought* 26, no. 2 (2009): 204–22.

Johnston, Ian, ed. *Galen, On the Constitution of the Art of Medicine, The Art of Medicine, A Method of Medicine to Glaucon*. Loeb Classical Library 523. Cambridge, MA, and London: Harvard University Press, 2016.

Jouanna, Jacques. *Greek Medicine from Hippocrates to Galen: Selected Papers*. Leiden and Boston: Brill, 2012.

Kallendorf, Craig W., ed. and tr. *Humanist Educational Treatises*. The I Tatti Renaissance Library 5. Cambridge, MA, and London: Harvard University Press, 2002.

Karvounis, Christos. 'Political Career,' in *The Oxford Handbook of Demosthenes*, edited by Gunther Martin, 321–35. Oxford: Oxford University Press, 2019.

King, John E., ed. and tr. *Cicero: Tusculan Disputations*. 2nd edn. Loeb Classical Library 141. Cambridge, MA, and London: Harvard University Press, 1945.
King, Margaret L. 'Caldiera and the Barbaros on Marriage and the Family: Humanist Reflections of Venetian Realities,' *Journal of Medieval and Renaissance Studies* 6 (1976): 19–50.
King, Margaret L. *Venetian Humanism in an Age of Patrician Dominance*. Princeton, NJ: Princeton University Press, 1986.
King, Margaret L. *Humanism, Venice, and Women: Essays on the Italian Renaissance*. Aldershot: Ashgate, 2005.
King, Margaret L., ed. and tr. *Francesco Barbaro, The Wealth of Wives: A Fifteenth-Century Marriage Manual*. The Other Voice in Early Modern Europe: The Toronto Series, 42. Toronto: Iter Academic Press; Tempe, AZ: Arizona Center for Medieval and Renaissance Studies, 2015.
Kristeller, Paul O. *Renaissance Thought: The Classic, Scholastic, and Humanistic Strains*. New York: Harper and Brothers, 1961.
Labalme, Patricia H. 'Sodomy and Venetian Justice in the Renaissance,' *Tijdschrift voor Rechtsgeschiedenis/Legal History Review* 52, no. 3 (1984): 217–54.
Labalme, Patricia H. 'Secular and Sacred Heroes: Ermolao Barbaro on Worldly Honor,' in *Una famiglia veneziana nella storia: I Barbaro. Atti del Convegno di studi in occasione del quinto centenario della morte dell'umanista Ermolao, Venezia, 4–6 Novembre 1993*, edited by Michela Marangoni and Manlio Pastore Stocchi, 331–44. Venice: Istituto Veneto di Scienze, Lettere ed Arti, 1996.
Lausberg, Heinrich. *Handbook of Literary Rhetoric: A Foundation for Literary Study*, edited by David E. Orton and R. Dean Anderson. Leiden, Boston, and Cologne: Brill, 1998.
Lazzarini, Isabella. *Communication and Conflict: Italian Diplomacy in the Early Renaissance, 1350–1520*. Oxford: Oxford University Press, 2015.
Lear, Gabriel R. 'Aristotle on Happiness and Long Life,' in *The Quest for the Good Life: Ancient Philosophers on Happiness*, edited by Øyvind Rabbås et al., 127–45. Oxford: Oxford University Press, 2015.
Lindberg, David C., and Katherine H. Tachau. 'The Science of Light and Color, Seeing and Knowing,' in *The Cambridge History of Science. Volume 2: Medieval Science*, edited by David C. Lindberg and Michael H. Shank, 485–511. Cambridge: Cambridge University Press, 2013.
Lorch, Maristella, ed. *Lorenzo Valla, De Vero Falsoque Bono*. Bari: Adriatica Editrice, 1970.
Maas, Martha. '*Polychordia* and the Fourth-Century Greek Lyre,' *Journal of Musicology* 10, no. 1 (1992): 74–88.
Mackie, Christopher J. 'The Earliest Jason. What's in a Name?,' *Greece & Rome* 48, no. 1 (2001): 1–17.
Mallett, Michael. 'Ambassadors and Their Audiences in Renaissance Italy,' *Renaissance Studies* 8, no. 3 (1994): 229–43.
Mattingly, Garrett. *Renaissance Diplomacy*. Baltimore: Penguin Books, 1964. First published in 1955 (London: Jonathan Cape).

McKechnie, Paul. 'Diodorus Siculus and Hephaestion's Pyre,' *Classical Quarterly* 45, no. 2 (1995): 418–32.

McLaughlin, Martin L. *Literary Imitation in the Italian Renaissance: The Theory and Practice of Literary Imitation in Italy from Dante to Bembo*. Oxford: Oxford University Press, 1995.

McManamon, John M. *Pierpaolo Vergerio the Elder: The Humanist as Orator*. Medieval and Renaissance Texts and Studies 163. Tempe, AZ: Medieval and Renaissance Texts and Studies, 1996.

Mensch, Pamela, tr., with James Miller, ed. *Diogenes Laertius*: Lives of the Eminent Philosophers. Oxford: Oxford University Press, 2018.

Moles, John. 'Livy's Preface,' *Proceedings of the Cambridge Philological Society* 39 (1993): 141–68.

Montuori, Mario. 'The Oracle Given to Chaerephon on the Wisdom of Socrates. An Invention by Plato,' *Kernos* 3 (1990): 251–9.

Moore, Bryan L. *Ecological Literature and the Critique of Anthropocentrism*. Cham, CH: Palgrave Macmillan, 2017.

Mueller, Ian. 'Mathematics and the Divine in Plato,' in *Mathematics and the Divine: A Historical Study*, edited by Teun Koetsier and Luc Bergmans, 99–121. Amsterdam: Elsevier, 2005.

Newton, Stella M. *The Dress of the Venetians 1495–1525*. Aldershot: Scolar Press, 1988.

Nisbet, Robin G. M., and Margaret Hubbard. *A Commentary on Horace*, Odes, Book II. Oxford: Oxford University Press, 1978.

Nisbet, Robin G. M., and Niall Rudd. *A Commentary on Horace*, Odes, Book III. Oxford: Oxford University Press, 2004.

Palmer, Richard. 'Physicians and Surgeons in Sixteenth-Century Venice,' *Medical History* 23, no. 4 (1979): 451–60.

Paschini, Pio. *Tre illustri prelati del Rinascimento: Ermolao Barbaro, Adriano Castellesi, Giovanni Grimani*. Rome: Facultas Theologica Pontificii Athenaei Lateranensis, 1957.

Pearson, Andrea G. 'Nuns, Images, and the Ideals of Women's Monasticism: Two Paintings from the Cistercian Convent of Flines,' *Renaissance Quarterly* 54, no. 4 pt. 2 (2001): 1356–1402.

Pease, Arthur S., ed. *M. Tulli Ciceronis* De natura deorum *libri tres*. 2 vols. Cambridge, MA: Harvard University Press, 1955–8.

Pellegrini, Marco. *Congiure di Romagna: Lorenzo de' Medici e il duplice tirannicidio a Forlì e a Faenza nel 1488*. Florence: Leo S. Olschki, 1999.

Pinkster, Harm. *The Oxford Latin Syntax. Volume I: The Simple Clause*. Oxford: Oxford University Press, 2015.

Pinkster, Harm. *The Oxford Latin Syntax. Volume II: The Complex Sentence and Discourse*. Oxford: Oxford University Press, 2021.

Pozzi, Giovanni, ed. *Hermolai Barbari Castigationes Plinianae et in Pomponium Melam*. 4 vols. Thesaurus Mundi 11, 14, 18, 19. Padua: Antenore, 1973–9.

Queller, Donald E. *Early Venetian Legislation on Ambassadors*. Geneva: Librairie Droz, 1966.

Queller, Donald E. *The Office of Ambassador in the Middle Ages*. Princeton, NJ: Princeton University Press, 1967.

Queller, Donald E. 'The Civic Irresponsibility of the Venetian Nobility,' in *Economy, Society, and Government in Medieval Italy: Essays in Memory of Robert L. Reynolds*, edited by David Herlihy et al., 223–35. Kent, OH: The Kent State University Press, 1969.

Queller, Donald E. 'The Development of Ambassadorial *Relazioni*,' in *Renaissance Venice*, edited by John R. Hale, 174–96. London: Faber and Faber, 1973.

Rackham, Harris, ed. and tr. *Cicero*, De finibus bonorum et malorum. Loeb Classical Library 40. 2nd edn. Cambridge, MA, and London: Harvard University Press, 1931.

Rackham, Harris, ed. and tr. *Pliny*, Natural History, *Volume III: Books 8–11*. Loeb Classical Library 353. 2nd edn. Cambridge, MA, and London: Harvard University Press, 1983.

Reeds, Karen M. 'Renaissance Humanism and Botany,' *Annals of Science* 33, no. 6 (1976): 519–42.

Rinaldi, Michele, tr. 'Appendice: Ermolao Barbaro, *De officio legati*,' in Luigi Robuschi, 'Il *De officio legati* di Ermolao Barbaro ed il pensiero politico nella Venezia di fine '400,' *Atti dell'Istituto Veneto di scienze, lettere ed arti: Classe di scienze morali, lettere ed arti* 172 (2013–14): 289–300.

Robuschi, Luigi. 'Il *De officio legati* di Ermolao Barbaro ed il pensiero politico nella Venezia di fine '400,' *Atti dell'Istituto Veneto di scienze, lettere ed arti: Classe di scienze morali, lettere ed arti* 172 (2013–14): 257–301.

Roskam, Geert. *On the Path to Virtue: The Stoic Doctrine of Moral Progress and its Reception in (Middle-)Platonism*. Leuven: Leuven University Press, 2005.

Ross, James B. 'Venetian Schools and Teachers Fourteenth to Early Sixteenth Century: A Survey and a Study of Giovanni Battista Egnazio,' *Renaissance Quarterly* 29 (1976): 521–66.

Ross, W. David, ed. *Aristotelis fragmenta selecta*. Oxford: Oxford University Press, 1955.

Ross, W. David, tr. *Aristotle:* The Nicomachean Ethics. The World's Classics. Oxford and New York: Oxford University Press, 1980. Revised by John L. Akrill and James O. Urmson.

Rothkamm, Jan, ed. *Three Speeches by Venetian Ambassadors 1433–1486: Francesco Barbaro, Ad Sigismundum Caesarem; Bernardo Giustinian, Ad universitatem Parisiensem; Ermolao Barbaro, Ad Federicum imperatorem/Ad Maximilianum regem Romanorum*. Wiesbaden: Harrassowitz Verlag, 2016.

Russell, Donald A., ed. and tr. *Quintilian:* The Orator's Education, *Books 1–2*. Loeb Classical Library 124. Cambridge, MA, and London: Harvard University Press, 2001.

Sandbach, F. H., ed. and tr. *Plutarch*, Moralia. *Volume XV: Fragments*. Loeb Classical Library 429. Cambridge, MA, and London: Harvard University Press, 1969.

Scaglione, Aldo. 'Review of Vittore Branca, ed. *Ermolao Barbaro*, De coelibatu, De officio legati. (Florence: Leo S. Olschki, 1969),' *Modern Philology* 69, no. 4 (1972): 338–9.

Schiefsky, Mark J. *Hippocrates*, On Ancient Medicine. Leiden and Boston: Brill, 2005.

Schroeder, Lea A. 'Replenishment and Maintenance of the Human Body (*Timaeus* 77a-81e),' *Apeiron* 54, no. 3 (2021): 317–46.

Sherratt, Susan. 'Feasting in Homeric Epic,' *Hesperia* 73, no. 2 (2004): 301–37.

Simkins, Ronald A. 'The Bible and Anthropocentrism: Putting Humans in Their Place,' *Dialectical Anthropology* 38, no. 4 (2014): 397–413.

Sinclair, Thomas A., tr. *Aristotle: The Politics*. Revised and re-presented by Trevor J. Saunders. London: Penguin Books, 1981.

Spencer, W. George, ed. and tr. *Celsus*, On Medicine: *Books I-IV*. Loeb Classical Library 292. Cambridge, MA, and London: Harvard University Press, 1935.

Strocchia, Sharon T. *Nuns and Nunneries in Renaissance Florence*. Baltimore: The Johns Hopkins University Press, 2009.

Swift Riginos, Alice. *Platonica: The Anecdotes Concerning the Life and Writings of Plato*. Leiden: Brill, 1976.

Takács, Sarolta A. *Vestal Virgins, Sibyls, and Matrons: Women in Roman Religion*. Austin, TX: University of Texas Press, 2008.

Taylor, Alfred E. *A Commentary on Plato's* Timaeus. Oxford: Oxford University Press, 1928.

Tredennick, Hugh, ed. and tr. *Aristotle*, Metaphysics, *Books I-IX*. Loeb Classical Library 271. Cambridge, MA, and London: Harvard University Press, 1933.

Tsouna, Voula. 'Epicureanism and Hedonism,' in *The Cambridge History of Moral Philosophy*, edited by Sacha Golob and Jens Timmermann, 57–74. Cambridge: Cambridge University Press, 2017.

Van der Eijk, Philip, and Maithe Hulskamp. 'Stages in the Reception of Aristotle's Works on Sleep and Dreams in Hellenistic and Imperial Philosophical and Medical Thought,' in *Les* Parva Naturalia *d'Aristote: Fortune antique et médiévale*, edited by Christophe Grellard and Pierre-Marie Morel, 47–75. Paris: Éditions de la Sorbonne, 2010.

van Rookhuijzen, Jan Z. 'The Parthenon Treasury on the Acropolis of Athens,' *American Journal of Archaeology* 124, no. 1 (2020): 3–35.

Wardle, David. *Cicero: On Divination, Book 1*. Oxford: Oxford University Press, 2006.

Waszink, Jan H., ed. *Quinti Septimi Florentis Tertulliani* De Anima. Supplements to *Vigiliae Christianae* 100. Leiden and Boston: Brill, 2010.

Willi, Andreas. 'Numa's Dangerous Books: The Exegetic History of a Roman Forgery,' *Museum Helveticum* 55, no. 3 (1998): 139–72.

Wohl, Victoria. 'The Sleep of Reason: Sleep and the Philosophical Soul in Ancient Greece,' *Classical Antiquity* 39, no. 1 (2020): 126–51.

Wolff, Hans J. 'Marriage Law and Family Organization in Ancient Athens: A Study on the Interrelation of Public and Private Law in the Greek City,' *Traditio* 2 (1944): 43–95.

Young, Charles M. 'Aristotle on Temperance,' *Philosophical Review* 97, no. 4 (1988): 521–42.
Zetzel, James E. G., ed. and tr. *Cicero:* On the Commonwealth *and* On the Laws. 2nd edn. Cambridge Texts in the History of Political Thought. Cambridge: Cambridge University Press, 2017.
Zorzi, Marino. 'I Barbaro e i libri,' in *Una famiglia veneziana nella storia: I Barbaro. Atti del Convegno di studi in occasione del quinto centenario della morte dell'umanista Ermolao, Venezia, 4–6 Novembre 1993*, edited by Michela Marangoni and Manlio Pastore Stocchi, 363–96. Venice: Istituto Veneto di Scienze, Lettere ed Arti, 1996.
Zorzi, Niccolò. 'Un feltrino nel circolo di Ermolao Barbaro: il notaio Tommaso Zanetelli, alias Didymus Zenoteles, copista di codici greci (*c.* 1450–1514),' in *Bellunesi e feltrini tra Umanesimo e Rinascimento: Filologia, erudizione e biblioteche*, edited by Paolo Pellegrini, 43–106. Rome and Padua: Antenore, 2008.

Index of Passages

Aelian
Varia historia
4.21 15 n.30

Apuleius
De dogmate Platonis
1.2.3 155 n.227

Aristotle
De anima
1.2 404a27-31, 405a8-13 101 n.28
2.3 414b12-14 67 n.203
2.9 421a21-6 119 n.100
3.4-5 429a14-18, 22-4, 430a14-19
    101 n.29

De generatione animalium
4.6 775a9-16 161 n.244

De partibus animalium
2.7 653a11-20 59 n.173

De somno et vigilia
3 456b17-34, 457b1-458a10
    59 n.173

Ethica Eudemia
2.1 1219b6-7 83 n.257
3.2.9-11 1230b36-1231a7 25 n.65

Ethica Nicomachea
1.6 1096a13-17 71 n.216
1.10 1100a10-11 83 n.257
1.10 1101a14-16 115 n.75
1.13 1102b13-1103a3 143 n.180
2.2 1104a11-27, 2.6-9 1106a24-
    1109b26 71 n.218
2.6 1106a26-b7 71 n.220
2.6 1107a.8-17 73 n.223
3.10 1118a23-6 25 n.65

10.7 1177a13-17, 1177b1-2, 19-20
    107 nn.50–2
10.8 1178b7-9, 21-3, 1179a24-32
    107 nn.53–4
10.8 1178b19-20 117 n.86

Historia animalium
1.6 490b8-14 13 n.26
2.15 505b26-32 13 n.26
4.1 523a32-b22 13 n.26
4.8 534b12-15 13 n.26
6.22 576a18-21 17 n.39
8.8 595b31-596a2 43 n.128
9.47 630b32-631a8 17 n.39
9.47 631a1-8 17 n.41

Metaphysica
1.1 981a1-7, 12-30, 1.2 982b7-21
    95 n.6
1.3 984b18-20 103 n.35
1.5 985b23-986a21 97 n.8
1.6 987b1-10 99 n.15
1.6 987b14-18 97 n.11
4.5 1009b12-17 101 n.28
6.1 1025b25-8, 1026a8-32 99 n.18
12.7 1072b13-30 99 n.18

Poetica
8 1451a16-35 13 n.24

Politica
8.3 1338a17-19, 40-b4 115 n.76
8.3 1338a37-40 113 n.65

[Aristotle]
Oeconomica
1.3 1343b30-1 161 n.244

Problēmata
28.2 949b6-12 25 n.65

28.7 949b37-950a16 25 n.65
28.7 949b38-950a2 27 n.72

Arrian
Anabasis
2.25.2-3 53 n.152

Artemidorus
Oneirocritica
1.70.2, 2.49-51, 3.23, 4.59.1 61 n.180
1.79, 80.3, 80.5 61 n.179

Athenaeus
Deipnosophistae
1 9a, 18a-b 69 n.208
2 55d, 10 419e-420c 37 n.111
5 219b 15 n.30

Augustine
De bono coniugali
3 19 n.48

Aulus Gellius
1.2.3-13 125 n.116
4.3.2, 17.21.44 15 n.33
4.11.3 31 n.92
4.11.11-13 33 n.95
6.16.6-7 67 n.202
15.2.1-8 29 n.79
19.2.3 27 n.72
19.2.5 25 n.65

Barbaro, Ermolao
Epistolae (as in Branca 1943)
LXXXII (to Jan I Carondelet) 179 n.2
LXXXVII (to Giorgio Merula) 167 and 179 n.3
XC (to Girolamo Donato) 167 and 180 n.8
XCI (to Marco Dandolo) 167 and 180 n.7
CXLV (to Antonio Calvo) 182 n.72
CXLVI (to Jacopo Antiquario) 182 n.72
CXLVII (to Ugolino Verino) 182 n.72
CXLVIII (to Antonio Calvo) 182 n.72
CL (to Jacopo Antiquario) 182 n.72
CLI (to Jacopo Antiquario) 182 n.72
CLII (to Antonio Calvo) 178 and 182 n.71, 72
CLIII (to Antonio Calvo) 182 n.72
CLIV (to Jacopo Antiquario) 176 and 182 nn.61, 72
CLVIII (to Antonio Calvo) 182 n.72

Orationes (as in Branca 1943)
IV 179 n.2

Barbaro, Francesco
De re uxoria (as in Griggio 2021)
I.7-8 19 n.46
IV.2 161 n.244
V.8 17 n.38
VIII.1 163 n.250
XVI 15 n.27

Catullus
83.3 43 n.128

Celsus
De medicina
1.3.13, 27-9 65 n.195

Cicero
Academica
1.23 141 n.176
1.44 97 n.12

Brutus
283 117 n.89
309 125 n.116

De divinatione
1.60 5
1.60-1 60–1
1.62 31 n.92
1.112 97 n.9
2.119 31 n.92

De finibus
1.61 117 n.89
2.17 125 n.116
2.24-5 15 n.28
2.39-41 29 n.82
3.16 23 n.59
3.45, 4.15, 41 105 n.43
3.72 123 n.113
3.76 83 n.257
4.68, 5.58 117 n.89
5.18 31 n.87

De haruspicum responso
32 5

De legibus
1.33 31 n.87
2.39 123 n.112
3.9.5 201 n.44

De natura deorum
1.4, 2.133-67 127 n.120
2.145 27 n.71
3.5 15 n.28
3.70 25 n.62

De officiis
1.15 143 n.182
1.16 101 n.27, 143 n.183
1.20, 31 133 n.139
1.22 133 n.140
1.29 133 n.143
1.42 137 nn.155–6
1.66 137 n.160, 139 n.162
1.67 139 n.161, 141 n.173
1.77-84 139 n.163
1.90 15 n.28
1.93 141 n.175
1.100-21 85 n.261
1.110 163 n.247
1.144 205 n.58
1.153 143 n.184
1.157-9 153 n.218
2.40 15 n.28

3.28 131 n.136
3.65, 69 5
3.96 89 n.272, 141 n.175
3.116 29 n.82, 89 n.272, 141 n.175

De oratore
1.165 117 n.89
1.217, 2.22 155 n.227
1.260-1 121 n.107
2.212 195 n.28

De republica
1.35 117 n.89

In Catilinam
1.2 63 n.190

In Verrem
2.4.55 63 n.190

Lucullus
74 97 n.12
91 123 n.113

Orator
13 117 n.89
113-14 125 n.116

Topica
78 15 n.28

Tusculanae disputationes
1.38 97 n.9
3.2 31 n.87
3.16 89 n.272
3.22 73 n.225
3.57 47 n.137
4.47 27 n.74
5.54 15 n.28
5.91-2 37 n.109
5.100 29 n.79

Q. Curtius Rufus
4.11.14-15 53 n.152

Dio Cassius
46.18.6 17 n.36

Diodorus Siculus
17.54.4-5 53 n.152
17.115.6 159 n.238

Diogenes Laertius
1.34 51 n.150
1.39 51 n.148
1.119, 8.2 97 n.9
2.6-7 85 n.263
2.19 15 n.30
2.26 15 n.32
2.37 15 n.29
2.86-90 29 n.82
2.109 121 n.107
2.125-44 37 n.111
3.4 155 n.227
3.20, 42 77 n.243
3.39 29 n.79
4.7 31 n.89
4.8 37 n.109
4.10 113 n.70
4.24 75 nn.232–3
5.52-3 77 n.242
6.2, 3 69 n.211
6.38 37 n.109
8.5 103 n.35
8.11-12, 25 97 n.8
8.19 33 n.95

Dionysius of Halicarnassus
Antiquitates Romanae
2.25.7 15 n.33

Ennius
Annales
206-12 Sk. 9 n.4

Euripides
fr. 892N² 67 n.202

Iphigenia in Aulis
16-19 47 n.137

Galen
Ars medica
24 91 n.281

De constitutione artis medicae
16 23 n.60

De sanitate tuenda
2.12 91 n.279

In Hippocratis prognosticum commentarii
2.11 59 n.169

Herodotus
1.32.7, 86.3 83 n.257
3.89-98 37 n.108

Hippocrates/Hippocratic Corpus
De morbis popularibus
6.6.2 91 n.279

De natura hominis
9 23 n.60

De vetere medicina
13.2 23 n.60

Prognosticon
10 59 n.169

Homer
Iliad
10.159 58–9 and n.170

Odyssey
10.156-84 69 n.208

Horace
Ars poetica
1-37 13 n.24
412-13 157 n.232

Carmina
2.10.5 73 n.224
3.30.14-15 196–7 and n.33

Josephus
Bellum Judaicum
5.418-19, 420-3 138-9 and
  n.165

Justin
Epitome
12.12.12 159 n.238

Juvenal
5.116-19, 14.7 31 n.91
6.166-9 163 n.248

Livy
Pref. 11-12 21 n.53
Pref. 13 9 n.4
6.1.1-3, 21.1.1-3, 31.1.1-5 9 n.4

[Longinus]
De sublimitate
44 117 n.91

Lucan
2.326-80 17 n.37

Lucretius
4.1-25 9 n.4

Martial
1 pref. 51 n.145
9.3.12, 34.2 37 n.107

New Testament
Mark 10.11-12 19 n.48
Matthew 19.9 19 n.48

Nonnus
Dionysiaca
25.1-10, 253-70 9 n.4

Ovid
Metamorphoses
10.1-85, 11.1-66 75 n.234

Persius
3.88-106 59 n.173

Plato
Apologia/Apology
21a 15 n.29
21b-22e 97 n.12

Epistulae
9 358a 133 n.140

Leges
637a-650b, 666a-e, 671c-672a
  29 n.79
808b-c 57 n.165

Respublica
398e, 403e 29 n.79
404b-c 69 n.208
439d-441a 61 n.178
441e-442b 61 n.178, 143 n.179
534c-d, 571d-572a 57 n.165
571c-572a 61 n.176

Theaetetus
174a 51 n.150

Timaeus 105–7 n.47
31b-32c, 35a-36d, 53c-57d
  113 n.66
77a-c 66–7 and n.204
86b-90d 81 n.251

Plautus
Aulularia
152 119 n.98
198 49 n.139

Pliny the elder
Naturalis historia
7.45 4
7.78 33 n.97
7.108 37 n.108
7.152 159 n.237
7.166 25 n.62
7.174 103 n.35
7.204 123 n.112
9.91 49 n.139
10.191 27 n.70

18.118 31 n.92
19.33-5 31 n.91
34.26 97 n.10

Plutarch
Homērikai meletai
fr. 122 33 n.95

Moralia
267c 15 n.33
331f-332c, 333b
    37 n.109
670d 33 n.95
831f 85 n.263
844d 79 n.245
1043e, 1044b 67 n.202

Vitae
  Alexander
  29.4 53 n.152

  Caesar
  10.1-5 47 n.138
  10.5-7 45 n.133

  Cato minor
  25 17 n.37

  Cicero
  41.5 17 n.36

  Demosthenes
  6.3-4, 11.1-2 121 n.107
  7.3 79 n.245

  Lucullus
  40-1 37 n.110

  Numa
  8.10 97 n.10

[Plutarch]
De liberis educandis
11 163 n.250

Porphyry
Vita Pythagorae
45 33 n.95

Quintilian
Institutio oratoria
1.4.5 111 n.62
2.11.7 13 n.24
9.2.26 63 n.190
10.3.25 79 n.245
12.1.33, 34-45 119 n.96
12.2.10-14 125 n.116

Sallust
Catilina
2.8, 13.3 57 n.165
9.1-12.5 21 n.53
10-13 63 n.190
60.5 41 n.123

[Sallust]
In Ciceronem
2 17 n.36

Seneca the younger
De beneficiis
2.18.8 25 n.62

Dialogi
1.2.5 157 n.232
1.3.6 31 n.91
6.16.3 163 n.248
7.4.4 33 n.98
8.6.4-5 133 n.147
9.17.5-6 57 n.165
12.16.6 163 n.248

Epistulae
8.1, 83.6 57 n.165
22.1 39 n.120
39.6, 110.9 33 n.98
45.5, 8-13, 48.4-12, 71.6 125 n.116
55.5, 77.6, 88.41 57 n.165
71.28, 75.10 43 n.127

78.23-4, 95.15-29, 110.12-13 63 n.190
88.20 111 n.62
88.27-8 45 n.132
89.22 31 n.91
97.8 51 n.145
114.1 119 n.97
115.3 89 n.272
116.2 43 n.127
121.17-21 23 n.59
122 59 n.169

Quaestiones naturales
4b.13.5-11 59 n.173
4b.13.11 33 n.98

Sextus Empiricus
Pyrrhoniae hypotyposes
2.229 123 n.113

Suetonius
Vitae Caesarum
   Claudius
     26.3 17 n.38

   Domitian
     1.1 37 n.107

   Iulius
     74.2 45 n.133

   Nero
     28.2 17 n.38

Tacitus
Annales
12.5-7, 14.2 17 n.38

Dialogus
28.5 163 n.248
36-41 117 n.91

Tertullian
De anima
48.3 31 n.92

Theophrastus
Characters
17 149 n.203

Valerius Flaccus
5.217-24 9 n.4

Valerius Maximus
1.8 ext. 6 25 n.62
2.1.4, 2.9.2, 6.3.10-12 15 n.33
2.10.8 51 n.145
4.3 ext. 3a-b 31 n.89, 37 n.109
4.3 ext. 4a 37 n.109
6.4 ext. 3 53 n.152
8.8.1-2 155 n.227

Virgil
Aeneid
6.847-53 21 n.53
7.37-45 9 n.4
7.45 9 n.2

Eclogues
6.1-12 9 n.4

Georgics
3.1-48 9 n.4
4.453-527 75 n.234

Xenophon
Memorabilia
1.3.5-6 29 n.79
4.5.9 29 n.83

Symposium
2.24-6 29 n.79

General Index

Achilles on Scyros 48–9
active vs. contemplative life 10–11,
    108–11 and n.59, 129 n.127,
    177
  superiority of contemplative life
    10–11, 110–11
Agamemnon 46–7 and n.137
Albert the Great 111 n.63
Alexander the Great 36–7 and n.109,
    52–3, 158–9 and n.238
ambassador as configured in *De
    officio legati*
  absolute obedience to mandate
    169, 177, 188–9 and n.11,
    190–1 and n.18, 196–7
  and Aristotelian 'middle way' 169
  brevity of speech desirable in
    before rulers 173, 196–7
  capacity for shrewd initiative
    (*prudentia*) 169, 173, 188–9
  correlation between inner
    condition and outer aspect 172
  his criminal behaviour harshly
    punished 202–5 and n.54
  duration of assignment 184–7 and
    n.5, 199 n.39
  financial burden upon 186–7 and
    nn.6, 8
  as incarnation of Venetian values
    169
  instructions to 184–5
  masking and dissimulation 169,
    173–4, 192–3 and n.25
  never seeks personal benefit from
    host state 177, 190–1, 200–1
    and n.44
  not a spy 192–3 and n.24
  as *orator* 195 n.28
  relazione of the Venetian envoy
    191 n.19

  'resident' ambassador 3, 169 and
    180 n.22, 171, 184–5 and n.4
  should never speak ill of
    predecessors or successors
    200–3 and n.45
  strategy of deliberate diversion
    and indirection 173
  and territorial disputes 196–9 and
    n.37
Anaxagoras 75 n.230, 84–5 and
    n.263, 103 n.35
animals
  care for their young 22–3
  free of human sins 34–5
  incest rare among 16–17 and n.39
  mules muddying water before
    they drink 42–3 and n.128
  senses of animals in comparison
    with human senses 25 n.65,
    26–7 and nn.70–1
Annius, Lucius 15 n.33
Antiquario, Jacopo 176, 178
Antisthenes of Athens 68–9 and
    n.211
Archelaus 15 n.30
Aristippus of Cyrene 28–9, 71 n.217
Aristotle 13 n.26, 31–2, 70–1 and
    n.216, 114–15, 167
  distinction between knowledge
    'from experience' and 'from art'
    95 n.6
  importance to Venetian civic
    ideology 169
  and mathematics 112–13
  the mean 2, 70–3 and nn.218, 220,
    193 n.23
  on mind and contemplation
    106–7
  nature of thought in 100–1 and
    n.29

on Pythagoreans 97 n.8
rational and non-rational parts of soul 142–3 and n.180
on sleep 59 n.173
Stagira restored at his request by either Philip II or Alexander the Great 138–9 and n.164
'theology' identifiable with 'primary philosophy' of metaphysics 99 n.18
on touch 118–19 and n.100
tripartite order of knowledge 98–9 and n.18
artistic conception/execution, unity of 12–13 and n.24
Asclepius, temple of 74–5
Athenian acropolis 36–7
atomism, nature of thought in 100–1 and n.28

Bacon, Roger 111 n.63
Badoer, Sebastiano 201 n.47
Barbaro, Ermolao
  ambassador to Milan, 1488–9 167
  ambassador to Papal Curia 1, 175
  botanical interests 129 n.128
  death in Rome, July 1493 1, 175
  delegation to Bruges, 1486 167
  devotion to humanistic studies 1, 167, 176, 177, 178
  familial ties to Papal Curia 176
  the Forlì incident 174–5, 177–8, 188–9 and n.13
  and holy orders 176
  masks his true self in *De officio legati*? 178–9
  nomination as Patriarch of Aquileia 1, 168, 174, 176, 178, 179
  role in frontier dispute between Venice and Milan 199 n.37
  work on Aristotle, Dioscorides, and Pliny the elder 129 n.128, 167

Barbaro, Francesco 78–9, 88–9 and n.271, 111 n.57
  ambassador to Milan, 1444 167 and 179 n.3
  favoured method of exercising 156–7
Barbaro, Zaccaria 13 n.21, 164–5
  ambassador to Milan, 1476 and 1485 167, 171, 179 n.3
  ambassador to Naples, 1471–3 186–7 and n.8
  ambassador to Rome, 1480–1 186–7 and n.7
  length and detail of his diplomatic dispatches 193 n.26
  portrayal in *De officio legati* 169, 172, 186–7 and nn.8–9, 192–3 and n.25
Biblioteca Comunale Ariostea, Ferrara 5
Bion of Borysthenes 20–1 and n.52
Biow, Douglas 171
Boeotia as byword for stupidity 43 n.128
Bon, Philippa 102–3
Branca, Vittore vii, 4, 168
  on *De officio legati* marking a shift in Ermolao's attitude to his Venetian civic calling 177–8
  'sapienza civile' 177
Bruni, Leonardo 121 n.108

Caligula 4
Calvo, Antonio 178
Carvilius Ruga, Spurius 15 n.33
Castiglione, Baldassare 170
celibate/celibacy
  akin to philosophical sage 47 n.135, 103 n.38, 130–1
  avoidance of potentially compromising places/situations 50–1, 74–9, 86–7
  blood, desirable nature of 150–1 and n.211

desirability of knowing theoretical medicine 128–9
disdain for emotions and scorn for pleasures 140–1 and n.176
drinking habits 32–3
female 2, 3, 160–3
four parts of the Panaetian *honestum* mapped on to celibate 3, 130–45 and nn.133, 137, 155, 160, 175, 181
four requirements in celibate-to-be 10–11
and friends 112–13, 152–5
god-like 3, 20–1, 94–5 and n.4, 103 n.38, 104–5, 106–7, 130–1, 134–5, 138–9, 140–1, 144–5, 156–61
and the golden mean 72–3
highest form of virtue found in 88–9
importance of exercise and relaxation 154–7
indifferent to popular favour, public honours, etc. 44–7, 86–7, 104–5, 138–9
principles for living chastely in celibacy 22–65
reflection of God's own distinction 8–9
self-control 2, 44–9
service to community even without engaging in public life 132–3 and n.147
shown special favour by God 134–5, 136–7
speaks in a natural, unaffected manner 118–19 and n.97
two classes of the unmarried 18–19
two obligations of 12–15, 94–5
vivacious and lively of mind 3, 148–9, 152–5
worthy of worship in life as well as in death 158–61

Christianity 16–19 and n.46, 103 n.38, 105 n.43, 113 n.69, 170–1
Chrysippus of Soli 66–7 and nn.202–3, 133 n.147
Cicero 46–7, 60–1, 72–3, 160–3
crushed by daughter's death 17 n.36
on decorum 140–1 and n.175
four Panaetian *personae* in *De officiis* 1 85 n.261
on generosity and kindness 136–7 and nn.155–6
on greatness of spirit 136–9 and n.160
on justice 130–3 and n.140
marriages 14–17
on truth as object of contemplation 100–1 and n.27
on wisdom and prudence 142–3 and n.181
Claudius 17 n.38
Cleanthes of Assos 133 n.147
Clodius Pulcher, Publius 45 n.133, 47 n.138
contemplation/the contemplative
aided by robust physical health 148–9
contemplative life as 'active' 35 n.105, 68–9 and n.209, 144–5 and nn.188–9
definition of 94–5, 108–9
out-of-body experience induced by 100–3
promotes good health 148–9
truth as object of 100–1 and n.27
Cornelia, mother of Tiberius and Gaius Gracchus 162–3 and n.248
Crantor of Soli 74–5 and nn.231–2
Cyrenaic school of hedonism 28–9 and nn.82–4, 71 nn.217, 219

da Rho, Antonio 73 n.226
Darius, king of Persia (both I and III) 36–7 and n.108, 52–3

De coelibatu
  avoidance of things harmful to sexual purity 22–65
  Ciceronian diction and style 31 n.87, 63 n.190, 117 n.89, 139 n.162, 141 n.176
  concession made to impoverished male reader 162–5
  content of Books 3 and 4 surveyed 2–3
  in counterpoise to Francesco Barbaro's *De re uxoria* 55 n.158
  date of composition vii, 1
  digression within 146–7 and n.192
  engagement in 4.1 with Aristotle's *Metaphysics* 95 n.6, 97 n.11, 99 nn.15, 18
  engagement with Cicero's *De officiis* 3, 85 n.261, 130–45 and n.133
  importance of heeding one's own nature 84–5 and n.261, 148–9, 164–5
  sequence of argument in 3.6.18-48 75 n.230
  as specialist treatise 54–5 and n.158
  treatments for preserving sexual purity in celibacy 64–93

De officio legati
  autobiographical component 170, 172–3, 199 n.37
  Ciceronian Latinity 171, 187 n.9
  its conciseness in keeping with ambassador's brevity of speech 173
  date of composition vii, 1, 168, 175–6, 177
  and dissimulation 169, 173–4, 178, 179, 195 n.29, 201 n.48
  Ermolao in Pavia (§§34–7) 172–3, 198–9 and n.40
  Ermolao spontaneously amends instructions from Venice (§§10–12) 173, 174, 188–9
  'how-to' manual in *institutio principis* tradition? 168–9
  incomplete? 168 and 180 n.16, 172 and 181 n.41, 175–6, 179, 207 n.63
  likely *terminus ante quem* 176, 177
  manuscript tradition vii, 4, 168
  'modern' diplomatic ethos in 1, 3, 171
  movement from public sphere to private 172, 204–7 and n.63
  novel emphasis on 'resident' ambassador 3, 169, 171, 180 n.22
  originality of 170–4
  patrilineal economy of 172, 173–4, 188–9 and n.14, 191 n.22
  print history 168
  three movements of 169
  tonal shift via interjections late in work 201 n.46
  the 'truth' about the Forlì incident (§§10–12) 174–5
  Venetian presence in 169, 171–2, 173, 175, 188–9, 194–7
  visual appeal of verbal portraiture within 169–70
  Zaccaria Barbaro's presence in 169, 172, 173–4, 186–7 and n.9, 190–1 and n.22, 192–3

De Rosier, Bernard 170–1 and 181 n.30
  his *Ambaxiatorum brevilogus* (1435–6) 170
  idealized view of diplomat's function 170–1 and 181 n.31
  no humanist 171

Democritus of Abdera 100–1 and n.28

Demosthenes 78–9 and n.245, 88–9 and n.271, 120–1

Diogenes of Sinope 37 n.109
Dionysius I of Syracuse 46–7 and
    n.136
Dioscorides 167
divorce 14–17 and n.33, 18–19 and
    n.48
Doglio, Maria 168, 169
Domitian 37 n.107
Donato, Nicolò 1
dreams of incest, murder, etc. 60–1
    and nn.179–80
dropsy 32–3 and n.97

eating
    consumption proportionate to
        individual needs/natures 66–7,
        72–3
    three dangerous habits in 30–1,
        32–3
eloquence as thriving in times of
    political strife, etc. 116–19 and
    n.91
Endymion and Selene 116–17 and
    n.86
Epicureanism 70–1
    and behavioural change through
        therapy/education 81 n.251
    hedonistic calculus 25 n.64,
        71 n.219
Euripides 47 n.137, 66–7
Eutimius/Euthymus 158–9 and n.237

Favre, Pierre 205 n.61
fixed and relative interpretations of
    the Aristotelian mean 71 n.220
four humours 80–1 and n.250, 90–1
    and n.281, 150–1
    relation between the elements,
        humours and temperament
        151 n.211
four parts of the Panaetian *honestum*
    decorum, restraint and modesty
        140–3 and n.175
    generosity and kindness (part of
        social virtue) 136–7 and n.155

greatness of spirit 136–41 and
    n.160
justice (part of social virtue)
    130–5 and n.137
wisdom and prudence 142–5 and
    n.181–2
Frederick III (Holy Roman Emperor)
    167
Fubini, Riccardo 176

Galen on sleep 59 nn.169, 173
Galli 48–9
gladiatorial training, defensive
    technique prioritized in 38–9
    and n.120
gluttony
    as pervasive blight 62–3
    shatters good health 26–9, 148–9
    tyranny of/slavery to 26–7, 32–3
the golden mean 2, 72–3
Grosseteste, Robert 111 n.63
Guarini, Guarino 111 n.57
Guarino, Battista 121 n.108

health
    application of expedients and
        avoidance of their opposites
        22–3
    both generated by and promoting
        liveliness of mind/spirit 154–5
    opposites as cure for opposites
        22–3 and n.60
Hephaestion 158–9 and n.238
Heraclitus 161 n.242
Hermotimus of Clazomenae 102–3
    and n.35
Homeric meat-eating 68–9 and n.208
Horace 196–7
Hortensius Hortalus, Quintus 16–17
    and n.37
humanistic curriculum 2–3, 108–31
    and n.57
    astronomy/astrology 2, 112–15
        and n.69
    dialectic 2, 122–5

eloquence 2, 114–21 and n.79
geometry 110–11
grammar 110–11 and n.62
historical study 120–1
mathematics 2, 110–11
medicine, empirical and
 theoretical 126–9
moral philosophy 130–45 and
 n.133
music 110–11
natural science 126–7
poetry 120–3
Trivium and *Quadrivium*
 109 n.57, 111 nn.62–3,
 123 n.113
in Venice 109 n.57
visual arts/optics 2, 110–11 and
 n.63, 114–15 and n.76
humans
 distinguished from other
  creatures by possession of
  reason 10–11
 natural divergence of life
  trajectories 10–11
 social by nature 153 n.218

iatroastrology 113 n.69, 114–15
incest 16–17, 60–1

Jason of Pherae 24–5 and n.62
Judeo-Christian anthropocentrism
 127 n.120
Julius Caesar, Gaius 44–5 and n.133,
 47 n.138
Julius Viator 32–3 and n.97

Labalme, Patricia 167–8
Laelius, Gaius 14–15 and n.28, 154–5
 and nn.226–7
Leucippus of Miletus(?) 100–1 and
 n.28
Licinius Lucullus, Lucius 36–7 and
 n.110
Loredan, Antonio 203 n.54,
 207 n.62

Marcia, wife of younger Cato 16–17
 and n.37
marriage, chaste living in 14–15 and
 n.27
Martianus Capella 109 n.57
Mattingly, Garrett 171, 179
Maximilian I (King of the Romans)
 167
melancholy 150–1
Menedemus of Eretria 36–7 and
 n.111
mental as well as physical
 impairment as responsive to
 therapy 80–1 and n.251
Merula, Giorgio 167
misogyny 3, 75 n.234
Mt. Olympus 74–5
Mt. Rhodope 76–7
Mucius Scaevola Augur, Quintus
 154–5 and n.227
Mucius Scaevola, Publius 155 n.227

Nero 4, 16–17 and n.38
Nestor in Homer 58–9 and n.170
'No man is happy until dead' 82–3
 and n.257
Numa Pompilius, books burnt 122–3
 and n.111

octopus 48–9 and n.139
Orpheus 74–7 and n.234
Ovid's *Art of love* 51 n.144

Panaetius 85 n.261, 101 n.27,
 131 n.133
Parmenio 52–3 and n.152
Pericles 36–7 and n.109
Peripatetics 73 n.223, 75 n.233, 76–7,
 98–9, 142–3
 Peripatetic mean 70–1, 73 n.225
Petillius Spurinus, Quintus 122–3
 and n.111
Petrarch's *De vita solitaria* 155 n.225
Pherecydes of Samos 96–7 and n.9
Phryne 30–1 and n.89

Piccolomini, Aeneas Sylvius
  121 n.108
Plato 28–9, 66–7
  Academy 77 nn.241, 243
  and Dionysius I of Syracuse 46–7
    and n.136
  on drunkenness 29 n.79
  intermediate status of
    mathematics in 96–7 and n.11
  on justice 130–1 and n.136, 132–3
    and n.140
  man as third product of divine
    construction in *Timaeus*
    104–5 and n.47
  recourse to numbers, musical
    pitch, and harmonic quantity
    112–13 and n.66
  on sleep 57 n.165, 60–1
  theory of Forms 13 n.26, 96–9
    and nn.11, 15
  on therapeutic psychological/
    physical rehabilitation
    81 n.251
  tripartite soul 60–1 and n.178,
    140–3 and n.179
  wrestling prowess 155 n.227
pleonastic negator 78 n.244,
  140 n.166
Plutarch 30–3 and n.95
Pompeia, wife of Julius Caesar
  45 n.133, 47 n.138
Popes
  Alexander VI 1
  Innocent VIII 1, 174, 175, 176,
    179
Porcius Cato, Marcus (the younger)
  16–17 and n.37, 50–1 and
  n.145
Praetorian Guards 40–1 and n.123
'proems in the middle' 8–9 and n.3
Publilia, Cicero's second wife 14–17
  and n.36
Pythagoras/Pythagoreanism
  certain foods forbidden 30–3
  eminence 96–7

number as essence of all things
  96–7 and n.8
as reincarnation of Hermotimus
  of Clazomenae 103 n.35
statue of at Rome, in Place of
  Assembly 96–7 and n.10

Quintilian on true orator as
  necessarily virtuous 119 n.96

Riario, Girolamo, assassination of 174
Roman values contrasted with Greek
  20–1 and n.53

Sabellico, Marcantonio 197 n.34
Scuola di Rialto, Venice 111 n.57
Scuola di San Marco, Venice 111 n.57
the senses 24–7
  and lust 26–7, 30–1
  smell 24–7
  taste and touch the most harmful
    senses 24–7, 38–9
  under 'soft' siege 40–1 and n.122
Sforza, Caterina 174
Sforza, Gian Galeazzo 189 n.15
Sforza, Ludovico 172–3, 174, 175,
  177–8, 188–9 and n.15, 198–9
  and nn.37, 41
Sibyl 160–1 and n.242
siege of Jerusalem, 70 CE 138–9 and
  n.165
Sizicaena, Lala 160–1
slavery metaphor 32–3 and n.98,
  36–9
sleep 54–65, 90–1, 148–9
  in Aristotle and Galen 59 n.173
  and dreams 58–61
  in Plato 57 n.165
  position in sleeping 62–3
  regular sleep prescribed in ancient
    medicine 91 and n.279
  sleeping by day, reveling by night
    56–9 and n.169
  three harmful factors in sleeping
    56–7, 90–1

unhealthy to go to sleep directly
  after eating 58–9
Socrates
  claim to ignorance 96–7 and n.12
  passion for symposia 28–9 and
    n.79
  pederasty implied in 15 n.30
  Renaissance efforts to make him
    'safe for Christianity' 15 n.30
  on sleep and dreams 60–1
  study of ethics 98–9
  two wives at same time 14–15
  and Xanthippe 148–51 and n.207
Solon and Croesus 83 n.257
sophistic quibblings, as corruption of
  dialectic 124–5
stade, length of 157 n.230
Stoicism
  anthropocentrism 127 n.120
  and behavioural change through
    therapy/education 81 n.251
  danger of temporarily indulging
    pleasure 42–3 and n.127
  doctrine of 'affiliation' (*oikeiōsis*)
    22–3 and n.59
  nothing more outstanding than
    virtue itself 102–5 and n.43
  'painted porch' 77 n.241
  reasonable affective responses
    25 n.64
  resistance to the Peripatetic mean
    72–3 and n.225
  sage's indifference to honours,
    wealth, etc. 47 n.135, 104–5
    and n.44

Tasso, Torquato 181 n.25
Teatini, Bernardo 203 n.54, 207 n.62

Terentia, Cicero's first wife 14–15
Thales of Miletus 50–1
Theophrastus 76–7 and n.242, 98–9
Thessaly as byword for gluttony
  43 n.128
Timotheus of Miletus 122–3 and
  n.112
Treaty of Lodi, 1454 171
Trotti, Jacopo 199 n.41

Valla, Lorenzo and his *De voluptate*
  73 n.226
Venice
  indirectly praised in *De officio
    legati* 194–7
  myth of 21 n.53, 171–2,
    195 n.30
  as 'new Rome' 21 n.53, 195 n.30
  patrician toga in 195 n.30
  sumptuary laws in 195 n.30
  unanimitas of 172, 182 n.73,
    202–3 and n.52
Vergerio, Pier Paolo 109 n.57,
  115 nn.76, 79, 121 n.108,
  127 n.122, 155 nn.226–7
Verino, Ugolino 178
Virgil 9 n.2, 141 n.172
Visconti, Filippo Maria 198–9 and
  n.38
Volterrano, Jacopo 176

Xanthippe 148–51 and n.207
Xenocrates of Chalcedon 30–1, 36–7,
  112–13

Zanetelli, Tommaso Didimo 168 and
  180 n.14
Zeno of Citium 77 n.241, 133 n.147

Index of Latin Words

animantes 67 n.204
appetitus 27 n.74
(*ars*) *designativa* 115 n.76
(*ars*) *perspectiva* 111 n.63
(*ars*) *spectativa* 111 n.63, 115 n.76
astrologia 113 n.68
auctoritas et gratia 187 n.9, 191 n.21

consenesco 125 n.117

dilargior 41 n.126
dissimulo 193 n.25

Eutimius poeta/Euthymus pycta 159 n.237
excitus/exercitus 5–6
expatior 57 n.167
exprimo 120 n.101

faces/facies 41 n.125
fax/faex 4
fractus 125 n.117

hercle/mehercle 6

igniculus 31 n.87, 33 n.96
illiberalitas 125 n.117
inanitus/inanimus 103 n.37
infreno/refreno 35 n.104
irretio/retiarius 51 n.143

lapides loqui 119 n.98
legati munus/officum 185 n.2
lucifugus 117 n.89

maius opus 9 n.2
mediocre ingenium 169 and 193 n.23
minutulae argutiunculae 125 n.116

ostium 35 n.103

polypus 49 n.139
proh tempora! proh mores! 63 n.190

quo circa/quocirca 76 n.235
quomodo/quocumque modo 65 n.196

rerum publicarum administratio 117 n.89

sanctum est . . . ut 5
Sibylla 161 n.242
speculor 95 n.6
sponte naturae 118 n.95
studia humanitatis 109 n.57
suae cervicis 59 n.172
sudor/studia 157 n.232
superbia 197 n.33

templum gentis Flaviae 37 n.107

unius manus 185 n.3

vas continentiae 205 n.61
Venus/venter 27 n.73
vetus proverbium 39 n.120

Index of Greek Words

ἀκρασία 29 n.83
ἀναθυμίασις 59 n.173

βούλησις 25 n.64

ἐγκράτεια 29 n.83
εὐλάβεια 25 n.64
εὐπάθειαι 25 n.64

ἡ γραφικὴ τέχνη 115 n.76
ἡ ὀπτική 110–11 and n.58

ἰάομαι/Ἰάσων 25 n.62

μεμψίμοιρος 148–9 and n.203
μεσότης 169

οἰκείωσις 23 n.59
ὁρμή 27 n.74

πανημέριος 59 n.170
πάννυχος 59 n.170
περιπατέω 75 n.233

στοὰ ποικίλη 77 n.241

τέλειος 115 n.75
τὸ ἐπιθυμητικόν 57 n.165,
  61 n.178, 67 n.204,
  143 n.180
τὸ θυμοειδές 57 n.165,
  61 n.178
τὸ λογιστικόν 57 n.165, 61 n.178,
  143 n.179

ὑγρῶν κρᾶσις 90–1 and nn.277,
  281

χαρά 25 n.64

www.ingramcontent.com/pod-product-compliance
Lightning Source LLC
Chambersburg PA
CBHW071826300426
44116CB00009B/1451